The Changing Church in Europe

The Changing Church in Europe

Wayne A. Detzler

ZONDERVAN PUBLISHING HOUSE
OF THE ZONDERVAN CORPORATION
GRAND RAPIDS, MICHIGAN 49506

THE CHANGING CHURCH IN EUROPE
Copyright © 1979 by Wayne A. Detzler

Library of Congress Cataloging in Publication Data

Detzler, Wayne A
  The changing church in Europe.

  (Contemporary evangelical perspectives)
  1. Europe—Church history—20th century. I. Title.
BR481.D47   274   78-11990
ISBN 0-310-37611-4

Printed in the United States of America.

To my family—
Margaret, Carol, and Mark
—for their love and encouragement

Contents

1

The Triumph of Secularism

Since 1960 the church in Europe has been plunged more deeply into the deep freeze of secularism, which had its beginning between 1870 and 1914 when the academic and labor world turned away from the church. From 1960 on, parish life in Protestant countries has quite dramatically lapsed into disuse and decay. By 1968 *Time* magazine could report concerning the continental churches: "In the traditional citadels of Christendom, grey Gothic cathedrals stand empty, mute witnesses to a rejected faith."[1]

Two years later the same international news weekly spoke of progressive paralysis in European religious life: "The churchgoer could once take comfort in the fact that he belonged to what was essentially a Christian society." *Time* writers had, however, discerned "a secular-minded culture that suggests the eclipse rather than the presence of God."[2]

No one is more astute in analyzing the European spiritual scene than Francis Schaeffer. It is his opinion that the "Christian consensus" in culture and life has melted away. Both in statistical adherence to the church and in practical attitudes, the modern European is essentially secular.[3]

In a more humorous vein, the British historian G.M. Trevelyan described himself as "a flying buttress of the Church." He supported the ecclesiastical establishment, but from the outside.[4]

European religious leaders are painfully aware of the declining fidelity of their contemporaries. A Salvation Army officer, Fred Brown, wrote *Secular Evangelism*—a book arising out of a thriving ministry in the inner city of London. Of the lads who frequented his youth club, he wrote, "For them, too, God is not dead: he never was [that is, he never existed]."[5]

Even the naive optimists who steer the unseaworthy ecumenical ship have become cognizant of the collapse of traditional religion. In the preliminary documents to the World Council of Churches' fourth Assembly at Uppsala (1968), the statement on worship lamented, "The secularization which predominates in many parts of the world offers a special challenge to our worship. . . . In worship God is affirmed—in secularization God is denied."[6]

The seed of secularism is humanism. It is the enshrining of human reason as the object of worship. All of existence is locked up in the narrow limits of human finiteness. Worst of all, it is assumed that this exaggerated humanism infuses virility into the human race. As Camus put it, "Man must choose between the tyrant God of Christian theology and being a *full man*" (italics mine).[7] Secularism is seen as a cosmic "fountain of youth."

Early in the period under discussion, leading churchmen began to register alarm. Bishop Hanns Lilje of Hanover concluded in 1962: "The era when Europe was a Christian continent lies behind us."[8]

From the traditionally liberal Union Theological Seminary in New York, the Dutch theologian Professor J.C. Hoekendijk assessed his native land. Hoekendijk described the "fourth man" in contemporary Europe. His great-grandfather had drifted away from the church. Grandfather had not even requested the baptism of his children. Consequently his father shrugged his shoulders whenever the lad asked embarrassing questions about God. Now the "fourth man" is not only a post-Christian. He is also a "post-atheist."

One is reminded of the oft-quoted quip of Søren Kierkegaard, the nineteenth-century Danish philosopher: "We are all Lutherans without having so much as a suspicion of what Lutheranism is."

Many modern writers have held up a mirror to show the state of contemporary continentals. Both serious scholars and popular periodicals portray European society as being devoid of spiritual foundations. The focus of thought and life is decidedly "this-worldly." In Europe today we see a vivid example of the conclusions reached by Harvey Cox in *The Secular City*. Modern man has a mental horizon that is coextensive with the limits of the physical universe. "He views the world not in terms of some other world but in terms of itself. He feels that any meaning to be found in the world originates in this world itself. Profane man is simply *this*-worldly."[10]

Francis Schaeffer feels that this frigid wave of despair has flooded most lands, especially those that at one time enjoyed the warming winds of the Protestant Reformation in the sixteenth century. But surely the despair is no less in Catholic Europe, as we observe in the turn to communism in Italy, France, Spain, and Portugal. Now committed Christians comprise a decided, sometimes pathetically small, minority. "Most Christians . . . continue on as if we were in the majority," Schaeffer concluded, "as though the *status quo* belongs to us. It does not."[11]

SIGNS OF SECULARISM

Secularism has reached deeper than mere theory in most European countries. Postwar generations have not only imbibed the secular spirit, they have put it into practice.

The Dutch journalist Jan van Capelleveen vividly summed up the situation when he addressed the International Congress on World Evangelization at Lausanne in 1974. Young people often regard the church as they do their own grandmother. She sits in a room full of portraits of the past. "It is wonderful to visit her for just a short time"; however, van Capelleveen conceded, "it would be impossible to live with her."[12]

Another gifted communicator is Horst Marquardt. In an article for the *International Christian Broadcasters Bulletin* he described the work-oriented West German. For him chasing the rising economic star of the *Deutsche mark* had diverted his attention from God. Most of Marquardt's contemporaries "regard Sunday not as a serious day of worship but as a break between two working weeks."[13]

This marked shift of emphasis from nominal Christianity to pragmatic atheism is seen throughout Europe. A plethora of illustrative material can be mustered to substantiate this thesis. The late American historian Kenneth Scott Latourette wrote, "The trend is toward de-Christianization of a predominantly nominal Christian population."[14]

In the Netherlands, military authorities already employ a "humanist chaplain" to serve men without religious persuasion. The Protestant chief of chaplains in Belgium is convinced that this trend will also spread to his country.

Danish secularism has snatched the headlines with reports of a film in production with the provocative title *The Love Affairs of Jesus Christ*. In it the Lord is blasphemously portrayed as a common adulterer. Does this not reflect the religious void in a country where about 2 percent attend worship regularly?[15] When the Danish national radio conducted an Easter week survey in 1974, this question was asked: "Do you think Easter and religion are related?" Only 10 percent of those interviewed saw any connection.

Even in England there is a growing secular mentality. The most widely publicized statement in this direction was the boast by Beatle John Lennon in 1966: "Christianity will go. It will vanish and shrink."[16] A decade later the Beatles have gone into liquidation, but Christianity is still alive.

A more serious analyst of the British scene is the Methodist peer and parson Lord Donald Soper. In a BBC radio interview during 1972 he lamented, "We are facing a serious decline in organized religion. I very much doubt that many of the existing organizations will survive for very long."[17] A *Daily Telegraph* report indicated in 1974 that proportionately more Russians attended church than did the British.[18]

A consequence of the religious recession in Britain is the abandonment of many church buildings. There are too many churches in Britain, due to the "Victorian orgy of church building." It is estimated that during the seventies and eighties between 2,000 and 3,000 churches will "become redundant," i.e., be closed for lack of use.[19]

When writing about continental vacations, one British travel correspondent referred incidentally to church life. The average English family abroad usually visits one or two churches in the country they visit. Bernard Hollowood, the writer, commented, "Strange really, that we usually consider one or two of them a must, because we're Church of England and therefore feel it unnecessary to underline our membership by attending more than one service a year at our local— on Christmas eve as a rule."[20]

A corollary of the surrender to secularism is seen in the visibly declining quality of life. The vicious circle of anxiety and tranquilizers is daily multiplied in many modern lives. According to medical estimates, one Briton in ten is taking tranquilizers. "Instead of religion being the opium [*sic*] of the people," Dr. Malcolm Loder of London University observed, "opium is the religion of the people."[21] This is reminiscent of of similar phenomena in America and some of the more industrialized European lands.

Prosperity has affected West Germany in a most obvious way. Small wonder that the architect of the postwar economic miracle, Ludwig Erhard, doubted the benefits of his boom. After becoming chancellor, Erhard confessed, "There is far too much German prosperity for the good of the German soul."

In the mid-sixties about 20 percent of German Protestants worshiped regularly. By the seventies this proportion had slumped to 5 percent. In the Berlin borough of Charlottenburg only .8 percent of the Lutherans are found in church on any given Sunday.[22]

Most Germans are members of either the Protestant or Catholic established church. It requires a legal act of separation to leave the church. Still during the period from 1961 to 1975 a record number of 1.2 million Protestants and 500,000 Catholics opted out of their respective churches. One bishop foresaw a further drain of 20% before the end of this century.[23]

When discussing this phenomenon of exodus, a Protestant spokesman summed up the situation frankly: "Church membership has always been considered a necessary part of man's standing in the community. As a result, our churches have just about the same public, institutionalized character as the municipal garbage collection."[24]

The mass defection from, and disaffection toward, religion can be explained by the sophistication of Germany's successful, industrialized society. Furthermore, World War II caused a serious disjuncture between the religious past and the present. Though there was a vigorous protest movement in the church against Nazi policies, there was complicity with Hitler on the part of many church leaders, and this seriously eroded popular confidence.

This explanation cannot, however, be applied to the Scandinavian countries. Still there is a strong secular flavor to life in many of those idyllic places. Recently a report leaked out that there had been formed in Norway an "Association of Heathens." This strange society embodied most of the tenets of secular thought: belief in man to the exclusion of "any higher divine power," sole human responsibility for good and evil, denial of life after death, and a utopian conviction "that man alone can realize his dreams of paradise."

It gives no cause for wonder that the Norwegian Lutheran Church should regard such developments with alarm. In the same periodical that carried the above report, Bishop Alex

Johnson was quoted as fearing that within fifty years Norway would indeed become a "nation of heathens."[25] It is possible, though not in the near future, that the Norwegian Lutheran Church may forfeit its favored position and become a "Free Folk Church." (This would involve the loss of a $16 million annual subsidy.)[26]

The next-door neighbor of Norway, Sweden, has evolved a rather sophisticated and extremely socialistic culture. In an intriguing report published by the *New York Times*, journalist Flora Lewis summed up Sweden pessimistically: "Swedes are helpful, considerate, tolerant. They ought to be the happiest, most contented people in Europe. They aren't."[27]

Alcoholism is on the increase in Sweden, especially among the young. Suicide outstrips traffic accidents as a cause of death. Between 1962 and 1971, highway deaths took 13,120 lives, but during the same period 15,993 took their own lives.[28] The Swedish government in its official publications revealed that during the two-year span of 1965 to 1967 those hospitalized for drug abuse multiplied from 828 to 2,476.[29]

As early as 1967 it was generally accepted that no more than 3 percent of all Swedes attended church more than once a year. (This even allows for the relatively lively Free Church movement.)[30] No wonder that the missionary leader Robert P. Evans estimated in 1973 that within a decade the Swedish Lutheran Church would lose its connection with the state and surrender its right to public patronage.[31]

In the face of this all-pervasive secularism, European churchmen have usually adopted a pathetic posture of capitulation. In his sermon at the anniversary of the Church Missionary Society, Dr. Colin Morris spoke disparagingly of the European church: "A 'domesticated' church can never express the plenitude of the gospel."[32]

British missionary leader Stuart Harris observed the rising tide of secularism in Europe. He laid the blame for this at the door of effete, rationalistic theology. "The decline has often been due to false and unsatisfying teaching," Harris observed. "People have grown tired of religion and the Church; they have embraced atheism, or become simply indifferent."[33]

WHERE THEOLOGIANS LEAD—OR FOLLOW

Theology in the secular seventies is reminiscent of the Lorelei legend. A massive rock towers over the Rhine River between St. Goarshausen and Kaub. The ancient poets believed that a seductive woman sat on the promontory, singing a siren song. She thus lured unsuspecting sailors to their death. Many contemporary continental theologians have exercised a similarly destructive influence.

Even Ernst Benz, professor at the Marburg University's ecumenical institute, assessed Teutonic theology critically. He spoke of a secularizing influence through which the content of religion had shrunk, stripped away by destructive critics.[34]

Professor Walter Künneth at Erlangen is much more outspoken in his criticism of the German theological scene. His caustic comments are so direct that the irreligious philosopher Joachim Kahl included them in his book, *Das Elend des Christentums* (English title: *The Misery of Christianity*). According to Künneth, "contemporary theology is characterized by a high degree of confusion."[35]

Many theologians have explained their humanistic taint by professing to adapt to modern society. They reason that secular man can accept only a humanistic religion. An American living in Belgium, George Winston, has correctly judged this trend: "Preaching that de-mythologizes the Bible also empties the churches."[36]

A German evangelical, Klaus Bockmühl, wrote about theological developments in *Christianity Today*. He spoke of the marriage between existential philosophy and Protestant theology, a union that relegates religion to realms of the mystical. In condemnation of these developments, Bockmuhl concluded: "It is the task of theology not to get drunk with foreign ideas and beat up God's children but to feed and strengthen them."[37]

After studying in America, Manfred Kober, a young German student, returned to sample the theology of his homeland. He wrote a vigorous critique in *Reformation Review*. He had studied mainly at Erlangen, but he also gained impressions of other faculties. He found that scorn was heaped upon any professor or student who accepted the miraculous elements in the Bible. Paul Althaus at Erlangen was a relative moderate in his criticism of the evangelical position. Nevertheless, when he spoke of Theodor Zahn, a defender of orthodoxy, Althaus was withering. Zahn was a very learned man, according to Althaus, "but his greatest mistake was that he tried to defend the authenticity and infallibility of the Bible."[38]

One professor sadly sized up the typical Lutheran parish. There are three thousand registered members. Of these, three hundred worship regularly, and thirty attend the midweek Bible study. Only three have a personal faith. "Unbelief is rampant," Kober concluded, "and the blame for this rests primarily with those who train the ministers—the university professors."[39]

This rejection of biblical Christianity is common to most continental theological faculties. In *The Church Before the Watching World* Francis Schaeffer concludes that the dominant tendency in current theological thought is unreconstructed rationalism. "According to rationalism, as I am using the term here, man can understand the universe by beginning from himself without any recourse to outside knowledge, specifically outside knowledge or revelation from God."[40]

Having surveyed modern theological thought in a general way, we will find a consideration of individual writers valuable. In most of them there is an abandonment of the "Godward" orientation and a "humanization" of Christianity. Since 1960 is the point of departure, a brief discussion of

Rudolf Bultmann is unavoidable. As the sixties dawned, his
star still shone in the theological sky.

During his long teaching tenure at Marburg (1921–1951),
Bultmann stood out as a pioneer of "Form Criticism." This
system of analysis breaks down the biblical text into the forms
that existed prior to the writing of Scripture, viz., pro-
nouncement stories, miracle stories, legends, Novellen
(tales), and myth. It is Bultmann's viewpoint that the gospel
narratives rest on myth. Strands of fact concerning Jesus have
been spun into an elaborate oral mythology and written down
in the Gospels. (A very late date for the Gospels allows time
for this mythology to develop.)

Concerning Jesus, Bultmann wrote, "At any rate, the
early Christians regarded him as mythological."[41] Stories of
the sick being healed, the demoniacs released, and the dead
raised are to Bultmann's thinking simply an intricate web of
fiction. Even the life of Jesus was largely fictional. The only
reality of Easter is the genuine "Easter faith" of the disciples.
They believed Jesus was alive, and he was "resurrected" in
their preaching.[42]

Since modern man cannot relate to these mythical concepts, they must be "de-mythologized." First, one must
realize that myths are bound up with an ancient world view.
Second, it is necessary to determine the meaning of these
myths for modern man and his faith.[43] The key to "demythologizing" the gospel was discovered by Bultmann in the
philosophy of Martin Heidegger, who also lectured at Marburg from 1923 to 1928. Bultmann declared his allegiance to
existential philosophy very clearly: "Existential philosophy
can offer adequate conceptions for the interpretation of the
Bible, since the interpretation of the Bible is concerned with
the understanding of existence."[44] In other words, the trick is
to determine what the biblical myth means in terms of
present-day life. Thus modern man can retain the essence of
Christianity without the "intellectual sacrifice" of believing
that miracles happened and Christ was God incarnate.

Ernst Käsemann, one of Bultmann's pupils, summed up

his mentor quite succinctly. "The constant is the self-understanding of the believer; christology is variable."[45] One can accept only present existence as reality; the life of Jesus must be trimmed and tailored to fit human life in the twentieth century. Since miracles are denied, they must be explained away. To quote Bultmann: "Jesus is not an historical fact which is capable of historical proof."[46] All that can be known is the *Dass* of Jesus' life. (One can know "that" Jesus lived and nothing else.)

If the views of Bultmann sound incredible, one can rejoice in the company of others who find them fanciful. The wise old bishop of Berlin, Otto Dibelius, accused Bultmann of bringing all spiritual truth "before the single standard of man's reason."[47]

Karl Barth, who himself was no evangelical, found Bultmann's theological gymnastics suicidal. He taunted the Marburger and exclaimed, "Thank God, Bultmann doesn't draw the consistent consequences and de-mythologize God."[48]

The biting cynic Joachim Kahl lumped Bultmann together with liberal theologians from the rationalistic past. "The theology of the de-mythologizer is no less irrational and no less authoritarian than the theology of all time." Kahl found Bultmann just as incredible as the myths he had committed himself to explain away.[49]

Speaking for many former students of Bultmann, Käsemann wrote, "As it is not uncommon today to speak of the 'school of Bultmann,' it may be allowable to emphasize that there are probably none of Bultmann's older and better-known pupils who do not adopt a thoroughly critical attitude towards the master."[50] This leads logically into a brief survey of continental, predominantly German, theology since the age of Bultmann.

According to John Macquarrie, the British chronicler of contemporary theology, Gerhard Ebeling at Zurich "may be regarded as the most influential representative of so-called 'post-Bultmannian' hermeneutics."[51]

Ebeling and many other "post-Bultmannians" reject Bultmann's sacrifice of a historical Jesus. They are confident that there is more to Jesus than simply the presumption of *Dass*, i.e., that he existed. Still skeptical, Ebeling stated his position in *Word and Faith*: "The fact that we cannot, as the 18th and 19th centuries imagined, reconstruct from the sources a biography of Jesus surely must not be confused with the idea that the historical Jesus is completely hidden from us behind the New Testament witness and totally unknown to us."[52]

Lest we be lulled into the false conception that Ebeling is an evangelical, he reminds us that Jesus is not the object of faith. He is simply an example of faith. We believe not on Jesus, but like Jesus. In this sense Jesus is the "ground of faith."[53]

A second representative of "post-Bultmannian" thought is Ernst Käsemann. Like Ebeling, Käsemann is certain that Jesus in some way represents historical reality. In fact, it was Käsemann who shocked the disciples of Bultmann at a Marburg reunion in 1953 by reopening the quest for a historical Jesus.[54]

To Käsemann, Jesus was not only a creation of apostolic proclamation. He lived and taught and his existence gave content to the apostolic *kerygma* (preaching). In his own words, "Every verse of the Gospels tells us that the origin of Christianity is not the Kerygma, not the Resurrection experience of the disciples, not the Christ-idea, but an historical event, to wit, the appearance of the Man Jesus of Nazareth . . . and His message."[55] While this sounds like a giant stride toward a biblical concept of Christ, one is disappointed by a deeper study of Käsemann. He regards much of the New Testament as fanciful embellishment of the kernel of history, which is Jesus. The miraculous acts of Jesus are not nearly as significant as the teaching of Jesus, which supercedes the Mosaic law.

Yet another example of "post-Bultmannian" thought is the theology of Ernst Fuchs. In the writings of Fuchs there is a great deal of emphasis on the "encounter" with God. We encounter the historical Jesus in the "proclamation" of the gospel. In a sense, preaching becomes not only a declaration of revelation but revelation itself. "The quest of the historical Jesus is now essentially transformed into the quest of the reality of the encounter with God in preaching."[56] Käsemann challenged this concept that the present is a revelation of God, but later writers, viz., Pannenberg and Moltmann, will show a return to this concept.

One final example of the "post-Bultmannians" is Günther Bornkamm. Like Ebeling, Käsemann, and Fuchs, he insists on the reality of a historical Jesus. To his way of thinking, there is an irrefutable link between the proclamation of the church and the historicity of Jesus. Like Bultmann, however, Bornkamm lays heavy emphasis on the existential interpretation of Scripture. One must determine how any given passage of the Bible meets the deep personal need. This cuts the heart out of any objective, historical-exegetical understanding of the text.[57]

After the sixties there developed yet another school of theology that went beyond the "post-Bultmannians." This is the so-called "Theology of Hope" represented primarily by Wolfhart Pannenberg and Jürgen Moltmann.

Pannenberg, according to the American professor John Cobb, "is fairly widely recognized to have published more substantive work in the past decade" than any other Protestant.[58] Pannenberg insists on the absolute, historical reliability of Jesus. Although the resurrection violates natural law, Pannenberg cites approvingly the historicity of the empty tomb, the post-resurrection appearances of Jesus, and the apostolic proclamation at Pentecost in Jerusalem.[59] Still Pannenberg hedged somewhat in an interview with *Christianity Today*. There were some elements, like Jesus' eating by the seaside, that were probably mythical.[60]

Pannenberg sees ultimate meaning in the hope of general resurrection. Drawing heavily from Ernst Bloch's *Das Prinzip der Hoffnung*, Pannenberg claims that man can cope with death only because there is hidden behind it "new life."[61]

Another determining doctrine in the thought of Pannenberg is the concept of history as a vehicle of revelation. It is an extension of natural revelation that embraces both the incarnation of Jesus and present time, thus universal history "can furnish the basis for a solution to the hermeneutical problem."[62]

Jürgen Moltmann is the second representative of the "Theology of Hope." He too sees the arena for divine activity and revelation in universal history. Because Jesus revealed God in history, we can face the future with hope. "Hope alone is to be called 'realistic,' because it alone takes seriously the possibilities with which all reality is fraught."[63] Because people have hope, Moltmann has dared to light again the revolutionary torch aimed at the goal of a utopia within history.[64] Moltmann speaks of steering history "on to the path towards earthly, corporeal, social reality."[65]

Although the "post-Bultmannians" and the representatives of the "Theology of Hope" differed from the relativistic existentialism of Bultmann, they continued to drag down European theology to the plain of humanism. Carl Henry has indicted contemporary theology for re-writing "the story of the Hebrew-Christian religion in terms of the naturalistic principle of unilinear evolution."[66]

Secular man has recast theology in the mold of secular, humanistic thought. Francis Schaeffer claims that Christianity "has nothing in common with either the old or the new secular rationalism."[67] Divine revelation no longer serves as the arbiter of truth. Man's reason, tainted by original sin, stands over the Bible as judge, jury, and executioner.

Samuel Külling, rector of the Free Protestant Theological Academy at Basel, addressed a gathering of Bible college teachers in 1967. His topic was "The Basis of Biblical Criticism." According to Dr. Külling, there are three motives for destructive scholarship. First, some reject the message of the Bible and they need to come to personal faith. Second, science provides the excuse for other critics. They need to have their old-fashioned view of science "de-mythologized." A final school of skeptics excises miracle elements in hopes of evangelizing secular man. These efforts have proved that a shrunken remnant of the biblical message is no more acceptable to modern man. Külling concluded, "Either the Bible is authority, or we are."

2

Ecumenism and Revolutionary Theology

The ecumenical movement was born in the early Victorian era as the offspring of evangelical piety. In 1846 European and American evangelicals met in London to form a loosely organized confederation of men committed to the foundations of biblical Christianity. Their aim was "not to create Christian union, but to confess the unity which the Church of Christ possessed as His body."[1]

In setting down its doctrinal basis, the Evangelical Alliance expressed its adherence to a rather explicit list of doctrines: the infallibility of the Bible, the immortality of the soul, the resurrection of the body, judgment by Christ, and the eternal damnation of the Christless.[2]

The Evangelical Alliance helped to maintain this unity by conducting a series of conferences. In 1854 the great Scottish missionary pioneer Alexander Duff fired the enthusiasm of evangelicals at the New York assembly. Gustav Warneck, the professor of missions at Halle, proposed at the London conference of 1888 that Protestants combine their forces to evangelize the world. When a conference took place in New York in 1900, no fewer than 162 missionary sending agencies participated, with aggregate attendance reaching 175,000. The featured speaker was Hudson Taylor, founder of the China Inland Mission.

Modern ecumenism, however, received its first major stimulus at the Edinburgh Missionary Conference in 1910. A total of 1,355 delegates met for ten days to discuss the motto "The Evangelization of the World in this Generation." John R. Mott was chairman, and he earned for himself the dubious distinction of being "father of the ecumenical movement."[3]

Out of the Edinburgh conference came the publication of the *International Review of Missions* in 1912. The continuing committee of Edinburgh was transformed in 1921 into the larger International Missionary Council. It must be noted, however, that the spores of dry rot were present in the structure from the beginning. At Edinburgh it was decided that "the missionary should seek for the nobler elements in the non-Christian religions."[4] Wrongly understood, this could lead to a toning-down of the absoluteness of the Christian message.

There was still an evangelical residue in the ecumenical movement, however, when the first Assembly met at Amsterdam in 1948. Most delegates approved of the statement "If the Gospel really is a matter of life and death, it seems intolerable that any human being now in the world should live out his life without ever having the chance to hear and receive it."[5]

From Amsterdam onward, however, the theology of the World Council of Churches began to turn from a God-centered to a man-centered alignment. In analyzing the presuppositions of the World Council of Churches, Robin Nixon penned a rather critical editorial in the *Churchman*, organ of evangelical Anglicanism. Nixon summed up the situation with this incisive sentence: "The tendency of modern theology is to be too man-centered, to concentrate too much on nature and too little on grace. This is seen again and again in the words and deeds of the World Council of Churches."[6]

The ecumenical movement as exemplified in the World Council of Churches had already slid a long way toward secularism by 1960. A brief survey of the theological decline of the World Council of Churches is germane to this work, because much of the philosophical and theological stimulus to the World Council's creed comes from European thinkers.

Pursuant to the assessment of the church in Europe, it is therefore worthwhile to examine the developments at the major conferences of the World Council of Churches since 1960.

NEW DELHI—1961

In 1961, for the first time, an assembly of the World Council of Churches was held outside predominantly Christian Europe and North America. The first assembly was the founding meeting in Amsterdam in 1948. Six years later a second assembly met in Evanston, a suburb of Chicago, where Northwestern University is located.

The third assembly at New Delhi was, therefore, a marked departure from the earlier gatherings. This was the first general meeting of the movement to take place outside the context of nominally Christian Europe and North America. Not only was the venue innovative, but the structure and composition of the World Council of Churches was also altered.

Over the New Year holiday of 1957/59, the International Missionary Council had conferred at Accra, Ghana. The World Council of Churches had urged the missionary council to become the missionary arm of the larger organization. Consequently, despite the resignation of a few evangelical members, the International Missionary Council voted at Accra to merge with the World Council of Churches. Three years later in New Delhi the merger was consummated.

The work of the International Missionary Council was taken over by the Commission on World Mission and Evangelism and the Division of World Mission and Evangelism. This merger was hailed as a needed infusion of missionary vision into the World Council. It was hoped that as a result both the missionary enterprise and the ecumenical movement would evidence a new spirit of evangelism.[7] Alas, the zeal that emerged was not according to the Scriptures, and the desire for a proclamation of the biblical message was soon eclipsed by a socially activistic concept of "presence." Peter Beyerhaus, Tübingen professor and articulate critic of the ecumenical movement, put it mildly when he wrote, "The great missionary awakening of the churches (which was expected from the 1961 merger of the International Missionary Council and the World Council of Churches) has not yet occurred."[8]

Not only was the structure of the World Council changed, but the complexion of the membership also took on a different hue. From the so-called "Third World," two Chilean Pentecostal churches and eleven African churches joined the Council. In all, twenty-three churches joined the Council at New Delhi and this expanded the number of church members represented by the movement by 71 million.

It was not the Third World churches that raised the eyebrows of World Council watchers, but the inclusion of the Russian Orthodox Church. Exiled Russians and those from other Eastern European countries raised objections to the membership of the Orthodox Church. Archbishop John of San Francisco, acting on behalf of the Russian Orthodox Church and Greek Catholics in America, abstained from voting in favor of receiving the Russian Orthodox members.[9]

Bearing in mind the recent repressive action by Russia against Hungarian freedom fighters, the refugee church in America was even more outspoken. Bishop Zoltan Becky of the Hungarian Reformed Church in the United States expressed the fear that admitting the Russians would turn the World Council's assemblies into a platform for propaganda. Bishop Becky reminded the delegates that the Russian government was "based upon the principles of an atheistic materialism and an undemocratic system of one-party dictatorship."[10] Obviously, the abstention of the refugee churches did not deter the Russian Orthodox Church from achieving recognition and membership.

Indeed the Russians did turn the World Council into a platform for preaching doctrinaire socialism. Furthermore, they abetted the ascendancy of humanism over biblical belief. Redemption soon was to be seen in terms of socialistic systems and salvation as a condition to be won by revolution. Religious persecution would no longer be defined in terms of communism's denial of freedom to worship. Instead, it would be applied to racism, sexism, and classism in Western countries.

The documents arising out of New Delhi represent an admixture of the more evangelical heritage with the politically activist elements. The Council accepted a trinitarian doctrinal statement that had the ring of biblical authenticity: "The World Council of Churches is a fellowship of churches which confess the Lord Jesus Christ as God and Saviour according to the Scriptures, and therefore seek to fulfil together their common calling to the glory of the one God, Father, Son and Holy Spirit."[11]

Another positive statement appeared in the document on "Service." Christian service was to be distinguished quite clearly from secular philanthropy. Service by the Christian "springs from and is nourished by God's costly love as revealed in Jesus Christ."[12]

Still there was the ominous whisper of a theology of liberation, which later captured the Council. Proclamation of the Christian message, according to the document on "Witness," "must mean to take seriously the secular causes of men's inability to hear or respond to our preaching." Among these qualifying elements were enumerated "the gods of this age, race, wealth, power and privilege."[13]

The stance of the Council toward these forces of oppression, real or imagined, was defined in the document on "Service." The church should employ every means short of violence to achieve racial justice. It should identify itself with the oppressed. On the subject of disarmament, it was stated that only total disarmament and the abolition of war could be considered satisfactory.[14]

By 1961 there had appeared the seeds of a theology of liberation within the World Council of Churches. To lay the blame at the feet of the South American and African Churches would be a naive simplification. Neither can one attribute the kaleidoscopic transformation of the Council to the infusion of the Russian Orthodox, or of the five Vatican observers who were first recovered at New Delhi. Rather, the political orientation in the Council's statements and actions arose from the teachings of American and European academics. Their political and theological liberalism caused them to recoil from cold-war polemics. Many embraced socialism as the only "fair" form of society. The New Left of the sixties had articulate spokesmen within the ecclesiastical establishment, and they appeared clearly at New Delhi.

UPPSALA—1968

When the fourth assembly convened at the Swedish university town of Uppsala in 1968, the theme was "Behold! I make all things new." Although the words were biblical, the concept was injected with a secular and political meaning. Philip Potter, the West Indian Methodist who now serves as general secretary of the World Council, claimed that at Uppsala the ecumenical movement turned from a "churchly" activity to a more "worldly" activity.[15] Dr. Potter meant this as a compliment, but the result for the World Council was weakness rather than strength.

Professor Hoekendijk wrote about this metamorphosis in *Planning for Mission.* "Here the idea of a *frontier* between Church and world, which serves as a line of demarcation between the saved and the unsaved, between belief and unbelief, is rejected."[16]

The application of this principle is seen in a positive attitude toward political and social revolution. The document entitled "Towards New Styles of Living" took up the subject. It declared that revolutions are to be regarded as an inevitable result of repression and that our Christian faith is relevant only when we encourage such revolutionary change.[17]

According to the framers of the document "Missions Today," political rebellion flares up when any class of people feels powerless to change its fate. It is incumbent on the Christian church to recognize the revolutionaries' plight and "the validity of their decision" to take up arms.[18] This type of situation was most evident in the area of racial prejudice.[19]

In fairness to the World Council leaders, one must also record their hesitance about using violence. In fact, it was a special contribution of the churches to develop "effective, non-violent strategies of revolution and social change."[20]

The most available application of the creed of social revolution was in regard to Vietnam. In 1968 the United States was carrying out heavy bombings of North Vietnam. Many of the American critics of the war were represented at Uppsala. Under the leadership of Paul Oestreicher, an associate secretary from the British Council of Churches, a resolution was passed in support of American army deserters, who "object to this war either because of the methods used to fight it or because, for other reasons, they believe it to be unjust."[21]

Robert McAfee Brown, a professor from California, roundly condemned the use of napalm bombs as antipersonnel weapons in Vietnam. He was joined by the Russian archpriest P. Sokolovsky who insisted that "the intervention of the United States was against the will of God."[22]

It was the implicit assumption of most delegates that the United States was a bully of international proportions. In the Vietnam war she was actively involved in repressing a popular revolution. Actually, the disciples of Ho Chi Minh were heralded as pioneers of a people's republic, a classless society free from external domination and internal injustice. The acceptance at Uppsala of this premise is an ignominious monument to the naiveté of many ecumenical enthusiasts.

Senator George McGovern, who was a candidate for the United States presidency in 1972, attended Uppsala as a Methodist layman. He commented incisively on the prevailing attitude and the use of America as a whipping boy. "No nation comes to this Assembly with clean hands," McGovern reminded the meeting.[23]

While McGovern's criticism was mainly political, others saw serious theological flaws in the work of Uppsala. John R. W. Stott was concerned that there was less interest expressed about the spiritual hunger of man than about his physical well-being. In the report "Renewal in Mission" is recorded this comment by the London Anglican: "The World Council confesses that Jesus is Lord. The Lord sends His church to preach the Good News and make disciples. I do not see the Assembly very eager to obey the Lord's command." In his valiant attempt to introduce biblical evangelism, Stott was supported by the British lay leader Sir Kenneth Grubb and R. Buana Kibongi, a pastor of the Evangelical Church of the Congo.[24]

In his annual sermon before the British and Foreign Bible Society during March 1970, Canon Douglas Webster was forthright in condemning the assembly at Uppsala: "I would hazard a guess that the time will come—perhaps soon—when those with the most knowledge and experience of real mission will consider the Uppsala report on mission to be little short of a sell-out to the diseased and confused spirit of our age." Six months after Canon Webster's solemn prophecy, there was solid evidence to substantiate his worst fears. The World Council of Churches decided to allocate $200,000 to the support of antiracist groups. Though the funds were earmarked for humanitarian purposes, among the recipients of these grants was a band of African guerilla fighters.[25] Although the Council had pledged itself to seek "non-violent strategies" of revolution, it pragmatically supported violence rather than the ballot box.

Why was Uppsala such a focal point in ecumenical history? First, there was a radical spirit abroad in the sixties. It was no less evident in Berlin than it was in Berkley. Second, evangelical Christians had begun to regard the World Council of Churches with suspicion. As they withdrew, the vacuum was filled by humanistic theologians and laymen. Third, the emotive presence of the Vietnam war on the international scene fanned the flame of discontent and disdain against establishments of both political and religious types.

BANGKOK—1973

To gauge the prevailing winds within the World Council of Churches during the sixties and seventies, it is important to discuss one conference that was not a general assembly. This is the meeting of the Commission on World Mission and Evangelism at Bangkok, which convened from December 29, 1972, until January 8, 1973. The topic of this working conference was "Salvation Today."

Only 326 delegates entered into the discussions at Bangkok, but the importance of their meeting surpassed the smallness of their number. Bangkok served to crystallize the transformation that had occurred in the World Council of Churches' concept of salvation.

One of the participants in Bangkok was Peter Beyerhaus, a professor at Tübingen. His thoughtful and devastating analysis of the conclusions reached there are presented in his book *Bangkok '73: The Beginning or End of World Mission?*

In his preface Beyerhaus summarized his conclusion concerning the conference: "Bangkok's understanding of salvation and missions was not the biblical one, but rather a syncretistic and social-political one; and further, where the Bible was apparently used, Christian assertions were ideologically undermined."[26]

As chairman of the central committee of the World Council, Mammen M. Thomas from India presented the current concept of salvation in an article in the *International Review of Missions* (April, 1973). There is a spiritual creativity behind both the technological and the socio-political revolutions occurring today. That creative spirit is the redemption of the human spirit by Christ. Ours is a day of pluralism that embraces various human situations and needs, different religious and secular societies, and various metaphysical and ideological backgrounds. To consider any single interpretation of the teaching of Jesus Christ or the salvation that he provides is impossible. Such a uniform view of Christian teaching would be possible only within the framework of religious imperialism.[27]

In the document dealing with salvation and social justice, there was explicit approval of revolution. According to the statement, many Christians serve Christ by engaging in political and economic combat against injustice and oppression. The churches must be redeemed from their bondage to the "interests of dominating classes, races and nations." There is no redemptive church unless it be liberated from complicity in institutional injustice and force.[28]

The goal of salvation is to "humanize" society, according to the prevailing viewpoint at Bangkok. This is defined in four propositions. First, salvation is freedom from the economic exploitation of man by man. Second, true redemption creates human dignity by releasing man from political oppression. Third, the result is the solidarity of all men and resistance to alienation caused by either economic or political repression. (This sounds strangely similar to the "classless society" of communistic utopianism.) Finally, the ultimate result of salvation is hope that overcomes despair.[29]

All of the statements that issued from Bangkok were united in the conviction that salvation was "this-worldly." Little was said concerning man's relationship with God. Jesus Christ was seen as a kind of super-revolutionary creating a classless utopia. The study group that defined "liberation" concluded, "We should at least be freed from the pietistic concept of salvation as primarily a private affair between an individual and God." The German report called for the *Entprivatisierung* ("de-privatizing") of salvation.[30] Ecumenical terms are subject to redefinition, depending on the prevailing theological and ecclesiastical winds.

Bangkok introduced a divorce that is horrendous in its

implications. The conference finally separated itself from the biblical view of salvation as a reconciliation of sinful man with a holy God. Salvation was redefined to bring it wholly within the confines of time and space.

Evangelicals were almost silenced by the dominant presence of those who support a socio-political view of salvation. During the preparation for the conference a detailed exegetical study of the subject was submitted by a Norwegian student group. This study was not included in the final conclusions.

A real sense of alarm pervaded the conclusions reached by Gunnar Stålsett, director of the foreign office of the Norwegian Lutheran Church. He threw out the pregnant question: "Is not the whole central message of salvation in the Christian church in danger of being made void of its biblical and historical contents?"[31]

For several years Christians in Germany had spoken out against the theological trends there. Following Bangkok, they met at Frankfurt to discuss the conclusions reached. Their meeting took place a scant six weeks after the Bangkok conference, and their opinion was predictable: "An alien understanding of salvation was presented [at Bangkok] under the influence of contemporary ideas. It has separated itself greatly from biblical foundations." The Frankfurt Konvent criticized especially the equation of redemption with the "God-is-dead" theological fad and the Maoist Cultural Revolution. It was especially alarming that Bangkok had considered the feasibility of a moratorium on sending missionaries to the Third World.[32]

By and large, David Johnson's compendium, *Uppsala to Nairobi*, is simply a statement of ecumenical thinking. It is thus worthy of deep consideration when spokesmen of the movement conclude that Bangkok will, "when viewed from the perspective of a greater span of years, prove pivotal in the history of world mission."[33]

Certainly Bangkok chiseled in stone the dogma of salvation by liberation. Biblical concepts of redemption were finally and completely subjugated to the socio-political purposes of the theology of liberation.

NAIROBI—1975

In 1975 the fifth assembly of the World Council was convened at Nairobi, Kenya. An entire edition of *The Churchman* was devoted to analyzing the study documents that had been distributed in advance. Bishop Stephen Neill contributed an article under the title, "Some Realism in the Ecumenical Illusion." This respected historian of the ecumenical movement concluded pessimistically: "Unless the Holy Spirit is very notably at work during the period which remains for preparation, and in the proceedings of the Assembly itself, Nairobi 1975 might well be the last as well as the fifth Assembly of the World Council of Churches."[34]

Neill, former professor of missions and ecumenics at Hamburg, was quite destructive in his assessment of the preliminary documents. "First impressions are of a certain theological naiveté in the material submitted," he wrote. The general tone was reminiscent of the "liberal optimism in the nineteenth century." Salvation was interpreted almost exclusively in terms of "political emancipation from alien rule."[35]

Although the general theme of Nairobi was "Jesus Christ Frees and Unites," the understanding of that theme was anything but unified. The editor of *Moody Monthly* spoke of a "minimum of unity in this most recent gathering of a diverse organization with conflicting goals and viewpoints."[36]

The keynote address at Nairobi was delivered by Robert McAfee Brown of Stanford University. His speech indicates just how perverted the theological fare was. Speaking of Jews, Hindus, Marxists, and Humanists, he said, "We can learn from them, rather than assuming that they must learn exclusively from us." His theological frame of reference was clearly the South American theology of liberation.[37]

The conclusion reached by the study group on "Confessing Christ Today" gave honor to biblical doctrine: "We are called to preach Christ crucified and risen again." A paragraph was added to interpret the proclamation of the gospel primarily in terms of social action. Just relations among men was given higher priority than justification by God.[38]

Writing for the *Daily Telegraph*, Cecil Northcott discussed "The Changing Face of the World Council of Churches." He recorded the phenomenal growth of the Christian church in South America. Half of the delegates to Nairobi came from the southern hemisphere. Then Northcott, a shrewd student of the ecclesiastical scene, warned, "The younger prophets of the southern hemisphere are said to be eager to claim the Church as a leader in their revolutionary campaigns for social justice and political freedom. Is it to be Karl Marx or Jesus Christ?"[39]

Although representatives of younger churches comprised a large bloc, they left the speech making largely to liberals from the West. Philip Potter, the executive secretary of the assembly, caused a stir when he accused Britain of "being responsible for the most racist system in history." Incensed, Sir Cyril Black, a Baptist layman and former Member of Parliament, rushed off a letter to the editor of the *Daily Telegraph*. "Surely it must now be clear that the time has come for British Churches and people to withhold further support from an organization that is so discredited as to be incapable of further useful activity," he fumed.[40]

When the prime minister of Jamaica, Michael Manley, addressed the assembly, he identified himself as "a humanist by instinct, an egalitarian in social philosophy, a democratic socialist by political commitment." Manley's dream of redemption was the triumph of Marxism over imperialism and colonialism.[41]

A concrete expression of the theological direction at Nairobi was the overwhelmingly-supported decision that money should continue to be supplied to "non-military programs of guerilla movements." The delegates defeated a motion designed to withhold funds from groups likely to "cause serious injury or the taking of life."[42]

Among evangelicals, the most eloquent spokesman at Nairobi was yet again the Anglican John R.W. Stott. He cited five fundamental beliefs that were endangered at Nairobi: a recognition of man's lostness, confidence in the gospel of God, a conviction about the uniqueness of Christ, a sense of urgency about evangelism, and a personal experience of Christ.[43] He concluded with an impassioned plea: "If justice means the securing of people's rights, is not one of their most fundamental rights the right to hear the gospel?"[44]

During the Nairobi assembly other issues arose that indicated the conservative delegates were not dormant. Two Russian laymen smuggled out a plea to the Nairobi assembly. They indicted the Council for silence in the face of severe Soviet religious persecution. The result was a resolution introduced to condemn the slaughter of Russian Christians and the imprisonment of believers.[45] When it came to the vote, the matter was buried in a subcommittee. In a show of sensitivity, Metropolitan Juvenaly from the Russian Orthodox Church stated that it was not the action of true Christian fellowship to criticize his nation.[46] It is small wonder that some delegates spoke of "a conspiracy of silence" to keep the Soviet issue from surfacing.

Some felt that there had been a serious attempt to placate the evangelicals at Nairobi. Harold Lindsell thought he detected a response to the criticism leveled at the World Council of Churches by the International Congress on World Evangelization at Lausanne in 1974.[47]

Noted missions professor Bishop Leslie Newbigin rose to the defense of the assembly. Admitting disillusionment with previous assemblies, Newbigin concluded that Nairobi had revealed "a deeper commitment to evangelism and a more profound sense of the adequacy of Jesus Christ."[48]

On balance, however, one is much less optimistic. Despite the valiant attempts of some conservative evangelicals such as John Stott, it seems as though they are very small fish swimming against a powerful torrent. In the words of N.T. Wright from Merton College, Oxford: "Particularly but sadly in the World Council of Churches, where 'salvation' has been given such a firm this-worldly orientation... evangelism often becomes simply irrelevant."[49]

CONCLUSION

Since 1960 the World Council of Churches has turned largely from a "God-centered" theology to one that is "this worldly." The most virile expression of this is its espousal of the theology of liberation.

The general secretary of the East Asian Conference of Churches, U Kyaw Than, portrayed the results at Bangkok. He spoke of a "spiritual infection which has started in Germany and... threatens to affect the whole world."[50]

Preaching at St. Paul's Cathedral in London, Bishop John Burrough of Mashonaland (with his seat in Salisbury, Rhodesia) warned of the inevitable fruits of the current theological climate: "Recently, the Church—notably the World Council of Churches and indeed the official Church of this country—has decided you must violently change the system in order to change the individual."[51] Perhaps the bishop tended to be an alarmist, but his fears are certainly not without foundation.

The marriage of Marxism and Christianity has been blessed by the World Council. The offspring are seen in the European churches. For instance, Pannenberg is losing students to Moltmann, who advocates a socialistic restructuring of society.[52]

Writing for the *Daily Telegraph*, Edward Norman, (Dean of Peterhouse, Cambridge) took as his theme "How Marx's Sirens Lure the Church." He traced the development of socialistic propaganda from Western clergymen and the World Council of Churches. Sadly, the dean declared, "Church leaders have read the signs of the times, concluded that socialism is about to succeed everywhere, and have judged it prudent, for the Church's survival, to be on the winning side."[53]

Since 1960 the fabric and pronouncements of the World Council of Churches have been systematically transformed into an instrument of social, political, and economic revolution. Consequently, the Council has created God in its own image. Philosopher Ludwig Feuerbach's fantasy has become reality in the sixties and seventies. "Man," Feuerbach said, "was the beginning, middle and end of religion; theology was anthropology."[54]

3

European Evangelicals Speak Out

At the dawn of the sixties Carl F.H. Henry bewailed the slumber of European evangelicals. His series of in-depth articles for *Christianity Today* proclaimed that winter had fallen on European theology. "The faithful remnant" was written off as a pietistic party imprisoned by "theological isolationism." Its influence was almost eclipsed by radical proponents of rationalistic European theology. In Carl Henry's very well-informed opinion, European evangelicalism was dead or dormant.[1]

A decade later, when the European Congress on Evangelism took place in Amsterdam, the chairman Gilbert Kirby declared, "I believe we have discovered authentic evangelicalism." He further defined the discovery by asserting that this was no "phony evangelicalism"; it was more articulate and influential than the "purely pietistic approach to life" that had prevailed previously.[2]

Many European churchmen have come to recognize the renaissance of evangelicalism. Bishop Stephen Neill, the chronicler of ecumenism and former professor at Hamburg, contributed to the *Churchman* on the eve of the Nairobi (1975) assembly of the World Council of Churches. "All over the world the Evangelicals are massing their forces, and in almost all churches," the bishop wrote. "The Pentecostal movement, the fastest growing movement in the Church, is still solidly anti-ecumenical. The ordinary man is just bored with the World Council of Churches."[3]

On one of his recent visits to the United States, John Stott was interviewed by *Eternity* magazine. The question was put to him: "Is the Evangelical church getting stronger?" The Anglican's answer was direct: "I think in Europe the quality is rising. . . . The standards are rising, if not the numbers."[4]

During the fifteen years under study, there has been a steady, almost spectacular emergence of an evangelical minority in Europe. From the Lutheran north to the Roman Catholic south, evangelicals have become more vocal and virile in the expression of their faith. Ecclesiastical authorities have been compelled to sit up and take notice. Fragmented for decades, the evangelicals now have discovered their unity and commenced to speak with one voice.

Evangelical Unity Rediscovered

In the early sixties European believers scarcely knew one another, yet by 1975 they had convened several significant conferences. The impetus came from overseas. During the sixties Billy Graham made strategic visits to Europe. Out of these emerged the World Congress on Evangelism in the autumn of 1966 at Berlin.

More than twelve hundred delegates from a hundred countries filled the famous *Kongresshalle* under the chairmanship of Billy Graham to discuss the theology and the practice of evangelism. From Ethiopia the venerable Emperor Haile Selassie came to address the assemblage. "The propagation of the Christian faith among nations has become a task of paramount importance in this age," the then-powerful statesman declared.[5]

Billy Graham spoke to the Congress at both the opening and the closing sessions. He felt the significance of the event very keenly and echoed the motto of the Edinburgh missionary conference of 1910. "It is my conviction," Graham thundered, "that here in Berlin could begin a movement of God that could touch the world in our generation."[6]

Indeed, the world did feel the impact of Berlin. It was Europe, however, that profited most from the Congress. Although the Berlin Wall remained, the walls of mistrust that divided European evangelicals began to crumble after Berlin.

Five years later (1971) in Amsterdam the European Congress on Evangelism took place. Under the chairmanship of London Bible College's brilliant principal Gilbert Kirby, 1,251 participants came from Europe and the Middle East. Non-Europeans comprised only 12 percent of the participants. It was a Congress led by Europeans for Europeans. The only non-European to speak was Billy Graham, whose organization underwrote the cost of the event. Half of the delegates were under forty years of age: half were laymen.[7] The dominance of aged European evangelical patriarchs was broken forever as a new class of younger leaders emerged. Most of these had been trained in the Bible colleges that have flourished in Europe since World War II.

On the dust jacket of the Congress report, *Evangelism Alert*, Gilbert Kirby explained the purpose of Amsterdam: "We will not be in Amsterdam to debate the validity of the Christian gospel but to search together for ways and means of communicating that gospel to the world today."

After Amsterdam there followed a dizzying succession of similar gatherings. Under the chairmanship of the Dutch children's evangelist Hermann ter Welle, 150 children's workers met during September 1972 in Vennes-Lausanne, Switzerland. Sixteen European nations were represented.

During June 1974 the Iberian Congress on Evangelism was convened at Madrid. One thousand evangelicals from Spain and Portugal met there to savor the heady atmosphere of freedom. The conference chairman, Reuben Gil exclaimed, "Evangelism in Spain and Portugal has entered a new day." He regarded the Congress as a "strategic and unprecedented event in the history of the Iberian church."[8] Although Spain has one of the smallest Protestant minorities in the world, more than three thousand turned out to hear the South American evangelist Luis Palau preach at a closing rally.[9]

Later in the summer of 1974 the International Congress on World Evangelization took place at Lausanne, Switzerland. In all, 2,371 delegates came, and almost a quarter of them were Europeans. Billy Graham set the tone by flinging out a challenge to the World Council of Churches: "I challenge the World Council of Churches Assembly, next year planned for Djakarta [actually held at Nairobi], to study" the Lausanne Covenant.[10] And the ecumenical meeting did, in fact, take note of that biblical statement on evangelism.

The theological voice of Lausanne was that of John Stott. In its laudatory report, *Crusade* magazine praised Stott for having "consistently managed to make both the profound simple and the simple profound." It remains an undeniable accomplishment that John Stott formulated the Lausanne Covenant in such a way that nineteen hundred delegates felt free to sign it.[11]

At Lausanne many Third World spokesmen challenged Europeans to more socially relevant missionary activity. Rene Padilla, a Manchester University Ph.D. doing student evangelism in Argentina, raised some hackles by declaring, "A Gospel that leaves untouched our life in the world . . . is not the Christian Gospel but cultural Christianity adapted to the mood of the day."[12] European and American evangelicals were well and truly shaken out of their slumber.

After Lausanne the spirit of evangelical unity continued to build. One year later Billy Graham was back in Europe for a youth congress at Brussels under the title of "Eurofest." A paucity of registrations and inept administration almost scuttled the event before it started. Still, 7,800 youngsters came from 40 European and Middle Eastern nations. The accommodations were spartan in the extreme, offering alternatives of sleeping on concrete floors or in tents. The food was served with the simplicity of a military bivouac.

Every morning the participants listened to solid Bible teaching from the Ugandan bishop Festo Kivengere and the South American evangelist Luis Palau. In the evenings, Billy Graham preached the gospel in Heysel football stadium. Serious spiritual activity was the sum and substance of the program, and the young people seemed to thrive on it. [13]

Yet another European gathering took place the following winter. Over the New Year holiday of 1976 more than 2,500 young people met at Lausanne. This conference was dubbed "Mission '76'" and organized by a committee of zealous young Bible institute graduates from the European Bible Institute at Lamorlaye, France. As students, they had participated in the European Student Missionary Association (now called The European Missionary Association). Out of this experience grew the vision for "Mission '76.'" The organizers raised $250,000 to cover all the costs, and several hundred committed their lives for missions. "Mission '76'" was yet one more evidence of evangelical stamina in Europe. [14]

One final conference must be mentioned as evidence for European evangelical unity. Under the chairmanship of John Stott, a conference of European theologians was held in the autumn of 1976 at the Belgian Bible Institute in Heverlee, Belgium. From sixteen lands, some of them in Communist eastern Europe, came more than ninety theologians. All of them claimed to be evangelicals. Among them were names that had risen to prominence during the past decade: Peter Beyerhaus of Tübingen, French theologian Henri Blocher, Klaus Bockmühl representing Switzerland, Jose Grau from Spain, and Josef Horak from Yugoslavia. An Evangelical Theological Society was formed to perpetuate this fellowship. [15]

There can be no doubt that the period of 1960 to 1976 marked for Europe the birth of a new spirit of evangelical unity. This transcended national and linguistic boundaries. It broke down for the first time the seeming impregnable barrier between the established churches and the free churches. Evangelicals have realized that the beliefs that unite them are far more weighty than the superficial matters that divide.

Evangelism, social action, and vocal opposition to rationalistic, humanistic, and ecumenical theology has forged a bond that ties together believers throughout Europe.

EVANGELICAL RENEWAL IN REFORMATION LANDS

Having surveyed the continent generally, let us now turn to individual countries. In the Reformation lands of northern Europe, evangelical life has found its most exciting expression. Germany, as birthplace of the Reformation, is a good starting point for this survey.

A phenomenon of German evangelicalism since World War II has been the relatively frequent visits of the American evangelist Billy Graham. In 1960 he returned to Europe for a series of crusades in Essen, Hamburg, and Berlin. About 700,000 heard him preach and 25,000 professed faith in Jesus Christ. In Berlin a tent was pitched just outside the Iron Curtain. This provoked protests from the Communist authorities and formed part of the malaise that ultimately led to the erection of the Wall a year later.[16]

Graham visited Germany again in 1963 and 1966. In 1970 a Europe-wide crusade was held under the title "Euro-70." Nightly meetings in Dortmund's "Westfalenhalle" were flashed by television relays to thirty-seven other cities across Europe and the United Kingdom. An aggregate of 838,000 heard Graham during the crusade. More than 15,700 professed conversion.[17]

German evangelicals not only engaged in evangelism, they also plucked up courage to confront the predominantly humanistic theology of their universities and churches. On January 12, 1966, thirty German pastors met in Hamm to found the "No Other Gospel" movement. They decided to stage a mass rally in opposition to the perverted preaching of their clerical colleagues. The theme was to be taken from Paul's protest that he could tolerate "no other gospel" (Galatians 1:6–7).[18]

The mass rally was scheduled for March 6, 1966, in the

"Westfallenhalle" at Dortmund. In preparation the committee printed 160,000 invitations explaining the new movement as "a marshalling point for all who stand true to the Bible and the confessions of the Church." On the appointed day more than 19,000 packed into the hall, while over 3,000 waited outside.[19]

From its inception the movement was something of a strange mixture embracing all who were "pietistic." For instance, Walter Künneth of Erlangen, who gave qualified credence to an inerrant Bible, nevertheless became a main spokesman. On the other hand, Heinrich Jochums, who is evangelical in the traditional sense of the word, held to an infallible Bible and the necessity for personal conversion.

In the decade since its birth, the "No Other Gospel" movement has grown steadily. The emphasis shifted from a battle against heresy to the defense of biblical doctrine. As theology became increasingly political during the late sixties and early seventies, the "No Other Gospel" movement called for a radical restriction of the church's message to the "fundamentally understood Biblical message."[20] The confessional movement resisted the inclusion of the liberal theologians Zahrnt and Käsemann in the German "Kirchentag" ("Church Day" Protestant rally). When their protest failed, the evangelicals boycotted the event in July 1967.[21] In 1975 they were strong enough to stage a counterevent to the "Kirchentag." More than forty thousand supporters of the "No Other Gospel" movement met at Stuttgart for a "Church Day Under the Word."[22]

The influence of the "No Other Gospel" advocates was expanded in 1970 through a special conference on missionary strategy in Frankfurt. Out of this meeting emerged the "Frankfurt Declaration." Salvation was declared to be a reconciliation of man with God by the death of Jesus Christ. Any theology of liberation embracing a political explanation of salvation was roundly rejected. Personal commitment to Christ was seen as the primary purpose of missions and a church composed of believers was the end result. All forms of compromise with non-Christian religions were repudiated.[23]

Over one hundred German pastors, professors, and theologians signed the "Frankfurt Declaration," and its impact was felt in mission circles worldwide. In a real sense this was a high-water mark of international influence for German evangelicals.

Less spectacular than the "No Other Gospel" movement and less well-publicized than the "Frankfurt Declaration" was the opening in 1974 of an evangelical faculty of theology at Seeheim. Speaking at the inauguration, Peter Beyerhaus hailed the new institution as a bulwark against the sociopolitical message of modern ecumenism. The leader of the new seminary is Cleon Rogers, a member of Greater Europe Mission. He remarked, "It was out of this morass of theological confusion that the call came for the founding of a theological seminary to train young people in God's Word."[24]

One further event in the German evangelical scene is worthy of comment in the limited space available. During June 1976 a youth conference was convened in Essen, Germany. From all over Germany ten thousand young people came to study the Bible and receive training in evangelism. This event, called "Christival," was climaxed by an evangelistic rally with Billy Graham. He acclaimed this "the largest evangelistic training session ever to be held on German soil."[25]

It is a small step culturally and linguistically from Germany to Switzerland. There also evangelicals have emerged as a force to be reckoned with. In 1966 Samuel Külling published a scathing attack on Biblical criticism. He noticed that it was even incipiently present in the "No Other Gospel" movement. Furthermore, he called for the establishment of a center for biblical studies.[26] It should be patterned on the Norwegian Free Faculty of Theology and the Free University of Amsterdam, he said. Further precedents for these independent institutions were the newly established Evangelical Seminary at Vaux-Sur-Seine, France, and the old Aix-en-Provence faculty that Donald Grey Barnhouse had supported.[27]

Külling persisted, and his vision became reality in 1970.

The Free Evangelical Theological Academy was opened on October 4, 1970. When he addressed the inaugural meeting, Rene Pache from Emmaus Bible Institute near Lausanne declared, "Our academy must take care to teach more than intellectual theology. . . . It must be a true prophets' school, which is competent to inculcate God's message with authority and power."[28] Time has proven the worth of this seminary at Basel, and by 1975 there were 128 young students enrolled.

A completely different training center sprang up in French-speaking Switzerland during the period under study. In 1948 Francis Schaeffer moved with his family to Huemoz. There he founded "L'Abri" ("The Shelter"). In his own words, "This is the place where the intellectual and cultural problems of the twentieth century are brought into contact with the Christian answers." By 1973, more than a million copies of Schaeffer's popular, apologetic books had been sold. They had been translated into fifteen foreign languages.[29] He also was featured in a powerful series of films depicting the decline in European culture. The title of this presentation is *How Should We Then Live?*

Yet another Reformation land is the Netherlands. There Christians have succeeded in penetrating the mass media on a scale unknown in Europe. In 1970, after prolonged negotiations with the government radio and television authorities, Dutch evangelicals were granted permission to broadcast two and a half hours on television and twelve hours on radio each week. They are allotted time on the basis of their strength in the Dutch population. More than 150,000 subscribe to the "Evangelische Omroep" (Evangelical Radio and Television, Inc.). In 1972 they leased an unused Roman Catholic Seminary and equipped it as a modern television center. The quality of their programs is such that one was selected by Dutch National Television as its entry in the Montreux Film Festival. The children's programs are popular to the point of drawing 15,000 letters for one particular presentation.[30]

The Reformation countries in central Europe have proven hospitable to evangelical activities. Germany shows the most promise, followed closely by Switzerland and the Netherlands. When one looks northward to Scandinavia, however, one discovers a very stubborn secular spirit. Still evangelicals are on the move.

By the early seventies in Sweden the so-called "Jesus Revolution" had surfaced. Newly converted young Swedes were appalled by the lame liberalism that characterized denominational Christianity. After a particularly poor Baptist Youth Conference at Gotland in 1971, an invitation was issued to a "Jesus Conference" during October in Eskilstune.

On the date announced, 250 appeared for the first "Jesus Conference." The speaker was an American—Don McFarland, dynamic leader of the Bible Club Movement in Sweden. From the beginning, heavy emphasis was placed on "teaching fundamental biblical principles for the Christian life." Seminars and teaching groups played a major role in the program.

From 1971 until 1974 two conferences were held each year. More than three thousand young people participated in these events and about eight hundred attended the ninth conference in 1976. Speakers represented every stream of Swedish Evangelical thought, but half the participants came from Baptist churches.[31]

The evangelical spirit among young Swedes has led to remarkable ventures. Perhaps the most unusual appeared in April 1974. A Norwegian coastal boat, *The Gideon*, was leased by several evangelical organizations in Sweden and fitted out with missionary and evangelistic displays. For several weeks the boat called at ports along the southern coast of Sweden. School groups, Sunday schools, and the general public came on board to see the displays and meet representatives of the missionary agencies, evangelistic organizations, and Bible institutes. This project, called *"Visionären,"* made an impact that was felt throughout Sweden. Many professed faith in Christ as a result of evangelistic meetings held on board, and missionary agencies and Bible institutes profited from the publicity.[32]

January 1977 marked yet another breakthrough for

Swedish evangelicals. Free churchmen in Gothenburg, Sweden's second largest city, organized an evangelistic crusade with Billy Graham. This was Graham's first crusade in Sweden, and the Scandinavium arena was filled, eleven thousand to thirteen thousand people attending each night. Landlines took a television relay to Stockholm, where four thousand came nightly to the Philadelphia Church. A summer crusade is projected for Stockholm before 1980, and this will be beamed by television to a dozen or more additional cities.

Finland stands out in bold contrast to secular Sweden. According to Bill Yoder, a veteran American missionary and observer of the Finnish scene, "The Finns are probably the most open people toward the Gospel in all of Europe. The State Lutheran Church has undoubtedly the strongest Evangelical, theologically conservative element of any European State Church." The Lutheran weekly paper, *Sana*, boasts a circulation of seventy thousand.[33]

In most Scandinavian countries, the Pentecostals are active. There are forty thousand Pentecostals in Finland, making them the largest free church. They send out more missionaries than the established Lutheran Church. The Pentecostal Finnish Free Foreign Mission Society has two hundred missionaries on the field, one missionary for every two hundred church members.[34]

Yet another force in the Finnish evangelical community is the People's Bible Society. Founded in 1945, it has flourished under the leadership of Veli-Pekka Toivianen. Over six hundred attend youth camps sponsored by the Bible society, and more than sixty thousand frequent retreat centers. In 1976 the People's Bible Society under Toivianen drew up an evangelistic strategy for five years. Its aim was the creation of an evangelistic outreach for each of the five hundred Lutheran parishes in the land. The potential impact can be assessed from the fact that 92 percent of all Finns are Lutherans.[35]

Like Finland, Norway is something of an evangelical northern light. In Norway 94 percent of the population is

Lutheran. There are 3,700 parishes with 1,100 pastors. The Lutherans support 17 missionary societies with 2,000 missionaries. Following the International Congress on World Evangelization in 1974, Bishop Erling Utman chaired a conference to determine the implications of the Congress for evangelism in Norway. Twenty Norwegians had attended the Congress, and 45 appeared for the follow-up session.[36]

Inter-Varsity Christian Fellowship reports strong interest among Norwegian university students. The Norwegian branch of that organization has twenty-five full-time staff members, and there are three hundred Christian Unions on campuses throughout the small country. Over ten thousand students are involved in these. Some of the opinions expressed by these students are a bit foreign to Anglo-Saxon thinking. One reporter wrote, "There is a growing group of students and former students who are politically radical and theologically conservative." A former staff member in Norway identified only by his first name, Jens, attributed spiritual awakening to the charismatic movement. "Five or six years ago we were too theoretical in our faith," he admitted. "The charismatic movement has been good for us because our faith in many ways has gone from our heads to our hearts."[37]

In bold contrast to the evangelical interest expressed in Finland and Norway, Denmark remains a continuing enigma to both Danish and foreign evangelicals. After several years of relatively successful work with Youth for Christ in Copenhagen, Mogens Larsen in 1965 organized a Billy Graham crusade for the Danish capital. Political activists tried to disrupt the meetings by throwing "stink bombs" into the "Forum." A Forum guard was hospitalized when acid was thrown into his face.[38]

Still Graham and his Danish committee persisted. As a result, more than 65,700 heard the evangelist and 681 responded to the invitation to confess Christ. The greatest result was not numerical. It was changed attitudes among Danish religious leaders. Paul Brodersen, Dean of Copenhagen Cathedral, exclaimed, "We have seen nothing like this in

Denmark since the revival of 1890–1900!" A Pentecostal minister, Kurt Mortensen of the Apostolic Church, concurred with his Lutheran colleague: "The future looks very promising now that so many different denominations are able to cooperate and the Folkskirche [established church] and free churches have shown they could stand together in this great evangelistic effort."[39]

As in most Nordic countries, the charismatic movement has gained ground rapidly. *Idea*, the information organ of the European Evangelical Alliance, commented on Denmark in its Autumn 1974 issue: "The charismatic movement has led to spiritual quickening in a number of churches, established and free."[40] This report was supported by an article in *Renewal*, the British charismatic publication. During February 1975 a charismatic conference took place in the historic Roskilde Cathedral, erected in A.D. 975. More than one thousand people gathered for the two-day event. Norwegians and Finns joined the Danes. It is not surprising that the charismatic movement has exerted such an influence in Scandinavia, for free churches are often influenced by historic Pentecostalism. To many Scandinavians the Pentecostal interpretation of sanctification is bound up inextricably with evangelical Christianity.

Although there are some bright spots in the Nordic lands, evangelicals are a small minority when compared with the total population. Furthermore, the linguistic restrictions prohibit publication of many evangelical books, thus limiting devotional and instructional literature for Scandinavian Christians.

EVANGELICAL EMANCIPATION IN CATHOLIC EUROPE

Over the recent history of Catholic Europe hovers the dominant spirit of Vatican II. When Pope John XXIII set out to lead the Catholic Church into the twentieth century, he could not have imagined the Pandora's box he was opening.

Not only the forms but to some degree also the content of Catholicism has since been called into question. This has given rein to the evangelical minorities that were held down for so long.

The post-conciliar climate has been especially felt in France. Small wonder, for since the Middle Ages France has demonstrated a puckish penchant for anticlericalism. During the past fifteen years, however, this national trait has been turned to the advantage of evangelical Christianity.

When he reported on the Billy Graham Paris crusade of 1963, Jacques Blocher estimated that the "total French Protestant 'active' community does not reach the 100,000 mark."[41] This has changed during the period under study. The annual evangelical conference meeting at Nogent Bible Institute in 1963 consisted of a few discouraged men huddled around a table, according to Jules-Marcel Nicole. In 1973 there were 300 and the conference had to be housed in the municipal hall.[42] When the first *Annuaire Evangelique* (annual report on Evangelicalism) was published in 1965, it included reports on 17 denominations with 764 churches. By 1973 this list had grown to embrace 46 denominations or associations representing 1,600 churches.

Yet another evidence of French evangelical virility is the increased interest in biblical training during the sixties and seventies. By 1962 a degree of cooperation between the foremost French Bible institutes had developed. Directors of the European Bible Institute (a Greater Europe Mission project), Nogent Bible Institute, the Brussels Bible Institute, and Emmaus Bible Institute in Switzerland met to consider the founding of an evangelical faculty of theology. Later, Baptist leader André Thobois and the Free Church's Samuel Benetrau were added to the committee. In 1967, with full accreditation by the Academie de Paris, a faculty was opened at Vaux-sur-Seine under the directorship of John Winston from the Belgian Gospel Mission. Within its first ten years enrollment has risen to a respectable fifty, with many students from the Third World coming to study there.[43]

Yet another free faculty of theology emerged in 1974. The Free Reformed Seminary was opened in Aix-en-Provence. Its confessional basis was the French (Huguenot) Confession of 1559, the La Rochelle confession. Faculty members were drawn from France, England, and Switzerland. About thirty students had registered by the second year of operation.[44]

The most visible expression of this new evangelical unity in France is "Impact '78," planned for 1977/78. A combined evangelistic effort, "Impact '78" is patterned on "Evangelism-in-Depth" and is seeking to mobilize evangelicals throughout France. Sharing the gospel with every French-speaking European is the goal, and Billy Graham will lead a climactic crusade. Operation Mobilization is printing two million tabloid Gospels of Mark for distribution on one weekend throughout France. "Impact '78" is seen as a direct result of the International Congress on World Evangelization in 1974.[45] One left-wing French author described the incipient awakening in a book bearing the title *The Corpse of God Is Wiggling*.

In central Europe, France presents a relatively encouraging picture of evangelical action, but neighboring Belgium also shows signs of life. In 1965 Bill Boerop reported that there were 36,400 Protestants in Belgium. Apart from the Reformed Church, the Belgian Gospel Mission was the most active. Founded in 1919 by Ralph Norton, the Belgian Gospel Mission had carved out a free church movement by 1965. There were 62 preaching centers serving an evangelical community of 3,810 Christians.[46] However, the evangelicals still suffered under strict legal and social restrictions. They were a disdained minority.

With the era of Vatican II a new freedom emerged. Not least among its by-products is the leadership of Cardinal Suenens, patron of the large Catholic charismatic movement. Freedom for Protestants is much more of a reality in Belgium today.

A dramatic example of this freedom was seen in 1975,

when the Belgian Bible Institute purchased the largest Jesuit Seminary in Belgium. Under the Jesuits, enrollment had slumped to the point where it was no longer feasible to operate the massive school in the Louvain suburb of Heverlee. The Belgian Bible Institute grew from 23 in 1969 to 146 in 1976.

It is one thing to see a reversal in Roman Catholic attitudes in relatively free central Europe, but even the tradition-bound nations of southern Europe have seen new liberty. By 1960 the evangelicals in Spain had gained some degree of protection before the law. The rights of evangelicals were vigorously defended after Don José Cardona became executive secretary of the Evangelical Defense Commission.[47]

Support for the evangelical cause in Spain came from an unexpected source in 1964, when Eugen Gerstenmeier, president of the West German Bundestag, visited Spain. He reprimanded the Spanish regime of Franco. "Sharing the anxieties over any restriction of Protestant missionary effort, [Gerstenmeier] stressed that evangelism is part of the very soul of Protestantism and that a denial of evangelistic opportunity infringes on Christian liberty." If Spain was sincere about entering the Common Market, Gerstenmeier insisted, she must grant religious freedom to Protestants.[48]

A combination of international pressure by men like Gerstenmeier and a revolution in Roman thought led in 1967 to a Religious Liberty Law. Under the new bill, Protestants can carry out the basic marriage and funeral ceremonies. Permission may be requested and received for public meetings outside church buildings. By 1971, the aggressive organization "Evangelism in Action" had succeeded in buying radio time on forty-four stations.[49]

Reporting on the liberalized laws in Spain, James Reapsome wrote for the *Greater Europe Report*. He attributed the freedoms to three trends: first, Spain desires to enter the European Economic Community; second, an annual influx of 20 million tourists has softened the resistance to Protestantism; and third, the Second Vatican Council declared that

Protestants are no longer heretics but "separated brethren."
Reapsome, who edits the *Evangelical Missions Quarterly*,
concluded, "Spain has the lowest percentage of evangelicals of
any Spanish-speaking country in the world, but it is as open to
Christian worship and witness as any Latin country. Spanish
Protestantism may be on the threshhold of unprecedented
opportunities."[50]

The Iberian Congress on Evangelism mentioned elsewhere helped to consolidate the gains guaranteed by the Religious Liberty Law. José Cardona, architect of the law, told
Congress delegates: "The law guarantees that authorities
must recognize the churches and their pastors, and it provides
for new schools, churches, seminaries, Protestant books and
magazines, radio broadcasts and public meetings."[51]

In neighboring Portugal freedom has come along a different route. Even during the sixties there was a good deal of
evangelical vitality in Portugal. As early as 1963 only about 10
to 30 percent of the Catholics were attending mass. More than
seventy thousand turned out to hear the Lebanese evangelist
Samuel Doctorian when he conducted a crusade in Lisbon. In
1963 there were an estimated six hundred Protestant
churches in Portugal with a total of three hundred pastors.
Evangelicals were thought to add up to about thirty
thousand.[52]

When the conservative dictatorship finally collapsed in
1974, religious change became the order of the day in Portugal. Jaime Vieira, president of the Evangelical Alliance in
Portugal, claims that they represent a total following of forty-
five thousand, a 50 percent increase over the sixties. Vieria,
hopeful for the future, says, "We now have more freedom
than ever, and we believe we should use it to spread the
Gospel."[53]

Like Spain and Portugal, Italy has long suffered severe
repression of religious dissent. Since World War II, however,
constitutional guarantees have helped to ameliorate this situation. One of the most dramatic fruits of freedom is the growth
of Pentecostal churches in Italy. At the end of World War II

there were 35 small, struggling Assemblies of God in Italy. Now there are 700 churches with a total membership of 150,000. There are not enough ministers to serve all of these congregations.[54]

Even the more traditional Protestants of Italy are enjoying new freedoms. After the European Congress on Evangelism in 1972, Italian leaders of the Plymouth Brethren called a special conference. Under a committee composed of Samuele Negri (Rimini), Paolo Moretti (Arghiani), and Georgio Brandoli (Florence), more than two hundred attended the gathering over the Easter weekend in 1972 in Florence.[55]

Following the same European Congress, Elio Milazzo, a Mennonite radio preacher, set up a provisional committee to organize an Evangelical Alliance. The purpose of the committee was threefold: first, to foster fellowship in the gospel; second, to defend the gospel against the cults; and third, furtherance of evangelism. At the Lausanne Congress in 1974 an Italian Evangelical Alliance was formed. Although there were some leadership problems in the beginning, it is now taking shape as a voice for Italian evangelicalism.[56]

THE BALANCE SHEET

While evangelicals in Europe have emerged as a powerful voice for the gospel, political liberalism has softened opposition in the southern European countries where dictatorship long petrified the political and religious scene. Since Vatican II the Roman Catholic Church has also taken a much more tolerant attitude toward Protestants in general. The evangelical emphasis on the Bible has capitalized on the climate of receptivity among many Catholics. Even the charismatic movement, which is not sanctioned by all evangelicals, has broken down walls of distrust between Catholics and Protestants.

During the sixties and seventies American missionaries have played an important role in supporting European evangelicals. Bible institutes have been formed to train leaders. Churches are being established in a few of Europe's 250,000 unchurched towns and villages. Literature has been produced and distributed, not least by Operation Mobilization. An entirely new radio ministry has been created by Trans World Radio, using leased facilities in Monaco.

If 1976 was for the United States the "Year of the Evangelicals," it was in a limited way also true of Europe. During the decades ahead there will be consolidation and creativity designed to expand still further the influence of the gospel. American missionaries will have fulfilled their mission when Europeans seize leadership of the evangelical movement.

4

Cults From East and West

"We've got Jehovah's Witnesses quite strongly, and the Mormons," British evangelical leader Morgan Derham told an *Eternity* interviewer. "We've also had Transcendental Meditation, but not in a big way."[1] Throughout Europe, from the British Isles to the Communist countries, the cults are advancing. Some are moving rapidly in an organized fashion. Others are creeping like a lava flow. Everywhere they are on the move.

In 1907 there were only seven cults in Germany, totalling about 35,000 members. By 1965 the picture had changed completely. There were 90 different cults boasting a combined membership of 800,000. This phenomenal growth occurred despite the fact that experts felt the cults had reached their peak in 1958.[2]

When one investigates more deeply, the cause for cultic growth emerges clearly. The spiritual stagnation of the religious establishment in many European countries has created a vacuum into which the cults intrude.

There are four further reasons why the cults succeed. First, they capitalize on the ignorance of nominal Christians. In European lands where church membership is often coextensive with the population (e.g., most Frenchmen are baptized at birth into the Catholic Church), there are many who have no clear idea of what their church teaches. Cults play on this lack of knowledge in winning converts.

Second, the representatives of the cults are well trained for their task of winning proselytes. Local leaders prime Jehovah's Witnesses to meet virtually all objections as they go from door to door. The young Americans who disseminate the Mormon message are likewise well educated to answer the superficial questions of nominal Christians.

Third, members of the cults exhibit a zeal that is unknown in traditional churches. Great personal affection is shown to any potential convert. Services tend to be much warmer than the liturgical worship of either established Protestantism or Roman Catholicism.

Fourth, the pseudo-Christian name of many cults confuses the uninformed. Who can tell that The Church of Jesus Christ of Latter Day Saints is not within the framework of Christianity? Is not the name of Jesus Christ enshrined in the church's official name? Again, how is one to know that the Children of God are not simply an enthusiastic collection of Jesus people?

Cultic confusion abounds in Europe and has done so since the early sixties. The multiplication of alternatives simply deepens the confusion. In this study, the cults are roughly divided into two groups: the older cults originating mainly in North America and the newer movements emanating from Asia.

THE APPEAL OF HISTORIC AMERICAN CULTS

The Jehovah's Witnesses

No cult has better adapted to the European scene than the Jehovah's Witnesses. Kingdom Halls abound throughout the continent, and they are not blighted by the typically American appearance of the Mormon churches.

In 1881 two Witnesses sailed from the United States for England. They brought 165,000 tracts with them.[3] Since then, this river of literature has swollen to become a flood. By 1965 the Jehovah's Witnesses had 345,000 "publishers" in

Europe. These are missionaries who are laymen and are almost without exception Europeans.[4] One-third of the Jehovah's Witnesses in the world are in Europe.

Statistics produced by the Jehovah's Witnesses are mind-boggling. There are 2,021,432 members throughout the world. In 1975 they conducted 1,351,404 Bible studies and baptized 297,872 new members. They spent a total of 371,132,570 hours in evangelism and distributed 273,238,018 magazines.[5]

In the 1973 edition of the *Yearbook of the Jehovah's Witnesses*, it was reported that there were 895 congregations in Britain. Some of the methods used to produce this number were outlined in the Yearbook. In 1960, 245 families moved to needy areas in an effort to establish the cult. During 1963 members spent 7 million hours in door-to-door evangelism and baptized 3,079 new converts. The Word of Truth Assembly attracted 31,501 to Edinburgh in 1965, and subsidiary conventions were held in Cardiff, Leicester, and London. At a mass meeting in Wembley Stadium during 1969, there were 88,416 present. Divine Rulership Assemblies were held in 1972 at nine different centers, at which attendance totalled 91,226.[6]

On the continent their work is not quite so easy. Joachim Heldt, in his popular survey of religion in Germany, devoted a chapter to the cults. It was his discovery that the Jehovah's Witnesses spent 1,700 hours to make one convert.[7] Still, the number of "publishers" in Germany grew between 1950 and 1965 from a substantial 26,805 to almost triple that number—76,393.[8]

Danish Jehovah's Witnesses have an aura of triumph about them. R.E. Abrahamson wrote in the 1973 Yearbook: "Regardless of what the problems are, the National [Lutheran] Church avoids confrontation, limping along between many opinions, itself a dying cause."[9]

While Protestant missionaries lament the difficulty in reaching Catholic Europe, the Witnesses seem to be successful. In secular and anti-American France, baptisms by the

Witnesses increased from 6,476 in 1973 to 8,679 in 1974. With 40,000 thoroughly indigenized home Bible studies, the French Witnesses have established a solid base for expansion.[10]

In Italy the growth rate is staggering. Ronald Fisher wrote about this in an excellent article for the *Evangelical Missions Quarterly*. Fisher states that "no church anywhere has achieved the growth rate maintained by Italy's Jehovah's Witnesses."[11] According to official statistics, the Jehovah's Witnesses in Italy have burgeoned from 2,587 "publishers" (or missionaries) in 1954 to an astounding 41,141 in 1974.[12]

Spain presents a similar picture of significant growth. In 1950 there were 93 members in that country. By 1970, despite the dictatorship, there were 10,086 members in 112 Kingdom Halls.[13] By 1973 it was estimated that the Witnesses had 40,000 Spanish members, compared with a Protestant minority of 30,000. Jehovah's Witnesses had established 200 congregations.[14]

The revolution in Portugal during April 1974 threw open the floodgates of freedom. By the end of that year there were in Portugal 13,111 publishers of the Jehovah's Witnesses' message.[15] One reliable observer estimated that seventy Kingdom Halls had been built between 1974 and 1976 in Portugal. Converts were being won at an average of ten per day.

In Communist lands, there are 100,936 publishers, according to Kurt Hutten.[16] In his excellent survey of Eastern Europe, Trevor Beeson devoted some space to the Witnesses. He concluded, "Persecution seems not to curb the activities of the Witnesses. Astonishingly, in the circumstances, they still engage in door-to-door visiting and even publish and distribute literature containing criticism of the government."[17]

Mormonism

The Jehovah's Witnesses have a thoroughly European operation and show success. On the other hand, the Mormons are also succeeding through the use of dedicated young

American missionaries. According to German expert Hutten, Mormon "missionary activity was always great. Since the second World War it has increased even more."[18] World membership in the Church of Jesus Christ of Latter Day Saints (Mormonism) has risen precipitously from 2.39 million in 1965 to a staggering 3.57 million ten years later.[19]

During the early sixties Mormonism commenced its meteoric growth. Between 1957 and 1964, worldwide conversions to Mormonism grew by 285 percent. By 1964 the Mormons were erecting three hundred chapels per year— almost one a day. At that time there were 13,371 missionaries in the world, most of whom were young Americans between nineteen and twenty-three years old, working without salary and supported by their families.[20]

In the sixties David O. McKay, the patriarchal president of the Mormons, declared a plan of action aimed at evangelizing Britain. First, every member was to function as a missionary. Second, young men were obliged to serve as full-time missionaries for two years. Third, every marriage was to be properly sealed in the Temple.[21] As a result, Mormonism in Britain mushroomed from ten thousand in 1956 to an astounding one hundred thousand twenty years later.[22]

The first Mormon missionaries, George P. Dykes and John Taylor, reached Hamburg in 1851. By 1960 there were twenty thousand German members. Combined membership in Germany, Austria, Switzerland, and Scandinavia was forty-five thousand.[23] Continental Protestants seem to be somewhat more reticent to convert to a cult than do either British or American Protestants.

Despite the relatively smaller size of continental Mormonism, the members are no less zealous than the Anglo-Saxons. When Spencer W. Kimball, the eighty-two-year-old successor to McKay, spoke at a conference in Helsinki, two thousand out of thirty-five hundred Finnish Mormons attended. In 1976 Kimball could report a total missionary force of twenty-four thousand, a doubling of the workers since 1960.[24]

A Greater Europe Mission member working in Copenhagen interviewed the leader of Danish Mormons, who reported that there were 150 in that super secular country.[25] According to the Emmaus Correspondence School in France, there are 600 American Mormons at work converting Catholics in that land. Mormons started their work in Spain in 1962, and by 1971 they had opened eleven chapels.[26]

In 1968 a missionary at work in Austria reported on Mormonism there. Although the Mormons had entered that country as late as 1960, they had made their presence felt with a massive one thousand missionaries. By 1968 that number had grown to twenty-four hundred. The young Americans spent up to seventy hours each week in their evangelistic work. According to David L. Brown, a law student from Salt Lake City, "Austria is a hard mission field, not because it is Catholic, but because it is tradition-bound."[27]

The *Dublin Sunday Press* carried a pictorial report on Mormonism in Eire during January 1976. The young zealots struck at the heart of Irish Catholicism when they argued, "Our President is infallible all the time. Your Pope is only infallible when he speaks *ex cathedra*, that is, on matters of dogma." During 1975 the 170 Mormon missionaries in Eire baptized 150 converts. Their aim for 1976 was 850. One Irishman in ten opens the door to talk with Mormons.[28]

Children of God
A new contribution to the confusion of cults is the Children of God movement. In 1971 six representatives, including leader Moses (David Berg), moved into a factory in Bromley, Kent. There they established a commune. Early press reports portrayed them as a happy group of Jesus People. They lived simply but apparently piously, and they taught only the Bible to their children. Moses' daughter Faith claimed, "We present an alternative way of life to the world-system of materialism, hypocrisy in established religion, and twentieth-century society."[29] It all sounded a bit naive and utopian, but generally quite harmless.

By August 1972 there were more reports in the papers. The *Daily Telegraph* carried an interview with Canaan, an erstwhile land agent from Lincolnshire. "I found a haven of peace in the Children of God center," Canaan professed. "Our mission is to spread the word of Jesus throughout the world."[30] Canaan appeared to be absolutely sincere, and his dedication was attested by the total denial of previous possessions and comforts.

The same month a report in the *New York Times* described the dimensions of the Children of God. There were 2,000 members in 115 colonies. Of these, 31 colonies with 500 members were outside the United States, mostly in England.[31] It is surprising that the Children of God commanded such spectacular press coverage for a relatively small movement.

Within a year of these reports, the clan started to go sour. In January 1973 John Hunt, M.P., protested to the British Parliament about the movement, which by then had between two and three thousand members in Europe. Hunt was acting on the complaint of a constituent from Bromley who lost both some property and his children to the cult. Scotland Yard could find nothing illegal in the movement.[32] Still there remained allegations of brainwashing and kidnapping against the Children of God.

The leader, who called himself Moses, disappeared from Bromley and hid away in Europe. From his seclusion Moses issues frequent revelations called "Mo Letters." By 1974 these had become increasingly sexual in their orientation. Moses sent his children Hosea and Faith, both in their early twenties, to visit Colonel Muammar Gaddafi, the Lybian strongman.

The Children of God pitchmen push pornography on the streets of England. From Stoke-on-Trent came reports that one young representative had attracted customers by calling, "Want to read something that is sexy, something that'll turn you on?" Called "Les Enfants de Dieu" in France, they pull out all the stops and make any necessary compromise to win converts. Moses instructed French pushers of the party line, "Kiss the Pope's foot if necessary" to woo followers. *Le Monde* naively praised them as "missionaries in blue jeans."[33]

Although the "Mo Letters" are still rolling off the presses and pitchmen stop passersby in most European cities, one has the impression that fewer are actually being taken in. Most now realize the implicit danger in the Children of God, and they are regarded more as a nuisance than a threat.

Armstrong's Worldwide Church

Another American invention is Armstrong's Worldwide Church. Playing the apocalyptic scaremongers, Garner Ted Armstrong and his father, Herbert, have deceived thousands. They have offices in London, Stockholm, Oslo, Århus (Denmark), and Utrecht (Holland).[34] *Plain Truth*, the propaganda organ of the Armstrongs' Worldwide Church, is given away in most railway stations and airports throughout Europe. Its slick appearance attracts a respectable readership.

During 1975 Armstrong's empire in England showed serious cracks. British leaders Charles Hunting and Richard Plache criticized Garner Ted Armstrong's well-known sexual escapades. Both of the Britons were suspended. Further points of conflict were numerous. Second marriages after divorce were ordered by Armstrong to be broken up. The faithful were forbidden to seek medical help, and when they did they were accused of lacking faith. Ministers lived in luxury, while the members suffered poverty. Armstrong claimed that only members of his church were true believers; all others were heretics.[35] This exclusivism almost always characterizes cults. In this way they justify their existence.

The New Apostolic Church

One further cult of western origin should be considered—Germany's New Apostolic Church. Arising out of the Catholic Apostolic Church in Holland in the last century, the New Apostolic Church places heavy emphasis on a self-perpetuating apostolate. All revelation comes through the apostles, and salvation is communicated by them through baptism. Capitalizing on most German Protestants' ignorance of the Holy Spirit, the New Apostolic Church has shown remarkable growth since World War II. In 1953 the New Apostolic membership in Germany was 343,113. Within a decade this had doubled to 700,000.[36] According to Trevor Beeson, there were 80,000 members in the German Democratic Republic during the mid-seventies.[37]

The traditional cults and their modern relatives have exhibited remarkable virility in Europe. The reason is simply secularism and the spiritual vacuum it causes. Historic established religion cannot win a hearing from many modern Europeans. Theological liberalism and the institutional character of the established churches have effectively repelled modern man. Daniel Jenkins, in his survey *The British: Their Identity and Religion,* pinpointed the appeal of cults: "English people join American sects like the Jehovah's Witnesses, whose tenets and style of life represent a sustained protest against many aspects of life in the modern world, and not least against nationalism."[38]

EASTERN CULTS POPULARIZE MYSTICISM

Since about 1970 a new wave of cultic activity has swept over Europe. These are the mystical eastern cults that originate in Asia, especially India. They are essentially self-hypnotic movements employing meditation to lift devotees out of the morass of mundane concern. Exploiting the counterculture's revulsion against bald materialism, they attract many young Europeans and not a few middle-aged seekers. Through this meditative activity one turns the back on both the egalitarian materialism of socialism and the aristocratic snobbery of capitalism.

The Divine Light Mission

One of the most well-known eastern cults is the Divine Light Mission with the young Guru Maharaj Ji at its head. In a helpful pamphlet, M.C. Burrell reports that the Divine Light Mission was founded in 1960 by Shri Maharaj Ji, father of the present Guru. At the tender age of eight, Guru Maharaj Ji succeeded his deceased father. The boy Guru took a world tour in 1971, and two years later he already had 10,000 followers in England. In 1973 the cult staged a "Summer Festival of Love and Light" at Alexandra Palace.[39]

The Divine Light Mission is marked by the patterns of traditional Sikhism. The individual follower, known as "Atman," has as his goal to achieve spiritual oneness with his "Brahman," Ultimate Reality. "Samsara," the transmigration of souls, plays an important part in achieving this state of mystical unity with the Ultimate. Salvation is defined in terms of release from reincarnation, the cycle of birth and rebirth.[40]

Salvation for the followers of Maharaj Ji is achieved through "constant meditation" that results in the merging of man's mind with the Divine Mind. Jesus is viewed as an early incarnation of Ultimate Reality, and the present pedestrian Guru is another revelation placed on the same level with the Lord Jesus Christ. The Divine Light Mission embraces all sacred writings, since "all Scriptures glorify Divine Knowledge." There is no qualitative difference between the Sikh Upanishads (800–300 B.C.) and the Bible.[41]

Followers of the Divine Light Mission are divided into about seventy Ashrams, or communities, throughout the United Kingdom and Europe. There are ten thousand followers in Britain, and half that number on the continent. Many have forsaken all that they possess to follow the Guru.[42]

The whole meditative empire almost collapsed in April 1975 when the teenaged Guru, then 17, was disowned by his mother, Shri Mataji. She castigated her son as "a playboy, not a holy man." In the previous year he had married a former airline hostess, twenty-four-year-old Marilyn Lois Johnson from the United States. From India, Shri Mataji issued the following excommunication of her wayward Guru son: "Therefore, with a heavy heart, I along with eight million followers in India devoted to this Mission denounce him and his activities and hereby remove him from the Mission as he has fallen from the spiritual path."[43]

This did not deter the young, enterprising Guru and his followers in America and Europe. Furthermore, the divine daughter-in-law did not revere the Guru's mother.[44] By February 1976 the storm had been weathered and a Guru spokesman, Robert Mishler from Denver, confidently asserted, "I think we've seen the last of her" (the Divine Mother of the Guru).[45]

The Unification Church

A second eastern cult that rivals the Divine Light Mission in flamboyance is the Unification Church. At its head is the Korean millionaire Sun Myung Moon. Its scriptures are his *Divine Principle*. Moon modestly describes himself as "the incarnation of God." It is his messianic mission to complete the unfinished work of Jesus Christ. Says Moon, "God is now throwing Christianity away and is now establishing a new religion." Some day all religions and societies will be unified under the messiah Moon.[46]

By the summer of 1976 Moon had gathered three thousand followers in Britain, and two thousand in the Netherlands. There were one thousand in France and the movement was popularized by an hour-long interview on French national television.[47] But it is especially in Germany that the "Moonies" have multiplied. Sun Myung Moon has said, "I am concentrating very much on West Germany, because Germany is the backbone of Europe."[48]

To win young converts, the Unification Church employs shady methods characterized by kidnapping and brainwashing. During May 1976 concerned parents in Britain formed an association called "Family Action Information and Rescue." Young people had been snatched from their families and brainwashed into a new allegiance to "their new Father," i.e.,

Moon. They were deprived of sleep for hours and indoctrinated by "Korean-style" lectures. Each day they were obliged to bow before a picture of Moon. In May 1976 Peter Rose, M.P. from Manchester, reported the Unification Church to the House of Commons in London: "Its sophisticated brainwashing techniques, its efforts to split youngsters from their families and give up their worldly goods are equally a danger to health and a matter of concern."[49]

In many European countries as well as the United States the Unification Church came into conflict with the law. Its financial machinations have aroused suspicion, as real estate has been amassed to give a financial basis. Reports of illegal and almost inhumane treatment of the faithful continue to arise.

The International Society of Krishna Consciousness

Both the Divine Light Mission and the Unification Church have commanded the notice of the mass media. Other eastern cults are not publicized as frequently. One of these is the International Society of Krishna Consciousness. As early as 1971, England's *Crusade* magazine reported the presence of saffron-robed Krishna followers. The movement was extremely nebulous in its doctrinal definitions. In fact, the disciples characterized their beliefs as "sublime and easy."[50]

Back to Godhead is the British organ of the movement, which acclaims the crusty old Indian A.C. Bhaktivedanta, Swami Prabhupāda, as its head. Their literature tries valiantly to bring Christianity under the umbrella of Krishna Consciousness. Snila Prabhupāda writes from Frankfurt: "'Christos' is Greek for Krsta, 'Christ,' Krsta Krsna. . . . Ultimately you are addressing the same Supreme Personality of Godhead."[51]

The same sort of syncretism mars their view of holy writings. Absolute truth is contained in all the great Scriptures. The oldest are the Vedic literature. The Bible is simply a later version. Salvation comes through the incessant chanting of "Hare Krishna," the "Krishna mantra." By this mindless means one achieves absolute unity with, and love for, God.[52]

The Hindu roots are seen in a strict prohibition against killing any living thing. "Thou shalt not kill" is violated, according to the spokesmen, in the slaughter house. True love to God means not killing his creation, especially dumb animals.[53] It is strange indeed, then, that a raid on the Taunus Mountains headquarters of the sect outside Frankfurt turned up several weapons. That German center produced a monthly income of $90,000 by book sales, incense peddling, and begging. Of the monthly income, $2,000 is sent to the headquarters of Hare Krishna in Bombay.[54]

Although its followers are not numerous, Hare Krishna has spread widely in Europe. Like other cults it plays upon the secular spirit of the age. The German leader Srila wrote, "In many places we have bought churches that were practically closed because no one was going there. In London I saw hundreds of churches that were closed or used for mundane purposes." Hare Krishna operates centers in Amsterdam, Berlin, Edinburgh, Frankfurt, Geneva, London, Paris, Rome, and Stockholm.[55]

Transcendental Meditation

One more mystical movement claims our attention. It is the more dangerous because of its seemingly innocent appeal to the public. In the sixties Maharishi Mahesh Yogi introduced the disillusioned Beatles to Transcendental Meditation. By 1975 he was in a position to hold a rally in the Albert Hall of London. Estimates are that thirty-four thousand practice Transcendental Meditation in Britain. "It's a simple technique of deep relaxation," declared one teacher in southern England.[56]

In 1974 Jack Forem, an American coordinator, wrote a general survey of the movement. Its roots are not very deep; they go back to 1961 when the Maharishi studied with his master in the high Himalayas. In 1972 a plan of action was drafted to organize thirty-six hundred teaching centers throughout the world. These centers would train one thousand teachers each and thus provide sufficient masters to reach the entire world population of 3.6 billion in 1972.[57]

The Maharishi said in January 1971: "We do not go by what the world has been. We go by what the world should be. We are planning today for the happiness of every man on earth."[58] The world began to take notice in the seventies. In 1971 a group of eight hundred new teachers met on Majorca for a conference. By the next year there were two thousand teachers of Transcendental Meditation in Italy.[59] The "Spiritual Regeneration Movement," the Maharishi's British branch, was enlisting an average of five hundred new pupils each month by 1973.[60]

In 1975 a Danish Conference on Transcendental Meditation was held. About ten thousand Danes were believed to have enrolled in courses designed to teach meditation.[61] Germany has fifty-four thousand meditators. The Maharishi European Research University is located at Weggis, Switzerland.[62] The world-wide expansion of transcendental meditation is masterminded by a computer headquarters at Seelisberg, high in the Swiss mountains.[63]

The eastern religions emphasize the exotic and thus attract many venturesome Europeans who are bored with the affluent society. They also proclaim a release from the anxieties and tensions of the twentieth-century rat race, and this captures the interest of the tranquilizer set. Declaring that they respect traditional Christianity, the eastern religions overcome any superficial resistance by nominal Protestants and Catholics. However, once inside, the initiates have demands placed on them—demands that rapidly alienate them from their Christian upbringing.

THE OCCULT: OLDEST CULT OF ALL

Documentary evidence concerning the occult must be used with great caution. This also applies to material taken from interviews with those who have been involved with it or have helped people disturbed by demonic activity. Accepting these limitations, there is still much that can be said about occultic experience in modern Europe.

Secular Europeans deny the relevance of religion and question the miraculous element in Christianity, but many seem to swallow uncritically the demonic manifestations. Germany presents the most obvious example of occultic power. Somehow the barbaric pre-Christian religion of Germany has survived over a millennium of official Christianity. It is estimated that there are eighty-five thousand occultic functionaries in West Germany, about twice as many as there are Protestant clergymen.[64] In his popular presentation of demonic phenomena, Peter Mayer estimates that three million West Germans are involved in spiritism.[65]

The occurrences of the occult are numerous. Many medical men prefer the pendulum to the microscope in the diagnosis of disease. The pendulum is allowed to swing over an ill person's body; the place over which it comes to rest is determined to be the affected part. It is strongly rumored that this method of diagnosis occurs even in university clinics.[66]

Heinrich Kemner, a well-known Lutheran evangelist, commented candidly in his autobiography: "Only after 30 years did I discover a sorcerer in my own church. Traditional religion is completely compatible with white magic. Many will pay any price to obtain healing."[67]

When "Teen Challenge" began its work in Germany, the youth workers discovered yet another example of the occult. Demonic possession was found to be closely linked with drug dependence. Addiction was often an external symptom of occultic connection.[68]

Even in England, where there is a large evangelical minority, there are cases of occultic oppression. In 1965 the Exeter Report exposed the extent of the occult in Britain.[69] Writing for the *Wall Street Journal*, London correspondent Richard F. Jensen claimed that exorcism in England was "quite literally an everyday affair." He further estimated that three million Britons were self-styled spiritualists. Jensen drew heavily on the experiences of Christopher Neil-Smith of Hampstead and also Henry Cooper, exorcism advisor to the Bishop of London. [70]

In the wake of a particularly dramatic exorcism at Barnsley in 1975, the exorcised man, Michael Taylor, killed his wife. This brought into national focus the whole question of exorcism. Bishop Treacy of Wakefield took to task the vicar of Barnsley, Peter Vincent, who carried out the exorcism. The bishop dismissed exorcism by saying "The film *The Exorcist* focused a great deal of public attention on this type of thing. . . . Suggestible people have come to see themselves in need of exorcism."[71]

Many people take demons more seriously than the bishop does. One Member of Parliament estimated that 78 percent of all secondary students had been in touch with a wizard or a witch.[72] At Hainault, Essex, Trevor Dearing conducted an exorcism service that was carried on Independent Television. Many were fascinated, but William Sargeant, the resident psychiatrist at Independent Television, dismissed the whole affair as "a tremendous show."[73]

Like Germany and Britain, Switzerland is the scene of frequent occultic experiences. While visiting Switzerland, Heinz Strupler of the Sonnenberg Bible School reported on interviews he had conducted. From Oberägeri came the report of an incident involving two women. Both faithful Catholics, they agreed that whoever died first would return to visit the second. In due time one passed away; then she came back to visit her friend in the church.

A piano teacher lured one of her pupils into the occult by playing a hypnotic tape recording. Thereafter, every time the young student heard a tape from a spiritist, she fell into a trance.

Like many young people, a girl in Zurich dedicated her life to Satan. She was to sign a pact in blood promising to serve the devil. The blood of a slain pig was used in this blasphemous ceremony.[74] Stories like these abound in Switzerland. The high mountains provide many isolated villages where pre-Christian paganism flourishes. Also, in many cases traditional religion has achieved something of a peaceful coexistence with demonic functionaries.

While many progressive Protestants and Catholics express skepticism concerning the occult, and not a few write this subject off as a figment of imagination, the official Catholic line is much more realistic. In a recent fourteen-column report published by the Vatican's official *L'Osservatore Romano,* the pope stated his position on spiritism. He called demonology "a very important chapter in Catholic doctrine that ought to be studied again, although this is not being done much today."[75]

In France fortune tellers have a thriving business. It is reliably reported that more than 100,000 Frenchmen visit a fortune teller every day. There are 6,000 known soothsayers in the land. In Paris there is one such charlatan for every 120 Parisians, compared with one doctor for every 514 and one priest for every 5,000.[76]

In his fascinating analysis of France, Frank Orna-Ornstein discussed the occult. He referred to the Black Mass, which was frequently celebrated in the Latin Quarter of the capital. A lawyer casts spells to help wealthy women dispose of their inconvenient husbands. Frenchmen were known to spend about $7.5 million per year on sorcery. Even rural priests were often practitioners.[77]

CONCLUSION

Even the most conservative analysis of Europe must take account of modern cultic and occultic advances. The cults appeal mainly to those who are disenchanted with traditional religious forms. They have found little or no relevance in either Protestantism or Catholicism, thus they turn to the intensely personal proclaimers of a new message, be it the older American cults or the new mystical eastern religions.

The occult is usually a spiritual spider web. In search of a word from a departed loved one, the unsuspecting person seeks out a medium. Serious sickness baffles the medical profession and the concerned loved one enlists the aid of a sorcerer. Since the spate of supernaturalist films, e.g., *The Exorcist*, *The Omen*, many mentally ill people have looked for a quick solution in exorcism. The end result is the same: bondage to the dark forces of spiritism. Though reliable documentation is difficult to obtain, the problem is serious enough to trap thousands of modern Europeans.

5

The Legacy of Vatican II

The Second Vatican Council (1962–65) was for the Roman Catholic Church a turning point. Conservatives regarded it as a precipitous plunge toward anarchy. For progressives it was a small step in the right direction. Millions of Catholics caught in the middle realize that the council has irrevocably changed the faith they hold.

Peter Hebblethwaite in his emotive book, *The Runaway Church*, presents a progressive interpretation: "At its best the transition from pre-conciliar to post-conciliar was one from arrogance to humility, from unjustifiable certainty to legitimate doubt, from swagger to stammer, from triumphalism to sharing 'the joys and the hopes, the griefs and the anxieties of the men of this age!'"[1]

Along with other Protestant scholars, Karl Barth was invited to attend the council as an observer. His impressions and questions were published in the delightful little volume, *Ad Limina Apostolorum: An Appraisal of Vatican II*. The Basel professor was quite enthusiastic about developments in the Catholic Church. He hailed the new emphasis on Christ and the authority of the Bible. Preaching was also expected to take a more prominent place in Catholic worship.[2]

When writing to Yves Congar, Barth said that mariology had been acknowledged only out of a sense of duty rather than conviction. Important statements were largely devoid of reference to the "Blessed Virgin." If Mary was mentioned, it was essentially a matter of window dressing to palliate the conservatives.[3]

On balance, however, Barth was under no illusions that "Roman Catholics might become 'evangelical.'" They had not finally abandoned the bones of contention: mariology and papal infallibility. Still, Barth urged his Protestant brethren to rejoice over the incipient signs of renewal in the Roman Church.[4]

Change was in the wind, and Vatican II exposed this to the eyes of the world. Hebblethwaite caught the atmosphere in a quote from Malachi Martin's *Three Popes and a Cardinal*: "Well before the year 2000," Martin theorized, "there will no longer be an institution recognizable as the Roman Catholic and Apostolic Church of today."[5]

There are 252,000,000 Roman Catholics in Europe. Some only nominally hold the faith. Others are hidden away in Eastern Europe. Many still are faithful to the mass and the practices of Catholicism. All are in some way touched by the revolution of Vatican II.

JOHN XXIII: THE PEOPLE'S POPE

The story of Vatican II began in the heart of Pope John XXIII. Most who knew Pope John were thoroughly enchanted by the man. In his authoritative and sympathetic biography, Lawrence Elliott painted a fine picture of the pope: "He radiated a charismatic warmth. He was interested in everyone, not in the detached, protocol-ridden manner of statecraft, but in the human way."[6]

Elected by the cardinals at age seventy-seven, John was expected to be a "provisional and transitional pope." However, he had been infected by the spirit of *aggiornamento*, not only a modernizing but rather a "reforming" of the church.[7] His ultimate aim was "the unity of Christian people."[8]

When a young American bishop complained about the curia, Pope John replied, "My dear young man, when you face Jesus Christ in eternity as one of his bishops, he is not going to ask how you got along with the Roman Curia, but how many souls you saved."[9] Perhaps he would not have vested those words with evangelical Protestant meaning, but he did show spiritual insight. On the lighter side, a diplomat once asked the pope: "Your Holiness, how many people work in the Vatican?" The papal reply was snappy: "I assume about half."[10]

Three months after his election, John suggested to his secretary of state, Domenico Tardini, that an ecumenical council be convened. Later he broached the idea to a small cluster of cardinals who had gone with him to one of his favorite churches, St. Paul's Outside the Walls. Afterward, when he was asked about the council, John walked to the study window and flung it open saying, "We expect the council to let some fresh air in here."[11]

Many advisors tried to dissuade John from the conciliar conception. In his vitriolic book, *Der Gefangene des Vatikans (Prisoner of the Vatican)*, Fritz Leist argued that the pope was a puppet of the curia, the Vatican cabinet. By locating the council at the Vatican, John had submitted to the conservative control by the cardinals.[12]

Even the pope's supporters were perplexed. One curial spokesman said, "We are paying for fifteen minutes of insanity in our pope." Cardinal Spellman of New York put a charitable interpretation on the affair: "I do not believe that the pope wanted to convoke a council, but he was pushed into it by people who misconstrued what he said."[13]

As preparations progressed, Pope John issued his encyclical "Mater et Magistra" ("Mother and Teacher of the nations—such is the Catholic Church established by Jesus Christ"). The tone of *aggiornamento* (modernization and reformation) was present as he argued for "socialization." Rich nations must sacrifice their affluence to aid the poorer lands.

Management must properly provide for labor. He also reasserted the papal prohibition of birth control, saying the pill was no solution to the Third World dilemma.[14]

On the opening day twenty-six hundred bishops were expected to fill St. Peter's basilica. John had created fifty-five new cardinals since his election in 1958. Expectancy filled St. Peter's as the pope welcomed his brother bishops. "Divine Providence is leading us to a new order of human relations," he began. Doctrines were to be studied in the light of modern scholarship. "Often errors vanish as quickly as they arise," he assured them, "like fog before the sun." The bishops were enjoined to seek a basis of unity among Catholics, with Protestant Christians, and even with non-Christians.[15] A gust of fresh air had blown indeed into the musty old structure, but John would not survive to see the end of his work. Death overtook him as preparations were underway for the second session in 1963.

THE VATICAN AND "SEPARATED BRETHREN"

At the second Vatican Council, Catholics took positive steps to heal the breach between themselves and Protestants. In fact, the French progressive Yves Congar claimed, "The principal achievement of the Council is that it aroused the entrance on a massive scale of the immense body of the Catholic Church into the ecumenical movement."[16]

Prior to the opening session, Pope John set up a Secretariat for Christian Unity. At its head was Augustin Cardinal Bea, who arranged for the pope to receive the Anglican archbishop Geoffrey Fisher in 1960.[17] In rapid succession the Catholic Church also established contact with the Greek Orthodox Church, Methodists, Lutherans, and the World Reform Alliance.[18]

In the Decree on Ecumenism submitted to the council, it was stated that Reformation churches have a unique connection with Rome. They are "bound to the Catholic Church by a specially close relationship as a result of the long span of earlier centuries when the Christian people had lived in ecclesiastical communion."[19] Absent from this statement is any reference to the fundamental difference of biblical doctrine that shattered the "ecclesiastical communion." Furthermore, the Catholic document implied that ecumenism is equated with a return to Rome.

Ordering a familiarization with Protestant outlook, the framers suggested various means for promoting contact with non-Catholics. Dialogue should be encouraged. Catholics also could share with Protestants in a "joint witness to our Christian faith." Participation in ecumenical organizations was encouraged. Prayers for Protestants were to be said.[20]

Protestant and even free-church baptism is rendered valid by the trinitarian formula, whether it is carried out by immersion, sprinkling, or pouring. The "minister's insufficient faith," or non-Catholic faith, never renders the baptismal act invalid. According to the Vatican documents, baptism is "the sacramental bond of unity binding all who are regenerated by it."[21] A denial of baptismal regeneration appears to be regarded as unlikely.

The delicate question of mixed marriages between Protestants and Catholics was answered with a certain moderation. Since there was to be more contact between the two traditions, it was assumed that more mixed marriages would result. Although certain ecclesiastical regulations could be softened, there could be no compromise on matters of divine law. Non-Catholic partners must permit all children to be raised in the Catholic faith. It is forbidden for a Catholic priest to share with a Protestant in performing the marriage. However, the non-Catholic clergyman may recite some prayers *after* the official ceremony. By way of concession, the excommunication of those who marry before a non-Catholic clergyman is abolished and retroactively revoked.[22]

Matters of contention were frankly discussed in the Decree on Ecumenism. Protestants fail to grasp "the role of Mary in the work of salvation." Also, they maintain a "love and reverence—almost a cult of the Holy Scriptures." (This is surely a bit naive in the light of liberal, biblical criticism!) Protestants decline to submit themselves to the "authentic teaching office" of the Catholic hierarchy. Finally, they have not "preserved the proper reality of the eucharistic mystery"; i.e., they fail to teach that Jesus is repeatedly sacrificed in the sacrament and that He is really present in the elements. For all of these reasons, the church cautioned the faithful "to abstain from any frivolous or imprudent zeal" in ecumenism.[23] Progress is the order of the day, but keep your hand on the brake! Hundreds of progressives, it was noted with dismay, have rushed headlong down the road of ecumenism.

A sampling of progressive thought can be garnered by looking at the Dutchman Edward Schillebeeckx and the Swiss theologian Hans Küng. Schillebeeckx wrote, "No longer are heretical books burnt amid general rejoicing at the entrance to the church." The Catholic now is compelled himself to "throw his own familiar traditions on the pyre." The faithful are expected to recognize the presence of Christian truth and a "more profound evangelical inspiration" in the "separated brethren."[25]

Hans Küng always seems to stick his neck out a bit farther than others do. He dared to assert that "Protestants are Christians too." Rome no less than Luther was responsible for the sixteenth-century schism, the Reformation. Küng calls his Catholic brothers and sisters to welcome the "separated brethren."[25]

The American Jesuit John McKenzie echoed the enthusiasm expressed by Schillebeeckx and Küng. Old issues and divisions had faded from the scene, wrote the liberal priest. "The most significant theological event here is the recognition of the Protestant churches as churches."[26]

While Catholic progressives sought to whip up interest in ecumenicity, some Protestant observers were less ecstatic. According to Karl Barth, the council dealt mainly with the "renovation of its own house." Therefore he viewed any reference to Protestantism as "peripheral and contingent."[27]

The German Catholic writer Ernst Fischer echoed Barth's caution. Protestants are to be considered a church only because of their past connection with the "True Church" of Rome. Their sacraments derive value solely because they imitate Roman Catholic sacraments. Unity must be created on Roman terms, and there is no room for middle-of-the-road compromise between Catholics and Protestants.[28]

Despite the limitations placed on concessions to Protestants, there has been since Vatican II a marked improvement in relations. Even Plymouth Brethren writers, in discussing Spain, conceded that "Vatican Council II, in its final session, made a clear declaration of religious liberty. Rome has not changed her dogmas, but it is not true to state that she has not changed her policy."[29] For oppressed Protestants in dictatorially Catholic lands, Vatican II switched on a light at the end of the tunnel.

Spanish Christians can now identify their place of worship with a name plate affixed to the building. Churches closed by the authorities in the fifties were reopened in the sixties, a case in point being Madrid's Second Baptist Church. Baptist pastors are invited to address Catholic seminarians, and some even hold ecumenical services. Still the fear lingers that Baptists are surrendering more than the Catholics in this ecumenical exercise.[30]

In a statement that would have caused Luther distress, the Lutheran Church agreed to recognize that the pope is the legitimate successor to Peter. A vague recognition of papal power was accepted without resolving the question of papal infallibility.[31] In return, a Lutheran World Federation delegation was invited in 1976 to meet the pope with a view to reversing the 1521 excommunication of Martin Luther. One wonders if the departed reformer would wish to have this belated acceptance by the prelacy he called the Antichrist.[32]

A *Common Cathechism* appeared in 1975 after five years of work by Lutheran, Reformed, Anglican, and Catholic theologians. It laid down a minimal basis of agreement in a maximum of pages, 700 in all. Then it referred to issues still being debated: papal infallibility, the role of Mary, the sacraments, etc. The *New York Times* praised this as "a key to understanding the direction that ecumenical theology has taken since it was inspired by Vatican II."[33]

Early in 1977 yet another ecumenical document appeared. This one was the result of study by the International Commission on Authority, an Anglican and Roman Catholic body. It had been agreed that any future unity would recognize the "primacy" of Rome and accord to the pope the role of universal patriarch. The Anglican *Church Times* took the occasion to call on Pope Paul VI to resign, making room for a "younger man with more zest for the last two decades of the twentieth century." Neither the pope nor the archbishop of Canterbury formally endorsed the document, and this raised a great deal of conservative criticism among Protestants.[34]

Although Vatican II opened the door to "dialogue" with Protestants, it also provided ground rules for the discussion. Change toward a more biblical form of doctrine was to be carefully circumscribed. The primacy of the Pope remained as a "Petrine" rock. Protestants were viewed as second-class Christians who had strayed, perhaps ignorantly, from the "True Church." Still, some freedom was gained by the hitherto persecuted minorities of southern Europe.

THE VATICAN AND THE BIBLE

If Vatican II took a new tack in ecumenical relations with Protestants, it was scarcely less revolutionary in its conclusions concerning the Scriptures. Karl Barth summarized it by saying that the trend to the Bible "is completely foreign to Trent and Vatican I. The footprints of these Councils lie far behind what Vatican II meant and said in this matter." The teaching office of the pope and priests no longer looms above the Bible, according to the Basel professor. Yet Barth carefully pointed out that this is a doctrine "not of the *sole* authority but of the *supreme* authority of the Scripture."[35]

In view of Barth's moderately enthusiastic analysis, it is worthwhile to have a firsthand look at the document of the council known as the Constitution on Divine Revelation. The Roman Church "has always regarded the Scriptures, taken together with sacred Tradition, as the supreme rule of her faith." For this reason "access to sacred Scripture ought to be open wide to the Christian faithful."[36] This is the phrase that has ignited a flame of interest in the Bible. That this was the aim of the conciliar bishops can be seen in supplementary instructions.

"Ignorance of the Scriptures is ignorance of Christ," according to the Constitution on Divine Revelation. Therefore, "the children of the Church" are urged to familiarize themselves "safely and profitably" with the Bible. They are to become "steeped in the spirit" of the Scriptures.[37]

Nevertheless, the faithful are reminded that only the hierarchy is qualified to interpret the Scriptures, since the Roman Church possesses the cumulative enlightenment of the church fathers as it is codified in tradition. "The task of giving an authentic interpretation of the Word of God . . . has been entrusted to the living teaching office of the Church alone."[38]

Catholics are admonished to avoid the use of paraphrases of the Bible. There was a proliferation of free paraphrases during the sixties and seventies, particularly in the Anglo-Saxon world. The conciliar documents maintained that it is in "the actual Biblical text" that God speaks to the world.[39]

Nevertheless, Vatican II laid stress on the popular reading of the Scriptures. The faithful were explicitly encouraged to read the Bible privately and in Bible study groups. Still the reminder came that only the "Church" was competent to interpret the text, and the footnotes containing Catholic tradition were to remain in the biblical text. All of these qualifications, however, had precisely the effect of bolting the stable door after the horse had fled. From 1965 onwards Catholic interest in the Bible burgeoned.

From Roman Catholic Europe came a veritable flood of

reports concerning the popularity of the Scriptures. In 1967 a senior Greater Europe Mission member reported from Rome that the Protestant minority had grown from 50,000 in 1945 to an estimated 250,000 in Italy. Since the Vatican Council, Pauline Sisters had sold hundreds of thousands of Bibles in a modern Italian translation. Fratelli Fabbri, one of the leading Italian publishers, sold more than a million copies of the Bible. He released these in weekly installments sold by supermarkets throughout Italy. In many parishes Bible study groups were meeting on a regular basis, often without the oversight of a priest.[40]

An Italian Baptist, Michele Foligno, was invited to address students in one of Rome's largest Catholic seminaries. He observed that a Bible and evangelical books were to be found in every seminarian's room.[41]

Another Protestant minister in Rome reported that evangelical books had become popular since the council. Priests eagerly buy Bibles and commentaries. According to Arthur Wiens, "Perhaps the greatest challenge resulting from the Vatican II Council is the need for evangelical literature."[42]

Another Catholic country, Austria, has experienced similar escalation in Scripture sales. The Austrian Bible Society was established in 1970, and soon it created a Bible exposition that is presented in city after city throughout the land. Often the Bibles are shown in Roman Catholic churches and schools. Up to 15,000 have viewed the display in the space of one week.[43] Catholic efforts to distribute Scriptures in Austria have met with unusual success. A *World Vision* journalist calls this "a startling breakthrough in a land where prayer books have far outnumbered Bibles."[44]

Lest optimism banish realism, one must take seriously the words of Hans Küng: "Tradition gets the better of Scripture, and the teaching office in turn gets the better of tradition, because it decides what the tradition is and hence also what Scripture is."[45]

Although there is a significant popular interest in the Bible and many Roman Catholics are studying it, one must never forget the role of the hierarchy in limiting scriptural interpretation to Catholic tradition. From Constantine to Vatican Council II, the church has remarkably adapted to its surroundings. It has been a religious chameleon. Also, it has shown itself ready to embrace virtually any movement that arises, whether from the direction of pietism or liberal rationalism. Still, one can rely on the Scriptures to be the dynamic and powerful Word of God—the sword of the Spirit.

THE POPE AND THE BISHOPS

At Vatican II even the ecclesiastical rock of the papacy seemed to soften. There was emphasis on the role of bishops in advising and consenting with the pope to determine doctrine. Some even hoped that the pope would become a kind of chairman acting in concert with a cabinet of cardinals.

However, the documents of the council defined limits to the role of the bishops. In the Decree on the Pastoral Office of the Bishops in the Church this relationship is set down clearly: "Together with their head, the Supreme Pontiff, and never apart from him, they [the bishops] have supreme and full authority over the universal Church."[46]

The bishops may determine dogma only within carefully prescribed limits. They must preserve among themselves and with "Peter's successor," the pope, a "bond of communion." Only in this close relationship with the pope can they then decree "that a particular teaching is to be held definitely and absolutely."[47]

This very carefully controlled role of the bishops did not find universal acceptance among Catholics. Fritz Leist took up a typically progressive position. "What does the pope mean, when Paul VI calls the bishops 'brethren'?" Leist asked. Then he answered his own question: "He may be absolutely candid in privately referring to the bishops as 'brethren'; alas they are not his brothers. They are subjects of the universal priest-king."[48]

From America David Wells echoed the same theme. The doctrine of collegial authority between the bishops and the pope was understood by some as a limitation on papal prerogatives. The bishops hoped, in vain, to gain control of authoritative teaching.[49]

In June 1968 Pope Paul VI stated his faith in God and church during a broadcast on Vatican Radio. This became known as his "Credo" ("I believe"). He affirmed his conviction that the college of bishops was infallible. There was praise for diversity in liturgical rites. Although the doctrines of original sin, purgatory, and the sacrifice of the mass were restated, he showed surprising flexibility in other matters, even leaving the door of salvation to sincere unbelievers open. Progressive theologians were briefly encouraged.[50]

Within days the bubble of hope burst. The encyclical letter "Humanae Vitae" exploded like a bomb on the church and the world. In it the pope smashed any hope of humanizing the teaching against birth control. "Every marriage act must remain open to the transmission of life," he wrote. Any artificial interruption of the procreative process was viewed officially as sin. As the papal critic Gary Wills wrote, "With 'Humanae Vitae'. . . Pope Paul did to his reign what Lyndon Johnson did with the Vietnam War."[51]

For years Catholics claimed that the papacy guaranteed unity. "Humanae Vitae" certainly wiped out that concept. In commenting on the encyclical, Herbert Carson wrote, "Possession of one who is claimed to be an infallible guide has not led to a condition in which unity in the faith is the hallmark, for the guide himself is assailed by dissident voices."[52]

As on the birth-control issue, Paul VI has taken a traditional view of the emotive subject of priestly marriage. According to the Vatican II documents, "By possessing virginity or celibacy for the sake of the kingdom of heaven priests are consecrated in a new and excellent way to Christ."[53] His hard line has caused many otherwise dedicated priests to give up.

The elite corps of the Vatican, the Jesuits, have fallen off in numbers from about 35,000 in 1965 to 29,638 one decade later. Thousands of them call for a softening of the iron discipline. One disenchanted Jesuit said, "Pope Paul is afraid that the order will disappear by becoming too secularized. But there's a danger that he might annihilate it by taking it over and turning us into dusty little papal valets."[54]

Yet another related question is the ordination of women. As the feminist movement gathers speed, the papacy can no longer close the Vatican shutters and forget it. Finally, in January 1977 the pope issued a ringing renunciation of ordaining women. "Christ was a man," the document argued, "and He did not confer the priesthood on his own Mother." Most Christians agree with this position, according to the pope's advisors. No quarter would be given to "intemperate feminism."[55]

Although the document was issued with full papal authority and enthusiasm, there were ripples even within the Vatican. The Secretariat for Christian Unity realized that this might hazard negotiations with the Church of England, which was steadily moving toward the ordination of women. "It was a pity that the Sacred Congregation for the Doctrine of the Faith did not see fit to consult us," the ecumenical office lamented. By this time, the condemnation of "petticoat priests" was already published.[56]

Pope Paul not only erected a fence of conservatism around the clergy and the contraceptive question, he also took an intransigent position on mariology and the eucharist. In 1974 a document was issued warning against "excessive and misguided devotion to the Virgin Mary."[57] This was sheer window dressing. In 1967 the pope already had undertaken an arduous pilgrimage to the shrine of Fatima in Portugal. On the eve of his departure he unveiled a new era of devotion to Mary. "All those who believe in the Gospel are obliged to venerate the Virgin Mary," the pope preached.[58]

Was he caught up with the excitement of a trip to Fatima? Hardly, for even in the well-planned presentation of his "Credo" on Vatican Radio in 1968 Mary played a prominent part: "We believe that Mary is the Mother who remained ever a virgin, and that by reason of this singular election she was, in consideration of the merits of her Son . . . preserved from all stains of original sin and filled with the gift of grace more than all other creatures." Here is the pure teaching of Pope Paul delivered for the edification of the faithful. Little moderation in mariology has occurred in this ecumenical age.[59]

When one turns to the teaching concerning the sacrament of the mass, there is also a strong strain of conservatism in Pope Paul's thinking. In his encyclical "Mysterium Fidei" he took up the battle against progressives who called it a "memorial feast," in which the cross of Christ is merely remembered. The teaching of the church, according to the pope, maintains that Christ is repeatedly offered in the mass. The elements become in reality his body and blood. Since Christ is the sacrament, the bread and wine must be venerated as the body and blood of the Savior.[60]

Since the Second Vatican Council, the pope has walked a tightrope between the conservatives in Rome and the progressives throughout the church. According to the sympathetic *Sunday Telegraph* writer John Organ, Pope Paul VI "has striven to mediate between progressive churchmen wanting more change, and conservative churchmen frightened of it." Organ concluded with admiration, "Paul VI will be remembered as the Pope who preserved unity in the Church after Vatican II."[61] One questions the premises here proposed. Has he really preserved the post-conciliar peace of the church?

SOW THE WIND; REAP THE WHIRLWIND

Vatican II was designed to produce *aggiornamento*, a modernizing and reforming of the Catholic Church. To some degree it succeeded, but still the secular spirit of the age has overtaken it. As John Allen Moore wrote, "In a secularized society the church is no longer the ruling force. . . . As a result the authority of the church decreases."[62] Even the late Pope Paul was forced to admit that he deplored the "doctrinal confusion and indiscipline" in the church.[63]

Many priests have renounced their vocation, the French clergy suffering the most dramatic losses. There were 40,000 priests in 1965, but ten years later this number had fallen off to 30,000.[64] In 1973 only 3 new priests were ordained in France. Seminary enrollment dropped from 920 new seminarians in 1966 to a startling 243 in 1972.[65]

Even in Italy, under the shadow of St. Peters, there is a defection from the priesthood. German television estimated that there were six thousand ex-priests in Italy during the spring of 1968.[66] An ex-Carmelite official of the Congregation of Justice and Peace is Marc Reuver. He left the priesthood because he became convinced that "it is almost impossible to be honest as a priest and stay in the Church."[67]

Pope Paul said, "Our suffering because of the many priests who are defecting is our crown of thorns." Between the close of Vatican II and the date of the papal lament in 1973, 13,440 priests worldwide had tendered their resignation.[68]

Not only has the number of priests declined; the laymen are also less faithful than they were prior to the council. For instance, in France an estimated 94 percent of the population are baptized Catholics. Yet only 16 percent attend mass frequently.[69] Small wonder, then, that missions professor Herbert Kane refers to France as "the most pagan country in Europe." He adds, "Fear and superstition abound, especially in the rural areas, and more and more people are turning to spiritism; so much so that the Roman Catholic Church now regards France as a mission field."[70]

Italy is also plagued by the same secular spirit. Although 99.4 percent are nominally Catholics, only about 20-25 percent are faithful to the church.[71] Since Vatican II, Italians have plucked up courage to defy the papacy openly. In 1974 a referendum overwhelmingly approved the institution of divorce as a right for Italian citizens. Three years later a liberal abortion law also passed handily in the Chamber of Deputies. It provided for the termination of pregnancy on demand during the first ninety days. Both of these bills were a public humiliation for the embattled Vatican.[72]

Like its neighbors, Spain also shows a rather blemished record of fidelity to the church. Only 26 percent are faithful in mass attendance, and only about 13 percent claim that their Catholic faith is a vital experience.[73] In the mid-seventies the death of Francisco Franco vastly weakened the alliance of church and state. As a result, the Concordat (treaty) governing relations between Madrid and Rome was rewritten. The state renounced its right to appoint Catholic bishops in Spain. At the same time, the church agreed not to block the trial of priests accused of criminal offenses.[74]

In Germany the disenchantment of Catholics is even more consequential. An estimated 500,000 officially renounced their church during the sixties and seventies. In the Catholic diocese of Rothenburg, "entire families are suddenly converting to the Jehovah's Witnesses."[75]

Even this relatively superficial survey of contemporary Catholicism reveals a progressive disintegration of the cultural and religious control of the church over its people. Addressing the Synod of Bishops in the autumn of 1974, Pope Paul frankly confessed, "The Church is in difficulty. It is more troubled than happy."[76]

By 1976 the pope had discovered at whose door the blame could be laid: "The identity crisis from which the Roman Catholic Church is suffering may be the work of the Devil."[77] The hoped-for modernization has not materialized in the decade since Vatican II ended its deliberations. Defection of priests and laymen has taken the place of dedication. The Anglican *Church Times* not long before Pope Paul's death called for his resignation and for the enthronement of "a younger man with more zest for the last two decades of the twentieth century."[78] Could any pope, young and zestful or old and conservative, turn the tide of decline that has followed Vatican II? As the Catholic Church looks to the future, it will require decisive and magnificent leadership from Pope John Paul II.

6

The Troubled Church

For centuries the river of Roman Catholicism flowed along in placid power. Since Vatican II, the river has turned into treacherous rapids. Trouble churns up from the lower levels of the church, and the sound of cataracts can be heard in the distance.

John McKenzie, an American Jesuit, summarized the situation when he wrote, "The Second Vatican Council, however, introduced changes some see as revolutionary, others as threats to the very identity of the Church. Furthermore, the celebrated monolithic structure of Roman Catholicism is now recognized as an illusion. Divisions within the Church have caused some apprehension of schism."[1]

McKenzie is liberal in his outlook, but the conservatives are equally concerned. From Britain the traditionally inflexible International Catholic Priests' Association echoed the same sentiments: "The erosion and final destruction of Papal power lies at the very heart of the power struggle now in progress within the Catholic Church."[2]

Before the council, traditional Catholicism remained unchallenged. Since Vatican II, however, the progressive party has been licensed for free expression. As one Irish writer said, "It is possible to think the unthinkable and speak the unspeakable."[3]

Alongside the progressive "Young Turks" there persists a

party of traditionalists. These seek to erect a wall of protection around the conservative Catholicism of preconciliar days. However, as if to add more explosive force to the bomb, the Catholic renewal movement has introduced Neo-Pentecostalism into the malaise.

David Wells summed it up in *Revolution in Rome*: "The pentecostals are not quite so eager to negate traditional authority as the progressives, and the progressives are not quite so interested in pursuing the inner light as the pentecostals."[4] In order to assess the state of affairs, each of the three parties, progressives, conservatives, and Pentecostals, will be considered.

PROGRESSIVES: COURAGE TO BE TROUBLESOME

When discussing the priesthood, Karl Rahner, an intrepid German Jesuit, wrote, "Real obedience includes the courage to be a troublesome subject."[5] Fidelity to the church can be expressed by a loyal opposition, according to Rahner.

From Milan the *Corriere Della Sera* used a medical metaphor to explain the church's plight. "Surgery can kill a sick man," he wrote; "but, if the surgeon is skilled, it can also make him whole."[6] Thus the progressive priests hack away at the body of Catholic dogma and practice hoping to restore health while running the risk of causing death.

In 1970 progressive thinkers congregated in Brussels under the auspices of *Concilium*, a respected Roman Catholic theological journal. At that meeting four major spokesmen for reform were present: Hans Küng, Karl Rahner, Yves Congar, and Edward Schillebeeckx. Their conclusions read like a declaration of independence as they pleaded for democratic election of the pope, academic liberty for theological studies, and the ordination of women to the priesthood.[7]

From Munich Fritz Leist called for a papacy free of dogmatic rigidity, legendary prerogatives, and political power. In other words, the pope must fill a pastoral role rather than that of a regal despot ruling a religious realm.[8]

The progressives do more than criticize the power structure of the church. They are really humanistic in their theology. They see salvation as social improvement. They regard the Bible as a human book fraught with multiple errors. According to Francis Schaeffer, they "believe and teach the same things as the existential theologians in the Protestant churches do, but using traditional Roman Catholic, rather than Protestant, terms."[9]

It is helpful to understand the progressive party by noting representatives of revolutionary Roman Catholicism. Because of his affront to the papacy, the Swiss theologian Hans Küng provides a particularly colorful example. Henry Chadwick, reviewing Küng's *On Being a Christian*, wrote, "He has the reputation of being out to rock the boat of traditional Roman Catholicism. His name brings a shiver of alarm to conservative bosoms, comfort to the progressives."[10]

In 1971 Küng burst upon the scene with his challenge to the papacy, *Infallible? An Enquiry*. In it he argued cogently that papal infallibility, which was declared in 1870 by the First Vatican Council, rested on shaky foundations. The New Testament did not declare the church infallible. Throughout history the papacy has promulgated its share of glaring errors. Indeed, neither the pope, nor the councils, nor the church, *nor the Bible* are infallible. Only Jesus is infallible and He is discovered through studying fallible Scriptures.[11]

The sparks flew, but Küng consoled himself. "It's improbable that I will be excommunicated," he told a *Time* magazine reporter. "I'll just go on with my work of demythologizing the church."[12]

Even Karl Rahner was appalled by Küng's attack on the papacy. Küng had, according to Rahner, placed himself outside the Catholic Church. Now the Swiss professor at Tübingen was to be regarded as nothing more than a "liberal Protestant."[13]

If Rahner was disenchanted, the pope was livid. On July

5, 1973, Pope Paul VI released a four-thousand-word document condemning "dogmatic relativism." In this "shot across
the bows" of Hans Küng, the pope declared that doctrinal
statements emanating from Rome were absolute truth, not
just "imperfect definitions of truth."[14]

When Küng persisted, the Sacred Congregation for the
Doctrines of the Faith chimed in. As watchdogs on doctrinal
matters, they "admonished" Küng. But Hebblethwaite was
right when he remarked, "Real problems cannot be banished
by the airy wave of an authoritarian wand."[15] The books au-
thored by Hans Küng were summarily banned from all
Catholic colleges and seminaries, a real boon to their sales
potential![16]

Another one of Küng's banned books was entitled, *The
Church*. It was first published in English in 1967. The church
is to be one, united by the "spirit of Christ." This abolishes
artificial distinctions, such as the barrier between priests and
laity. "All Christians are priests," Küng declared, echoing
Luther. This universal priesthood extends to preaching and
even sacramental celebration.[17] Küng declared that the
church is never to become a mediator intruding between God
and man. The priesthood is a rusty remnant of Judaism. Historical tradition is the only basis that the list of seven sacraments rests on. Only two are known to the New Testament—
baptism and the Lord's Table.[18]

In his book, *That the World May Believe*, Küng opens his
arms to Protestants. "Whoever is saved is saved through
Christ in the Church," he claims, and thus every believer
"belongs in some way [often a very hidden way] to the one
Church." He is accordingly critical of "the superstition and
miracle-fever and apparition mania in so many of the faithful,
devotion to our Lady swamping the thought of Christ, Vatican
politics, persecution of Protestants in Spain and South
America."[19]

Recently Küng came out with yet another broadside at
papal power and pomp. This book's title is *On Being a Christian*. After dismissing papal infallibility, apostolic succession

of Catholic bishops, the sinlessness of Mary, and priestly celibacy, he turns his critical powers on the Scriptures. The birth of Jesus is enshrouded in myth. His miracles were legendary. The preexistence of Jesus is a product of Hellenistic philosophy. Being a Christian is not assenting to a body of doctrine, Küng concludes. It is the "acceptance of faith in Christ and imitation of Christ."[20]

Küng is enamored with the triumphant hope of Christ's return. In it he sees the proclamation of resurrection for the entire human race. The world will be renewed, and in a cosmic sense mankind "will live happily ever after." Judgment is just a figment of fundamentalist imagination.[21]

Küng is the most radical of European progressives, but Rahner too is sharply critical of the Catholic doctrinal and ecclesiastical system. In *The Christian of the Future* Rahner declares his allegiance to the church, but it is a church of his own creation. "The Church is always in the flux of history," therefore its form changes while the content of faith remains. In this statement, at least, Rahner is much less radical than Küng.[22]

The true church is not the ecclesiastical establishment, according to Rahner. It is the body of Christians that stands out in distinction from the clerical clique. Rahner warns Catholics against two dangers: clerical triumphalism and lay defeatism. Priests often think all would be well if the church's commands were kept. On the other hand, laymen often despair because the church changes so slowly. The Christian is a missionary of God's grace, not a shock troop of ecclesiastical dominance, Rahner declares.[23]

Rahner's revolutionary tendencies are contained within the boundaries of Catholic dogma. The same is true of his book *The Priesthood*. The priest must "be a nonconformist when the occasion requires it," but he must always speak within a Catholic framework. Yet in the same book Rahner defends traditional Catholic values. The "Virgin Mary" is "an irremovable and necessary factor in God's plan of this salvation history." "Devotion to Mary . . . is somewhat essential for the Christian." Dialogue with non-Catholics is a vehicle to develop understanding of them, but the Catholic "remains convinced of the absolute claim of the Roman Catholic Church."[24]

With deep affection for the church, Rahner lamented, "We live in a land of heathens, a land with a Christian past and certain Christian leftovers."[25] He desires reform but shies away from the revolutionary incitements of Hans Küng. It is no wonder that he rebuked his academic and philosophical colleague for falling into the trap of "liberal Protestantism."

Turning from Germanic Catholicism, one finds progressive thought in a particularly virulent form among Dutch and Belgian Catholics. According to Herbert Carson, "Dutch Catholicism is famous—or for the conservatives, infamous—for its radicalism."[26] A "soul brother" of Küng is Edward Schillebeeckx, the Dutch writer. According to him, the doctrinal statements of the church are true, but they are merely signposts pointing to greater, indeed absolute, truth about God.[27]

For Schillebeeckx, God is identified as an inner feeling that assures men that the future has meaning. At the end of the road man will be rewarded rather than punished. This eschatology is embodied in two of his writings: *God the Future of Man* and *The Problem of Eschatology*.[28] Despite these radical ideas, when it comes to the doctrines of mariology and the sacraments, Schillebeeckx is traditionally Catholic.[29]

Another evidence of the ferment in Dutch Catholicism was a meeting of priests held at Noordwijkerhout in January 1973. Progressive priests launched a verbal attack against Bishop Jan M. Gijson of Limburg, spiritual head of one million Catholics. In protest against this indignity, the papal nuncio Bishop Angelo Felici walked out of the meeting. The vicious attack by progressives embraced such emotive issues as birth control, priestly celibacy, and biblical criticism.[30]

The same fire flared up again in 1976 and 1977. Many priests had deserted their vocation and become lay teachers in Catholic theological faculties. They had also taken advantage of their freedom to marry. In 1972 the Vatican demanded that these men be dismissed, but the Dutch hierarchy and academic authorities demurred. A pitched battle between the Vatican and Dutch Catholics ensued. Finally, in the face of falling mass attendance and a desperate decline in ordinations, the Vatican backed down. Now there are even married priests in some liberal parishes.[31]

One further spokesman of Benelux (Belgium, Netherlands, Luxembourg) progressives must be considered. He is Joseph Cardinal Suenens of Belgium. He is mainly known for his outspoken defense of charismatic Catholics. However, he is also a progressive thinker. Regarding the papacy, Suenens agreed with Rahner, that "the Pope should be elected by a representative body of the world's bishops." The pope was a captive of curial graybeards, and thus he is cut off from the body of the church.[32]

Less dramatic than continental progressives are their British brethren. In 1975 Hubert Richards resigned from the priesthood and surrendered his post as principal of Corpus Christi College, London. He had come to question the miraculous stories of Christmas and Easter as well as the miracles of Christ's life. In a move of unusual honesty he resigned his vocation.[33]

One of the most articulate spokesmen of British progressives is Peter Hebblethwaite. The author of *The Runaway Church*, Hebblethwaite had edited the Jesuit periodical, *The Month*, during the years after Vatican II. In 1974 he resigned from the Jesuits, married, and settled down in Oxford to pursue a writing career. In *The Runaway Church* Hebblethwaite argues against the prevailing feeling of "resignation" in Catholicism. The danger is that Catholics will resign themselves to a traditional *status quo* and back down from the reforms that were introduced at the council.[34]

A practical progressiveness appeared in the dioceses of Shrewsbury and Nottingham in 1976. On the threshold of Lent, a general absolution for lapsed Catholics was proclaimed. The obligatory secret confession was waived, and

Catholics were invited to take communion. All that was required was regular attendance at the "station masses" of Lent. This was a desperate plea, intended to woo back disenchanted devotees, but it was not notably successful.[35] Regular mass attendance continued to slip. There are 5.5 million Catholics in Britain. In 1974 an average of 4.2 million (76 percent) went weekly to mass. By 1976 this had been halved to two million (36 percent).[36]

Across the Irish Sea, the Republic of Ireland appears to be the last bastion of Catholic power. More than 90 percent of Irish Catholics go to mass each week. Even there, however, there is a growing defection from the traditional teachings of Rome. In an interview, Stanley Mawhinney, a veteran Irish preacher, outlined some symptoms of Catholic decline. Theological liberalism had penetrated Catholic colleges and seminaries. Young people were deserting the church and turning to cults.[37] The government even introduced a bill approving the sale of contraceptive pills.[38]

Throughout European Catholicism the progressive party is making its power felt. On the surface it appears to be a biblical, almost Protestant, movement. Underneath, it is nothing more and nothing less than rationalistic humanism. As Karl Barth warned the French progressive Yves Congar, "You are travelling down . . . the steep path to Schleiermacher and Bultmann, where you cannot in the end expect to harvest good fruit."[39]

Although at fundamental disagreement with the Vatican and the national hierarchy, the progressives persist within the pale of the church. As Jose Borras, a Spanish priest turned Baptist, said, the progressives remain inside the Catholic Church in spite of disagreements, because they "feel the need of reforming the church from inside."[40]

Although the progressives are humanistic and rationalist in their philosophic outlook, they eventually fall back into traditional dogma. They query the claims of the papacy. Looking to the New Testament, they support their criticism. "But constantly they are drawn by their committal to Rome back into the old dogmatic orbit," concluded Herbert Carson. [41]

Many see in the progressives the intellectual offspring of the French philosopher-theologian Teilhard de Chardin, who died half a decade before the council. He attempted to synthesize modern science and Christian theology, but he erred on the side of secularism. Thus the progressives strive to unite the sacred and the secular, the natural and the supernatural. At the end of their efforts, however, they are compelled to admit that "the reality of God has been lost in the Church." [42]

CONSERVATIVES: APPLYING THE BRAKE TO CHANGE

In the wake of Vatican II many conservative Catholics have tried to retard change and resist progress. There is a feeling that the church is like a car careering out of control. Pope Paul personalizes this dilemma; he is a man "being led where he would not go." [43]

It is small wonder, then, that the pope has "publicly and definitely put himself on . . . the side of conserving superannuated structures," according to the Frenchman Jean-Marie Paupert. [44] In August 1966 Pope Paul published his progressive ruling that bishops should resign at the age of seventy-five. The pope's conservatism showed, however, when he stipulated that this ruling did not apply to members of the conservative curia. [45]

The Irish church is another stronghold of conservatism. After news of Vatican II appeared in the Irish press, the Archbishop of Dublin smoothed the ruffled feathers of his flock by saying, "Allow me to assure you. No change will worry the tranquility of your Christian lives." It is understandable, therefore, that some call Irish Catholicism "the crotchety mother-in-law of the Church of Rome." [46]

Just as a picture of progressive thought can be painted by a selection of colorful figures, so also a survey of conservative leaders illustrates the conservative cause. No conservative has received more flamboyant press coverage than the French archbishop Marcel Lefebvre. He hit the headlines during the summer of 1976 when he celebrated the traditional Tridentine mass in Latin at Geneva, Switzerland. He likened his little seminary at Econe to the boy David. Perhaps the David of Econe would slay the Goliath of progressive thought in the Roman Church.[47]

A month later he again said the Tridentine mass, and this time six thousand attended in a hall at Lille, France. *L'Osservatore Romano*, the official Catholic paper, declared that Lefebvre had rendered himself liable to excommunication, since the vernacular mass was declared to be the only valid mass. A left-wing priest from France, Guy Gennesseaux, viewed Lefebvre as a puppet of political conservatism, sneering that "the old, conventional Right is seeking to arise from its ashes, as it does whenever a conservative regime [viz., that of Giscard d'Estaing] is in difficulty."[48]

Lefebvre was undaunted. His sermon was a tirade against Catholic progressives. "The only true Catholic Church is the traditional one," he declared. At Vatican II a marriage had been consummated between Catholicism and revolutionary thought, and this was an "adulterous union." When the church ordered that mass be said in the vernacular instead of Latin, it had forced upon the faithful a "bastard rite." Archbishop Donald Coggan and all Protestants were heretics, not "separated brethren." Furthermore, it was estimated that a quarter of all French Catholics concurred with Lefebvre.[49]

The pope suspended Lefebvre for his mutiny, but this did not stop the seventy-year-old primate. He knew that twenty-five thousand Frenchmen were loyal to his viewpoint.[50] Even Hans Küng, the archprogressive came to Lefebvre's defense. "I demand justice also for our traditionalists," Küng wrote. "They should not be faced with Roman highhandedness and insolence of office. In word, there must be no inquisition against Econe."[51]

Political and church authorities quickly tried to cool the conflict. President Giscard d'Estaing expressed his "concern

over whatever can divide the Church in France."[52] Writing in
London's *Sunday Telegraph*, Desmond Albrow warned that
the excommunication of Lefebvre would create an ugly scene,
"nothing less than a schism: a church within the Roman
Church."[53] Undaunted by threats of excommunication and a
ban on the sacraments, Lefebvre and his followers persisted.
Early in 1977 a thousand of his traditionalist disciples stormed
the church of St. Nicolas du Chardonnet in Paris and installed
temporarily two conservative priests, who celebrated the
Latin mass.[54]

Another lone preserver of traditional Catholic thought
was Oswald Baker, parish priest at Downham Market, Norfolk in England. When he persisted in celebrating the Latin
Mass, he was suspended by Bishop Charles Grant of North-
ampton. When required to turn over the keys to the parish
church, Baker set up an altar in the town hall and celebrated
the outlawed mass. Ninety attended his service, while seventy heard the vernacular mass in the parish Church.[55]

In a dramatic statement, Baker declared, "I shall never
say the so-called new Mass though it cost me my life to refuse.
I am being persecuted and victimised. The allegation is that
my ministry is harmful."[56] But Baker did not bleed for his
cause, he simply faded into obscurity. A brief column in the
Daily Telegraph in November 1976 indicated that he had
been invited by the traditional Una Voce Association to say
the Latin mass in Glasgow.[57]

A more organized offensive by conservative Catholics is
being carried on by the British organization known as the
International Catholic Priests' Association. One of their main
targets is Teilhard de Chardin, whom they view as the villain
in the progressive movement. He was a pantheist who made
God identical with His creation. His political viewpoint was
that of a "collectivist," for he advocated socialism. Furthermore, he was a "secularist" who elevated science to the
level of religion.[58]

Concurring with the standard conservative viewpoint,
another conservative named Albers wrote *The Hidden*

Schism. According to Albers, "it is absolutely impossible to quote any other modern Modernist who has raised his voice against the Church from within, who was not deeply influenced by Teilhard." Condemning the progressives with one list of ecclesiastical expletives, Albers wrote: "No doubt, many minds poisoned by Teilhardism, Modernism and Marxism were present during the deliberations of Vatican II."[59]

In the *News Letter of the International Catholic Priests' Association*, Albers reported on the Australian tour of Bishop Alan Clark of Elmham. Like many progressives, Clark claimed that infallibility and authority were prerogatives of the entire Catholic Church. At the same time he questioned the concept that Christ is repeatedly sacrificed in the mass. "This man is obviously no longer a Catholic," said Albers. He condemned Bishop Clark for using his office as bishop "to subvert the Catholic Faith."[60]

The International Catholic Priests' Association is quick to protest against progressive thought. When Basil Cardinal Hume became Archbishop of Westminster, the Association published an open letter to him in their *News Letter*. This letter was an appeal to determine the progress of secularism: "The schools called 'Catholic' in your Archdiocese are in urgent need of investigation to discover the true extent to which Modernism has eaten into the lives of the young."[61]

Another example of conservative reaction comes from certain laymen. In an article Honor Tracey, an articulate Catholic woman, attacked post-conciliar changes in the church. "What the 'aggiornamento' has done to Catholics is daily becoming clearer," she began. In some European cities mass can be heard in five different languages every day. This is "like a new tower of Babel." This behavior by the church is like a mother assuming a new "persona." Her skirt is hiked up above her knees, her speech is teenaged jargon, and she takes up smoking. "The children are bewildered, bereft and, as it were, orphaned."[62]

Conservatives fight on valiantly for the church of their fathers, but one wonders if they are not jousting at windmills.

Writing in *L'Osservatore Romano*, the French Dominican Georges Cotter concluded, "Traditionalists in the Church today are a minority who suffer from a complex of being exiled."[63]

Although there are many moderates who support traditional practices and doctrines, the extremes of conservatism—viz., retaining the Latin mass, condemnation of non-Catholics, etc.—are a lost cause. Many feel that the church will move even more toward the vocal and influential left, leaving conservatives like pitiful little boats stranded on tidal mud flats.

Charismatic Catholics: Renewal or Revolution?

Both the progressives and the traditionalists enjoy a degree of popular support, but it is the Catholic Charismatic Renewal movement that has caused the most excitement. Joseph Cardinal Suenens claimed that "the charismatic movement is a revival of a form of prayer which the rationalism of liturgy has driven out of the Church."[64]

Despite his enthusiastic leadership of the charismatic movement, however, Cardinal Suenens roots it firmly in Roman Catholic dogma. "What's spoken about and experienced in the Charismatic Renewal as baptism in the Spirit, is what we're looking for. It's what we need to be able to lead the people to. We partake of the Spirit through baptism and confirmation."[65]

The Catholic Renewal movement is true to its name. It is both Catholic and a renewal. The American priest and sociologist, Andrew Greeley, was probably correct when he declared the Catholic Pentecostals to be "the most vital movement in Catholicism."[66]

The truth of Greeley's assessment can be demonstrated. From a highly skeptical Reformed journal, *Present Truth*, comes confirmation of charismatic strength. "In 1967, neo-Pentecostalism penetrated the bastions of Rome. In Catholicism the charismatic movement has been met with open arms."[67]

A high point in the charismatic movement's continental history came on Pentecost Sunday in 1975. More than twenty-five thousand crowded into St. Peter's in Rome. At least ten thousand were delegates at the International Conference on Charismatic Renewal. Cardinal Suenens, together with twelve bishops and eight hundred priests, celebrated the mass. There was dancing in the Spirit. When the Pope addressed them, he urged that they be faithful "to the authentic [Catholic] doctrines of the faith."[68]

It is estimated that there are 600,000 charismatic Catholics in the world, a minute but vocal minority among 252 million European Catholics.[69] In Ireland, Catholic Pentecostals outnumber their "soul brothers" and sisters in Protestantism. About 5,000 attend annual Renewal conferences in Dublin. Weekly almost 700 pray together in the Friends Meeting House at Dublin.[70] Tom Flynn, chronicler of the Irish renewal movement, traced the Pentecostal popularity in Eire to the publishing of David Wilkerson's book *The Cross and the Switchblade.*[71]

Although Ireland is the strongest center of Catholic Pentecostalism in Europe, the movement is also recognized elsewhere. There are an estimated 58 charismatic prayer groups in Britain and 100 in France.[72] By 1974 there were 10,000 French Catholics involved, and a multiplication of 40,000 was predicted within the year.[73]

The Catholic charismatics are emphasizing informal ecumenical relations with Protestants and they justify this on the basis of Vatican II. Cardinal Suenens claimed in 1973, "The charismatic renewal has extraordinary ecumenical implications.... Many important breakthroughs are happening in a wonderful way in the charismatic renewal."[74]

Although the Catholic Pentecostals are more ecumenical and more literal in their view of the Scriptures, they also hold tenaciously to Catholic dogma. Tom Flynn explained this incongruity by writing, "The Eucharist has taken on a new depth" for Catholic Pentecostals.[75] The devotional contemplation involved in charismatic prayer leads to a deeper awareness of sin and desire for confession. Also, according to O'Connor, a growing and deeper appreciation of Mary is found among charismatic Catholics.[76]

Despite the charismatics' professed allegiance to the Catholic faith, some bishops view them skeptically. In his celebrated 1974 meeting with leaders of the Renewal movement, Pope Paul VI warned them. Charismatic communities, he insisted, "cannot be exempted from legitimate ecclesiastical authority and be left to the arbitrary impulse of individuals."[77]

After the mass at St. Peter's in 1975, Alfred Cardinal Ottaviani spoke for the Vatican and warned against the divisive side effects of charismatic renewal. "The aggressive spiritualism of the neo-Pentecostals over the long haul risks producing a split," he said, "dividing the Catholic world into those Catholics who possess the fervor of the Holy Spirit, and those who are just common Catholics."[78]

Cardinal Willebrands of the Secretariat for Promoting Christian unity was hardly more cordial than Ottaviani. He warned of the "individualism, separatism, and triumphalism that could emerge from the movement if its perception and practice of the charismatic gifts were made normative in the life of the entire church."[79]

Predictably, the International Catholic Priests' Association in England has vehemently challenged the charismatic renewal movement. Its members speak of the masses held by charismatic priests as "wierd liturgical 'happenings.'" They regard Cardinal Suenens as a self-appointed "Pentecostal Pope," but the conservatives accuse him of being a "faithless prince of the Church." In their *News Letter*, the British traditionalists even make oblique reference to the supposed connection between Pentecostal meetings and sexual orgies. Their dogma may be traditional and conservative, but their polemics are reactionary and risky.[80]

A final word of Catholic assessment is found in the writings of Schillebeeckx. He is aware of his neighbor Cardinal Suenens, who regards the charismatic renewal as an essential element to the reformation of Roman Catholicism. However, Schillebeeckx appeals to the hierarchy, "as the principle of leadership and guidance . . . to supervise this kind of charismatic expression as it has to supervise all expressions of the life of the church"[81] It is strange indeed that Schillebeeckx would appeal to the hierarchy and concur almost verbatim with Pope Paul.

If Catholic observers are somewhat ambivalent about their charismatic brethen, so also are Protestant commentators. Protestant charismatics are predictably enthusiastic in analyzing their Catholic friends. Michael Harper, writing in his magazine, *Renewal,* enumerated several aspects of change in the Catholic Pentecostal movement. Laymen have risen to positions of leadership on a par with clery in the movement. There is a penetration of the entire church with the charismatic message. Charismatic Catholics show sincere obedience to their religious superiors, thus refuting the frequently leveled charge of spiritual anarchy. Priests, bishops, and even Cardinal Suenens have lent their support to renewal. Finally, under the leadership of Suenens a doctrinal conference was held at Malines, producing a statement of faith.[82]

Much less laudatory was the article in *Crusade* magazine by the noted English Pentecostal preacher W.T.H. Richards. He declared that because the Catholics are confirmed in their nonbiblical doctrinal position by their spiritual experience, one must doubt the validity of that experience. It is just as suspect as a "Christian Scientist who [might] claim an experience of the Holy Spirit and speak in tongues, yet stay within the beliefs of Christian Science."[83]

The Canadian church historian W. Stanford Reid echoed the criticism of many concerned Protestants. After experiencing the "baptism in the Spirit," many Catholics take up practices that had formerly been discarded. In the words of Reid, "Catholic Pentecostals tend to go back and begin using av-

enues of contact with God that they had abandoned—the ro-
sary, the Real Presence [of Christ in the sacrament], devotion to Mary."[84]

Most Protestant students of modern Catholicism concur
in their assessment of the renewal movement. There is a renewed appreciation of the sacrament, leading even to some
priests recommending that the worshiper spend time in ad-
oration of the served sacrament. Mary is venerated as the one
who "presided" over the events at Pentecost. One writer,
Simon Tugwell, is so taken with the potency of experience as a
source of divine revelation that he admits as legitimate vehi-
cles of spiritual truth such anti-Christian sources as Marxism,
Zen, and Transcendental Meditation.[85]

PROGRESS THAT IS SUPERFICIAL

Considering the delicate balance of power in modern
Catholicism, it is extremely difficult to predict its future
course. The progressive party is vocal and articulate and includes some of the best thinkers in the church, viz., Küng,
Rahner, and Schillebeeckx.

On the other hand, the conservatives have the powerful
curia on their side. Obviously colorful characters like Marcel
Lefebvre cause concern to their conservative colleagues, but
there still remains a sizeable and respectable body of traditionalists who are influential. Pope Paul VI was the titular
head of this movement.

The charismatic Catholics have aroused a good deal of
popular support and press coverage. They regard Joseph Cardinal Suenens as an active and convincing leader. Even the
pope has given reserved approval to renewal.

One might expect rather rapid changes in Catholicism,
but this is not the case. The future is by no means within the
grasp of any one party. David Wells astutely observed, "The
future of Roman Catholicism depends on the outcome of the
struggle between the people and the Pope."[86]

After several years of service with the Southern Baptist Foreign Mission Board in Europe, J. D. Hughey summarized the scene: "What is the future of the Roman Catholic Church? My guess is that it will be cleansed and strengthened for its role in the new world which is emerging. It will not look or act quite like the old Roman Catholic Church. Much of its theology will be changed but not its basic dogmas."[87] One thing is certain, the church will never revert to its preconciliar form.

7

Catholicism and Communism:
Detente?

Historically Communism and Christianity have been at odds. Karl Marx and Friedrich Engels scoffed at Christian social action in the nineteenth century. They called the activities of Christian reformers "the Holy water with which the priest consecrates the heartburnings of the aristocrat."[1]

When the American preacher D. L. Moody came to Britain in 1874, Friedrich Engels lashed out against him. Engels, who collaborated with Marx in spreading Communist propaganda, fumed, "The whole business [of revival] is a plot of the British bourgeoisie to import Yankee revivalism to keep the proletariat contented."[2]

Communism and Christianity, especially of the evangelical variety, were presumed to be totally incompatible. In the nineteenth and early twentieth centuries little attempt was made to reconcile the two. However, within the short span of the last two decades a new attitude has arisen. Communism has bloomed into a garden of diverse forms. In western Europe a new word has been coined: "Eurocommunism." This is carefully distinguished from the Bolshevic and Stalinist streams of Russian communism. Coexistence with the church, both Catholic and Protestant, is now hailed as a *modus vivendi*.

FROM CONDEMNATION TO COEXISTENCE

In 1949 Pope Pius XII categorically condemned communism. From the Holy Office came a statement castigating all who professed, defended, or spread Marxist doctrine. Excommunication would follow if this ruling were violated.[3] It was hoped that this threat would thwart the rise of communism outside Russia, but it failed.

When Hungarian freedom fighters tried to gain liberty from Russia, they were brutally repressed. Neither western politicians nor church authorities could intervene. Pope Pius XII simply stood by, expressing his distress. Communist authorities ignored the Vatican, and this revealed its impotence to roll back the Red wave.[4]

John XXIII was both more realistic and more diplomatic than his predecessor, Pope Pius XII. His conciliatory stance was most evident in his last encyclical, *Pacem in Terris* (Peace on Earth). It was directed not only to the priests and people, but to "all men of good will." In it, the pope declared that though communism was a false teaching, those who espoused it were to be respected and accorded all human dignity. Turning his attention to western vices, he deplored the colonial powers and their attendant racial discrimination. The arms race was decried as a cosmic suicide pact, and he called for it to be halted forthwith. Pope John quoted Pius: "Nothing is lost by peace; everything is lost by war."[5]

During that same year, 1963, Pope John had received the son-in-law of Nikita Khruschev. He was Aleksei Adzhubei, editor of the government newspaper, *Izvestia*. After a relaxed and friendly audience with Adzhubei and his wife, the pope said, "You say you are atheists. But surely you will receive the blessing of an old man for your children?" Obediently, the Adzhubeis bowed their heads to receive the papal blessing.[6]

A storm of public protest arose in the wake of this audience. Some claimed that the pope had clothed the Communist cause with a mantle of respectability. Others dubbed

him the "Red Pope." When Pope John heard this, he wept.[7]
It was estimated that the Italian Christian Democratic party
lost over a million votes because the pope met the Russian
editor.[8]

Even Nikita Khruschev spoke warmly of Pope John. Writing in the *Saturday Review* during December 1962, Norman
Cousins quoted the Communist leader. "The Pope and I have
differences of opinion on many questions," Khruschev admitted, "but we are united in our desire for peace. I would like to
have contacts with the Pope. I believe it is true that the Pope
and I have things in common, because we are both of humble
origin."[9]

Under the influence of Pope John even the documents of
Vatican II reflect an open door toward the East. Dialogue was
encouraged between Catholics and Communists (who were
described as "unbelievers"). Indeed, it could not be avoided
in the pluralistic society that now exists. The document on
"Dialogue with Unbelievers" declared that conversation must
not always be "apostolic," i.e., have as its aim the conversion
of the unbeliever. On the other hand, unbelievers can be
helped through dialogue toward faith.[10]

In May 1971 Pope Paul issued his papal letter *Oc-
togesima Adveniens*. Freely he admitted a "pluralism of op-
tions" in social structure. The church could no longer create a
pattern of society that would be universally applicable. Every
"Christian community" must adapt to the culture in which it
lives, even if it be communistic. In this letter addressed to
Cardinal Roy, president of the International Justice and Peace
Commission, Pope Paul broke forever "the taboo on socialism."[11]

Pope Paul also had referred to communism in his first
encyclical letter, *Ecclesiam Suam*. He said that Communists
make liberal use of concepts embodied in the gospel, viz., the
brotherhood of man, mutual aid, and human compassion. In
fact, the pope seemed to hint that communism was something
of a "secularized form of Christianity."[12]

Chiefly responsible for relations with Communist governments since Vatican II has been Archbishop Agostino Casaroli, head of the Vatican's Council for Public Affairs. He attended the 1973 summit conference on European Security at Helsinki. He also visited Moscow and invited Communist heads of government to come to the Vatican. In fact, the Russian foreign minister Gromyko and the president of the Supreme Soviet, Podgorny, have had audiences with the pope. Tito also visited Rome, as did the Rumanian chief of state, Ceausescu. Small wonder indeed, that Casaroli has earned the nickname of the "Henry Kissinger of the Vatican."[13]

Not only was Casaroli active in forging links between the Catholics and Communists, Franz Cardinal König also was engaged in bridge building. As chief of the Secretariat for Relations with Non-Believers, Cardinal König maintained lively contact with Catholics in eastern Europe. He spoke optimistically of the survival of Catholicism in Russia: "The continuing existence of religion after 58 years of atheistic propaganda and discrimination in a country where the economic conditions have changed completely is an embarrassment for the Marxist-Leninist theory."[14]

In this day of dialogue, many Catholic thinkers have imbibed Marxist ideas without being aware of having done so. French writer Roger Garaudy wrote a book entitled *From Anathema to Dialogue*. He concluded that the shaping of society cannot afford to ignore either Communistic or Christian alternatives. Neither the Christian nor the Communist model for society was universally applicable.[15]

To divorce the fortunes of the church from those of the Communist cause is no longer a historical option open to modern Europe. Co-existence is not just an ideal to be striven for, it is already reality—from Russia to Rome. The observer of contemporary continental church life reluctantly concludes that a compromise has been found that is more favorable to communism than to Catholicism.

POLAND'S PERSISTENT CATHOLICS

Poland is the largest Catholic country in eastern Europe, and the church has endured there with a reasonable degree of success. As one high school teacher put it, "The church has been in Poland for 1000 years and Communism only for 30.... Allegiance takes a long time." After three decades there are two million card-carrying Communists, but there are 30 million Catholics.[16]

This Catholic persistence does not go unnoticed by the Vatican. In 1975 Pope Paul received a delegation of three thousand Poles led by their venerated primate, Stefan Cardinal Wyszynski. The pope encouraged them by saying that he had "followed with admiration the 'ardent work' of the Polish churchmen in their Communist-led country."[17]

Attendance at mass serves to substantiate claims of Catholic faithfulness. In rural areas about 87 percent of the population attend weekly, and urban areas show an average of 77 percent. About 95 percent of the children take their first communion. One schoolgirl said, "Religion is taken very seriously in my home."[18]

Since Vatican II, there has arisen a wave of home Bible study groups in Poland. Here laymen and priests study the Scriptures on an equal basis. Bible-study programs were started by a priest who learned how to conduct them while he was living in Rome.[19]

A further sign of Catholic virility is the missionary outreach of the Polish church. According to recent statistics, more than two thousand Polish missionaries work in the Third World. They serve in Africa, Latin America, Oceania, and Asia.[20]

The cornerstone of Catholicism in Communist Poland is the vigorous Cardinal Wyszynski, now over seventy years old. His ascension to political and religious power began in 1956, when the party chief Wladyslaw Gomulka released him from house arrest.[21]

Thanks largely to the cardinal's pressure, the faithful

have resisted government efforts to "atheize" them. There are fourteen thousand churches and chapels operating, and they are served by nineteen thousand priests. An additional forty-five hundred novices are in training for the priesthood, and there are twenty-eight thousand Polish nuns. In 1973 Edward Gierek, the party secretary, handed over to the Polish church deeds to several thousand churches in the territory taken from Germany after World War II.[22]

In 1976 Cardinal Wyszynski lodged a complaint against the proposed Polish constitution, which would forge closer links to Communist lands and enshrine communism as the exclusive political ideology. Claiming that this rendered Poland a "vassal state" of Russia, he emphasized that "the prosperity of Poland cannot be built by one social group."[23] In a pastoral letter he asserted that the constitution would "limit the sovereignty of the Polish people."[24]

Later in 1976, when the cardinal reached seventy-five, the mandatory retirement age for bishops, he submitted his resignation in accordance with Vatican policy; but the pope persuaded him to stay on. The pope and the political leader, Edward Gierek, both recognized the cardinal's genius in steering a "moderate course between compromise and intransigence." One retired West German diplomat explained the mystique of Wyszynski by saying, "What makes the Cardinal such a great success is that he is, above all, a good Pole. That means he is anti-German, anti-Russian, and anti-Communist."[25]

When Gierek pushed up prices for food by 50 percent, the cardinal rushed to defend rioting workers. The police had arrested many workers who participated in antigovernment riots. Through Wyszynski's intervention, some of these were released. The cardinal lamented in a pastoral letter issued by the Polish bishops' conference: "It is painful when workers have to struggle for their rights with a workers' government."[26]

The power of the Polish primate is clearly recognized by Gierek's government. In early 1977 a report reached the West that forged sermons attributed to the cardinal were being circulated by the government. Under the magical power of Wyszynski's name fake sermons that made the cardinal appear to support Marxism in general and Gierek's government in particular were published. Certainly this is a weird twist to the old adage that imitation is the sincerest form of flattery. [27]

Thanks to the charismatic presence of Wyszynski, Polish Catholics have enjoyed unparalleled liberties. Ordinations of Polish priests have risen from 480 in 1971 to 606 four years later, and this occurred at a time when ordinations were plummeting in the West. As one Polish church official says, "Young people here become priests because it is an act of herosim."[28]

In 1966 the Polish Catholics celebrated one thousand years of Christianity in Poland. Gierek had vetoed a papal visit, because he feared that popular demonstrations would be inevitable and uncontrollable. The Communist party tried to challenge the church's strength by staging public protests, and 250,000 Communists joined in. Wyszynski combatted this by scheduling counter-demonstrations, which attracted half a million. It is reliably rumored that Gierek's wife is a discreetly practicing Catholic. The party boss's mother has a photograph of her famous son on the table, but behind it hangs a large picture of Our Lady of Czestochowa.[29]

Gierek's minister of religion, Kazimierz Kakol, has gone on record as advocating "the long-term existence" of the church in Poland. In July 1974 he opened regular diplomatic discussions with the Vatican. There have been 263 building permits for churches granted since 1971 in Poland. No government inspection is imposed on religious education, and the teachers are not required to report to the government on the students who attend.[30] Since 1945, the Polish government has aided in the repair or rebuilding of 5,000 Catholic churches.[31]

The publishing of religious books and Bibles is also remarkably free from restraint in Poland. In 1975 a new translation of the Polish Bible appeared. An initial edition of fifty

thousand copies sold like the proverbial "hot cakes." In the
first two days fifteen hundred copies were bought.[32] Still, one
young priest lamented, "Even though the Catholic Church in
Poland regularly receives permission to print Bibles, in our
city we don't have enough to give one to all who are asking."[33]

Despite the uncharacteristic liberty given to Polish
Catholics, there are disturbing signs of political pressure. As
the editor of London's *Daily Telegraph* stated in December
1976, "Yet, even in so overwhelmingly and proudly a Catholic
country as Poland . . . discrimination is so systematic and severe as to amount to a clear policy of persecution. Inevitably,
in the satellite countries, the Church is widely seen as a patri-
otic rallying point against foreign oppression. As liberal ideals
percolate in, the confrontation seems bound to become more
acute."[34]

In 1973 the issue of religious education became a source
of irritation between the church and the Communists. The
government reorganized the schools in such a way that all-day
education was introduced. This effectively precluded continuation of Christian education by the priests. Since there
was no slot in the curriculum for religious education, priests
had been catechizing children after school hours. The revised
schedule would rule out even such extracurricular efforts.[35]
In January 1977, Catholic bishops were still protesting attempts by "authorities to weaken the influence of parents and
the Church over children."[36]

Even more imperious was the government action in pulling down Catholic chapels. In preparation for Easter 1976, a
wooden chapel was erected in the forest near Warsaw at the
village of Gorki. No sooner had the peasants put up the building than the police appeared and tore it down. The authorities
also confiscated the farmers' axes, saws, and hammers to pre-
vent them from rebuilding the chapel.[37]

Earlier, in 1974, a chapel in Warsaw had been subjected
to a flying raid by government order. The priest was shut out
of his church, and an effete former priest who had renounced
the faith was pressed into action to carry out the sacrament.

This was certainly a bizarre twist to the Communist desecration. Then the chapel was razed to make room for a redevelopment scheme. [38]

Despite the popular strength of Catholicism and the personal magnitude of Wyszynski, Polish Catholicism is far from free. Liberty hangs by a thread, and the thread may well snap when Wyszynski dies. Perhaps the Polish Pope John Paul II is the best guarantee of continued freedom.

SOVIETS AND THEIR SATELLITES: NORMALIZING RELATIONS

Pope Pius XII called Russia the "northernmost outpost of Catholicism in Europe." Indeed, in the Baltic republics of Lithuania, Latvia, and Estonia more than 90 percent of the population are Roman Catholic. [39]

In their excellent little book *Young Christians in Russia*, Michael Bourdeaux and Kathleen Murray marshall dramatic evidence to show that young Russians are rallying to the church. In Lithuania most young people exhibit significant fidelity to the Catholic Church. In fact, "teachers wage a lone battle against whole classes of Catholic children who are prepared to stand up for one another." When a petition against the repression of religious education was handed to the government during 1973, it contained 14,238 signatures of Lithuanians. One-quarter of them were school pupils. In Lithuania Catholicism is both a deep-seated "religion" and a rallying point of anti-Soviet feeling. [40]

From the time of Pope John XXIII and Nikita Khruschev there have been attempts to keep cordial relations between the Vatican and the Kremlin. In fact, Khruschev and Pope John had several personal contacts. Although an official treaty known as a Concordat has not come into being, there has been sufficient freedom to facilitate papal communication with the Catholic faithful in the Baltic States. [41]

The lines of communication have at times been strained. For instance, in 1971 two Lithuanian priests were sentenced to prison for indoctrinating (i.e., instructing) children. In protest, six hundred irate Catholics demonstrated outside the courtroom doors. A year later, one young Catholic turned himself into a torch at Launas, Lithuania's second largest city. Thousands took up the martyr's call and rioted through the streets with signs screaming, "Freedom for Lithuania."[42]

Another element of stress in the relations between Rome and Moscow is the persistent Ukrainian gadfly, Cardinal Slipyi. Through the good offices of Pope John he was released from a Russian prison in 1963 and exiled to Rome. From there he now fights relentlessly to publicize the plight of his Ukrainian flock. Late in 1976 Slipyi used an audience with the pope to request that he be created Patriarch of the Ukrainian church. Pope Paul refused, because he did not wish to risk damaging ecumenical relations with the Orthodox Church.[43]

Thus the uneasy peace between the Kremlin and the Vatican continues. It is generally conceded that the Soviets desperately need papal support in controlling the Catholic dissidents in the Russian domains. On the other hand, Catholic cooperation with the Russian regime also buys for the faithful a degree of freedom from oppression. At best, the situation is tenuous, and it could at any time erupt into severe repression and even bloodshed.[44]

Hungary presents yet another textbook case of knife-edge relations between the pope and the Communist overlords. During the Stalinist era, atheistic authorities almost succeeded in abolishing Catholic education. Enrollment in parochial primary schools fell from 86 percent to 27 percent, and secondary school students declined from 80 percent of the eligible children to a miniscule .7 percent.[45]

In 1964 an agreement was forged between the Hungarian government and the Vatican. Church officials were given a larger role in the selection of bishops. There was also to be a cessation of the repression of Catholic children and an easing of restrictions on priests. One has the impression that Communist authorities were negotiating from a position of unquestioned and unassailable power. Hungary's 67 percent majority of Catholics seems to have been crushed once for all in the ill-fated 1956 uprising.[46]

Substantiation of this assessment can also be derived from the tragic tale of Joszef Cardinal Mindszenty, archbishop of Esztergom and primate of Hungary. During the fifties he was jailed for six years and afterward he spent fifteen years as an exile in the American legation at Budapest. Quietly he was lured to Vienna by papal diplomats in 1971 to allow the Vatican and Hungarian officials to normalize relations. The pope issued a florid statement to him: "The crown of thorns has been placed upon your head. . . . We bow before you with profound respect."[47]

In 1975 the pathetic old hero of Hungarian Catholicism died in Vienna. He had "fallen victim to *detente*, and his *Memoirs*, published in 1975, record his bewilderment as he went off into 'complete and total exile.' "[48]

A year later Laszlo Lekai was installed in the seat hallowed by Mindszenty's courage. Lekai appears to be much less of a man of God. He is a "realist" who advocates cooperation with Communist powers. The minister of religious affairs, Imre Milos, is confident that he now has total cooperation from the Hungarian hierarchy. As the German evangelical Heinrich Jochums wrote, "Under the cover of a totally new hierarchy the annihilation of the church rushes on."[49]

In Yugoslavia a maverick form of communism exists under the independent leadership of Tito. About six million Yugoslavs claim allegiance to Catholicism—32 percent of the total population. In 1962 the archbishop of Zargreb published the magazine *Glas Concila* (Voice of the Council). His primary purpose was to explain the changes that had come to Catholicism during the Council. In the years since its publication this periodical has persisted, and its readership has grown to 180,000. In 1972 the editor even included in *Glas Concila* a potent letter from Alexander Solzhenitsyn.[50]

Further indication of the respect with which Tito views the church was seen in 1966 when a document was signed by both Tito and the Vatican. This led to the exchange of envoys.

Furthermore, it insured the separation of church and state. Freedom of conscience and religion was likewise guaranteed.[51] In exchange for all of these concessions to the church, the pope promised to help control terrorism in the incendiary multiracial climate of Yugoslavia. Bishop Franc Franic of Split hailed the document as a basis for peaceful coexistence. Others were more skeptical, however, and decried the document as a "slow form of death" for the church.[52]

A new edition of the Bible in Serbo-Croatian appeared in 1969. It was produced over three years by a translation team headed by the national poet, Jure Kastelan. Although it was patterned loosely on the *Jerusalem Bible*, and most of the translators were Catholics, the new version bears no episcopal imprimatur. It is hoped that it can be used by all Christians in Yugoslavia.[53]

Despite the unusual degree of freedom accorded to Catholics in Yugoslavia, a program to discourage dissidents was instituted in 1973. According to a 1975 report, "legal and police pressures against churches have mounted during the year, and new laws limiting church activity are expected to come into force." Some issues of *Glas Concila* have been suppressed.[54] Clearly, as Tito nears the end of his rule and the fear of political disruption grows, less freedom can be given to Yugoslav Catholics. One can expect either internal pressure to limit Catholic freedom or Russian intervention in the wake of Tito's passing. The grim precedents of events in Hungary, Eastern Germany, and Czechoslovakia must always color the observer's expectation of the Communists' future performance.

Czechoslovakia is yet another example of a predominantly (75 percent) Catholic country in the Eastern European block of nations. In 1967 the Catholic professor Giulio Girardi challenged Czech Communists to discussions. They met at Marienbad, and Girardi challenged the Communists to humanize their system. The end result was Alexander Dubcek's short-lived experiment.[55]

As 1968 dawned, a sunrise of justice came to Czechoslovakia. "Espionage" convictions against scores of priests were overturned. Bishops who had been jailed during the fifties were "rehabilitated" and released. Bishop Frantisek Tomasek of Prague reported that there prevailed "the best climate for religious freedom since the country went Communist in 1948."[56]

Then came the tanks! One unforgettable August morning Russian forces overran the country, crushing forever the Dubcek regime and its attendant hope for freedom. From that point onward, a calculated program removed Catholicism from every avenue of influence in the land.[57]

Roman Catholic faculties sympathetic to the "Spirit of 1968" were quickly replaced with orthodox Communists. Any vestiges of Vatican II were likewise wiped out. In 1970 government propaganda directed against Catholicism was intensified. Three years later socialist rites were introduced to replace baptism, confirmation, marriage, and funeral masses.[58]

By the mid-seventies many dioceses were not occupied by bishops. In fact, only two bishops served the country's thirteen dioceses. The Vatican had simply refused to accept the "assortment of puppets and stooges" offered by the government as episcopal candidates. Many priests were likewise jailed, and an order of monks had been disbanded.[59]

When one considers Catholicism in Communist lands, it is a picture of steady decline and church concessions to atheistic powers. What rights Vatican diplomats extract from Eastern governments are simply an aspirin to provide temporary relief from pain while the cancer of state control gnaws away at the church's vitals. Hope of triumph or even meaningful cooperation appears to be a fool's fantasy.

ITALY: COMMUNISM ON THE DOORSTEP

Since the sixties there have developed in many Catholic countries reasonably virulent Communist parties. These Western socialists call themselves "Eurocommunists." They profess to espouse a mixed economy of private enterprise and state control. In France, Spain, and Portugal recent political developments have contributed to a consolidation of Communists. They are a force with which both priests and politicians must reckon.

Nowhere in Western Europe is Communism so strong as it is in Italy. Already in 1963 the Italian party boasted a membership of two million, the largest Communist concentration in the West.[60]

When Italian bishops conferred in 1973, the issue of Communism arose. Die-hard conservatives insisted that "one cannot be a Christian and a Marxist at the same time." Some of their colleagues, however, sought to demonstrate the invalidity of that categorical claim.[61]

Giovanni Franzoni, abbot of the Benedictine Community at St. Paul's Outside the Walls in Rome, nailed his red colors to the mast. He condemned America's earlier involvement in the Vietnam war. Announcing his intention to resign from the community, he proclaimed his intention to live with and fight for the rights of Roman shack dwellers. "Paradoxically, social reconciliation can today only mean a struggle for a classless society," Franzoni said, echoing the Communist line.[62]

Antonio Cardinal Poma, Bishop of Bologna, sought to mollify the left-wing criticism by advocating a greater emphasis on the social gospel. He recognized that the sacraments and traditional sermons simply did not meet modern man's needs. He urged a more personal proclamation of Christianity. But his moderate demeanor was not appealing to the socialistic bishops.[63]

Meanwhile communism was gaining at the polls in Italy. In 1972 the Italian Communist party polled 27.9 percent of the votes, while the staunchly Catholic Christian Democrats captured 37.8 percent. Two years later the Communists pulled up to 33.4 percent and the Christian Democrats dropped back to 35.3 percent. At the same time, Catholic voters, despite a threat of excommunication, advocated divorce as a right for every married couple.[64]

As 1976 began, the impending threat of even greater gains for the Communists grew. Pope Paul arranged to meet Rome's Communist mayor and the Communist-controlled city council. The pope begged Signor Giulio Argan, the mayor, to protect the city's "unique Christian character." (Previously Pope Paul had warned that a Communist council and mayor would turn the "eternal city" into a "godless city.")[65]

When the election campaign was reaching its apex, Pope Paul issued his famous injunction to the faithful: "Remain, remain in my love." This meant in simple language, "Vote Christian Democrat."

Premier Aldo Moro also joined in the rhetoric against the Reds. "What divides us from the Communists?" Moro asked. His answer was predictable: "It is our conception of man and our Christian belief, which is an important part of our heritage."

An estimated five million laymen turned into political vigilantes determined to stop the Red wave. Their slogan was wildly emotive: "If you vote Communist, it may be the last time you get a chance to vote."[66]

As a show of force for the church's position, the Italian Synod of Bishops opened their meeting in Rome during mid-May, 1976. Cardinal Poma, chairman of the Synod, issued a general warning that any Catholic campaigning on the Communist ticket risked excommunication. This was, however, too little too late, and thousands of the Catholic faithful declared their fidelity to Marxist social and political theory.[67]

When the dust settled after the election, the Communists controlled fully one-third of the local governments in Italy. *L'Osservatore Romano*, the official voice of the Vatican, reported in September 1976 that Communist authorities had initiated a concerted attack "against Catholic educational and welfare institutions." Municipal nursery schools were being opened, and the subsidy previously paid to Catholic schools was cut off.[68]

Further inroads into the ethic of Catholicism continue to

emerge. Early in 1977 the Italian Chamber of Deputies approved an extremely liberal abortion law. Under its provisions women were allowed to make the decision to keep or destroy the baby within the first three months of the life of the fetus. *L'Osservatore Romano* criticized the bill as the "easiest and most indiscriminate of all such laws, because it allows abortion for the most indefinite and indefinable causes."[69]

There seems to be little doubt that Catholicism and Communism are destined to become strange and reluctant bedfellows. Historically, Catholicism has compromised only on nonessential issues. This time it may have to surrender some basic principles of ethics and ecclesiastical politics. As the British parliamentarian Julian Critchley wrote, "The 'historical compromise' between Christian Democracy and Communism may already be taking place."[70]

RED MARKS ON THE BALANCE SHEET

A survey of Eastern and Western Europe since 1960 reveals sizeable gains for communism. The balance of power between Rome and Moscow has steadily tilted against the Catholic Church.

One wonders why communism is so attractive to European working classes. Writing at the outset of this period, the mission strategist and Europe-watcher, Robert Evans, suggested five possible reasons for communism's popularity. First, surging secularism has undermined the influence of both Catholicism and Protestantism. Second, the legacy of the French Enlightenment and Revolution lingers in the historical memory of modern Europeans. Third, materialism has become the working philosophy of most continentals, and things have become an end in themselves. Fourth, since the end of World War II an entire generation of political leaders has died, leaving political instability throughout Europe. Finally, from Britain to Berlin and Sweden to Sicily, labor unions have aligned themselves with socialist politics.

Catholicism has embarked on a road of compromise. It learned this lesson during the nationalistic nineteenth-century revolutions. The principle was refined as it adapted to Fascism in the thirties and forties. Now communism commands further compromise.[71]

8

Repression of Soviet Saints

Communism is at its very heart revolutionary. According to the gravestone of Karl Marx in London's Highgate Cemetery, "Philosophers have interpreted the world. The point is to change it."[1] For over a century the teachings of Marx and Engels have been changing it.

From the outset of revolution in Russia, Christians came under the heel of oppression. In *Gulag Archipelago*, Alexander Solzhenitsyn quoted a protest by Patriarch Tikhon directed at the Council of People's Commissars in October 1918: "Many courageous priests have already paid for their preaching with the blood of martyrdom."[2]

Since 1960 there has been a veritable flood of literature portraying the pitiful state of Soviet believers. In *Discretion and Valour*, British researchers enumerated the measures employed to crush Christians. Denominational bodies are systematically stifled. The Eastern-rite Catholic Uniates were forced to unite with other bodies, thus sacrificing their distinctive doctrines. Mennonites have been denied the right to form a central committee. When Reformed Baptists tried to convene a conference, they met a stone wall of governmental prohibition.[3]

If denominational bodies have suffered, there has been even more pressure exerted on local churches. Ministers have been compelled to register with the government and to sub-

mit to scrutiny and interrogation. Churches have been summarily closed down. All types of Sunday schools and children's services are banned.[4]

Christian believers are bearing the brunt of this opposition. Vocational promotions are withheld from Christians, and
university training is out of reach for most who profess faith in
Christ. Christian families often find it impossible to secure
housing. On the pretext of protecting children, the state often
spirits them away from Christian parents and consigns them
to state-run orphanages. In the public media Christians are
repeatedly subjected to defamation of character.[5]

In 1969 a document against the persecution of children
was compiled by the so-called "Union of Christian Baptist
Mothers," a protest movement spearheaded by the separatist
Reformed Baptists. The petition was sent to party chief
Leonid Breshnev. It was backed by forty pages of signatures,
1,453 in all. Still this protest against antireligious repression
fell on deaf ears.[6]

An ecumenical protest, the first of its kind, was submitted to the Supreme Soviet in June 1976. This petition against
persecution of religious bodies was signed by several leading
clergymen representing the Russian Orthodox Church,
Lithuanian Catholics, Baptists, the Church of Christ, and the
Seventh-Day Adventists. Their conclusion was a slap in the
face for contemporary post-Stalinist Communist chiefs. Their
spokesman, Igor Shafarevich, wrote, "In many ways the situation of the Church in Russia now is as bad as under Stalin. . . .
Although big changes have been made in Soviet society since
the death of Stalin in 1953, the position of the Church has
been left untouched."[7]

It is the persistent persecution of Christian believers that
repeatedly draws attention to Russia. Lenin said that the Revolution would lay to rest forever "shameful laws against
people of other beliefs."[8] In 1973 Soviet diplomats hypocriti-
cally initialed the Helsinki agreement guaranteeing the right
of religious belief and practice. Still the harsh hammer of

communism pounds away at believers in all of the Soviet republics.

PATTERNS OF PERSECUTION

Although the tyranny of Stalin's Russia was renounced by his successors, the persecution of believers did not stop. In 1959 Nikita Khruschev launched a five-year program aimed at the destruction of Christianity. The primary target was Soviet youth, and religious instruction for all under eighteen was ruled out. Parents were forbidden to compel children to attend worship, and ministers were enjoined to discontinue religious instruction.[9] At the same time, Nikodim was chosen to be Metropolitan of the Orthodox Church. He was a man who could be relied upon to "cooperate" with Communist authorities.[10]

In January 1960 Khruschev addressed the Communist Party Congress and demanded that laws limiting religion should be strictly enforced. A year later a Communist Party circular gave details of measures to be taken against Christians. Intelligence information concerning the existence of churches and their attendance was to be forwarded to the Central Committee. The sociological composition of churches would be studied. Ministers who had refused to register with the authorities were exposed, and the government ordered special vigilance against prohibited domestic rites such as the baptism of infants.[11]

At the twenty-second Party Congress in 1961, Khruschev fumed that Christians were still flourishing. He urged greater ruthlessness in rooting out this weed in the socialist flower bed. Later on that year it could be reported that since Khruschev's ascension to power in 1953, more than ten thousand churches had been closed. Seminaries for training Orthodox priests had been reduced in number from eight in 1958 to three by 1965.[12]

Realizing that the family is the strongest link to the church, Khruschev took steps to replace family festivals with socialistic ceremonies. Later he introduced secular services for baptism, marriage, and burial.[13]

The years from 1953 to 1964, when Khruschev dictated the policies of Russian government, were indeed "black years" for the church. Not only the Orthodox Church and the Baptist churches were systematically suppressed. Smaller religious minorities such as the Seventh-Day Adventists, Pentecostals, and the Jehovah's Witnesses were also attacked without mercy.[14]

There were three main reasons for Khruschev's pogrom against Christians. First, he feared for the internal security of the state. Second, churches were regarded as an unproductive drag on the already weak national economy. Finally, churches harbored representatives of reactionary thought who could upset the socialist applecart.[15]

With the passing from politics in 1964 of Nikita Khruschev, Christians hoped for a respite from repeated attacks. But there was no respite. In 1970 William Fletcher wrote, "The anti-religious campaign which has been waged by the Soviet State for the past decade has created a general condition of extreme tension for all believers."[16]

After 1968 there was an increasingly vocal civil rights movement in Russia, one of whose main aims was religious liberty. This was countered by increased pressure on the nonregistered churches, those who refused to submit to scrutiny by the local "Soviet" (council). This provided official churches with a breathing space, and the government even allowed them to print one edition each of the Bible and a hymn book.[17]

The intensity of this persecution was documented during 1975 by Amnesty International researchers. Although Article 24 of the Soviet constitution guarantees "freedom of religious worship," in practice this permission is regularly denied. Christians, Buddhists, and Moslems alike are imprisoned for religious crimes. In fact, a large proportion of so-called prisoners of conscience are in jail for religious reasons. When the police burst in upon a forest prayer meeting near Mogilev, Belorussiya in 1974, Nikolai Loiko of Minsk was shot and seriously wounded. Religious literature was rigorously sought out. Christian prisoners failing to work on religious holidays were locked up in solitary confinement. At the very minimum, Amnesty estimated that in 1975 there were approximately ten thousand religious prisoners in Russia.[18]

An editorial in London's *Daily Telegraph* during December 1976 aptly summed it up: "Never before has the assault by an intolerant and all-mighty secular power on religious faith and observance been so sustained, scientific and insidious as during the past 60 years in Russia. . . . In the place of the dramatic fire and sword of less sophisticated tyrants, who provided the Church with renewed life-blood at the cost of that of its martyrs, there is a grim relentless threat to livelihood, education, family and status."[19]

As the Red wave rolls over Russian Christianity, it is the young people who are most maligned. This lends a particularly diabolical aspect to the whole dirty business of persecution. Urging that children be nurtured "in the Moral Code of the Builder of Communism," the government has attempted since the sixties to cut children off from all Christian instruction. It is felt that a movement robbed of its young will sooner or later die out.[20]

The rationale for persecution is reminiscent of Roman reasons for attacking the early Christians. Christians force their children to become "socially withdrawn," since they are not allowed to mix socially with other children. According to socialistic propaganda, a Christian child "will inevitably be morally, psychologically, and socially stunted." Furthermore, according to I.I. Ogryzko's book *Children and Religion*, "Religion suppressed the striving of children towards knowledge, science, and culture."[21]

This irrational approach is pushed to ridiculous extremes. One recent report "demonstrated" that one-tenth of all children develop a middle ear infection after christening. In

Orenburg province one town was supposedly swept by an epidemic of scarletina among recently christened children. Some babies allegedly had even drowned in Orthodox baptismal fonts. Jews too have been objects of this kind of unfounded and ridiculous criticism. During the past decade twenty thousand baby boys were reported to have died from infection related to circumcision.[22]

In Russian schools specific attempts are made to dissuade Christians' children. Teachers are urged to undertake "personal work" to convert their charges to atheism.[23] One kindergarten teacher took her class to a park. When the youngsters became hungry, she mockingly told the believers' children to pray for their food. When no food came, she scoffed, "There is no God. You are stupid to believe on such a fairy tale." Then she told the others to say this prayer: "Lenin, give us something to eat." By previous arrangement, a van with snacks drove up as soon as they finished "praying."[24]

The governmental department for atheism has converted many closed churches into museums of atheism. These crude exhibitions are designed to break down confidence in Christianity. Although adults may visit them, they are mainly designed to convince young people of the irrational nature of religion.[25]

Since Christians normally do not join socialist youth movements such as the Komsomols (Young Communist League), their participation in academic life, sports, and the professions is severely limited. Olympic athletes, for instance, are uniformly drawn from the ranks of young Communists. University training is not open to non-party members. If students are discovered to be believers, they are usually expelled.[26]

In the sixties, deputy minister of education, Mikhail Petrovich Kashin, described Christianity among school children as "a terrible enemy which we often underestimate." "We do not want our boys and girls to grow up merely ignorant of religious questions," he went on to say. "We want them to become convinced, militant atheists."[27]

Still young people turn to Christianity. The *Fraternal Herald*, organ of the registered churches, claimed that "old methods of atheist propaganda" were losing their sting. Even highly educated youngsters were turning to Christianity. This included the offspring of both believers and atheists, and it was especially true in the centers of traditional religious strength, such as the Ukraine.[28]

Although some still turn to Christianity, the grim fact of persecution persists. Since the time of Stalin there has been little light streaming into the black torture chamber of Communist repression. Churches are closed. Pastors either register or become refugees stalked by Soviet authorities. Still it is the children who bear the brunt of constant atheistic bombardment. When all else fails, they are snatched from their parents and sent away to a state-run orphanage.

EMBATTLED BAPTISTS

Because of their illegal position as unregistered churches, the Reformed Baptists present the most cogent case study of Communist pressure and its results. The Reformed Baptists took on identity in about 1961. Concerning them William Fletcher wrote in 1971: "In 1961, a formidable opposition movement arose within the Russian Baptist community, which claimed at its peak to represent twice as many congregations as did the legalized Russian Baptist organization."[29]

The source of this virile company of Christians was the "Action Group," which formed under the leadership of Alexii Prokofief, Gennadi Kryuchkov, and Georgi Vins. (The latter has since become a personification of the plight shared by these Soviet saints, and his incredible story will be treated in depth.) One year after the "Action Group" formed, more than 100 of the Reformed Baptists had been jailed.[30] In fact, 524 had been rounded up at the beginning of 1962, and 400 of these had been held for a period of fifteen days.[31]

In May 1966, 500 Reformed Baptists from 130 congregations converged on Moscow to petition the Party for religious liberty. Their approach to the Central Committee of the Communist Party was rudely rebuffed. Five days afterward the congregation in Kiev was raided during a worship service. On May 23 there was a second armed attack. The officer in charge was unusually high-ranking, Major-General Degtyarev. (This reveals the serious light in which the authorities regard Reformed Baptists.) The general sought to defame the religious prisoners by depicting them as "criminals against the state, debauchees, thieves, drunkards, and murderers."[32] The presentation of proof to substantiate such wild accusations seems to be completely irrelevant to Soviet jurisprudence.

A few months after this shocking incident a group of Reformed Baptists formed the Council of Relatives of Prisoners. Their purpose was to publicize the plight of imprisoned fellow believers. A letter of protest was prepared and smuggled out to U Thant, the late Secretary General of the United Nations. There was an exact listing of 202 Protestants then in prison for their beliefs. In eighteen cities chapels had been confiscated and the congregations expelled. Two private homes (if that phrase has any meaning in a socialist state) that had held Christian meetings were bulldozed into rubble. There was a plea to the United Nations to force the Kremlin to give freedom to Christians.[33]

During December 1969 a conference of Reformed Baptist leaders convened at Tula. At that gathering there were 120 delegates from 47 different areas of the Soviet Union. Gennadi Kryuchkov, one of the founders of the "Action Group," was chosen chairman of the Reformed Baptists. Representatives of the officially registered All-Union Churches were present. Despite the completely open nature of this convention, the Reformed Baptists were still refused the right to register. Their political and legal exile and the persecution of their leaders, such as Georgi Vins, continued.[34]

The British Baptist leader David Russell attended a Baptist congress in Moscow in 1976. On that occasion he was granted a two-hour interview by Victor N. Titov, Deputy Chairman of the Council of Religious Affairs. During that discussion he made "a strong plea for clemency to be shown to those still in prison." Obviously, this appeal fell on deaf bureaucratic ears. After the meeting in Moscow, Russell visited Georgi Vins's congregation in Kiev. Up to 80 percent of the men in the church were under thirty years of age. The Reformed Baptists' vitality left a lasting impression on the British clergyman.[35]

Fifteen years after they united, the Reformed Baptists are the most harassed group of believers in the Soviet Union. Mrs. Yakimenkova said to one visitor from the West: "Tell the United Nations that we hear nothing from them. . . . Our prayer meetings are broken up by the police. They send our men to the camps. We, the wives, our aged parents, and our children are left to die from starvation."[36]

In 1975 a subterranean printing shop operated by the Reformed Baptists was raided. A group of Christians had worked there for long periods of time. Because they were deprived of sunlight, they existed on high potency vitamin tablets. Over 300,000 pieces of Christian literature had been produced. Then the K.G.B. got wind of it. They arranged to have a supply of radioactive printing paper sent to the Baptists. Then they simply sniffed out the site with a James Bond style of helicopter operation. The presses were shut down, the literature confiscated, and the printers imprisoned.[37]

No one leader symbolizes the stamina of the Reformed Baptists better than Georgi Vins, the persecuted pastor from Kiev. *Time* magazine even praised him for his "stubborn and courageous" stand for the faith.[38]

In 1976 an autobiography by Vins was smuggled to the West and published in London. Vins set the scene for understanding the Reformed Baptist movement when he referred to the Soviet situation in the previous decade: "By the sixties the voice of the Church had become very faint. Witness to Christ was bounded more and more by the walls of prayer houses, but inside these houses, the number of which was catastrophically decreased, ministers who had been false to God under the pressure of atheism led the task of curtailing the work of the Gospel."[39]

A doctrinal basis of the Reformed Baptists was carefully set out by Vins. By and large, it was similar to that which the Anabaptists of the Reformation era had used. There was emphasis on a "gathered church" of Christians identified by believers' baptism. The Scriptures were the sole standard of faith and practice. Church and state were to be completely separate, with each congregation autonomous under the rule of the Bible. In true Reformation style, the priesthood of all believers was reiterated.[40]

Georgi Vins was first arrested and sent to the Anyusha corrective labor camp in Siberia in 1966. He remained there for three years. Prison officials tried to force him into collaboration against the Christian community, but Vins responded with a hunger strike. Meanwhile he infected the entire compound with his Bible teaching and zealous Christian witness. Prisoners soon stopped smoking and swearing, and many were converted. So serious was this threat that the camp commander lamented, "Another six months and half the camp will become Baptists."[41]

Released in 1969, Vins proceeded with pastoral work. This so incensed the Communist authorities that they again arrested him in 1974, sentencing him to an additional five years in Yaktutak, Siberia.[42]

In 1976 a tape-recorded message from Vins to his persecuted mother, Lydia, was reported in London's *Sunday Telegraph*. Vins was suffering imprisonment for "violating church/state laws, defaming the state and infringing personal rights." All of the family's furniture had been confiscated, leaving Vins's wife and children virtually homeless. The Baptist General Secretary, Aleksei Bichkov, condemned Vins in Communistic tones: "[He is] an extremist with a martyr complex. . . . He is the most zealous of our opponents. He has called us atheists." This vitriolic attack against Vins ironically substantiates the suspicion that some of the official Baptists are collaborators.[43]

During the summer of 1976 several major demonstrations in the West pleaded for Vins's release. At Bonn 12,000 paraded through the German capital calling for Vins's discharge from prison. On the same day between 6,000 and 10,000 Englishmen marched to the Russian Embassy in London. There the M.P. Michael Alison tried to present a petition bearing 300,000 signatures. The Russians refused to receive the list of names.[44]

Russian reaction to these protests produced a crafty ploy. An unofficial news release reached the West at the end of 1976, stating that Vins had been set free. Far from being a fact, this was only a clever Communist ruse designed to take the sting out of Western protest. In reality, the Baptist martyr was still suffering in Siberia.[45]

TAMING THE ORTHODOX CHURCH

Western observers might be excused for entertaining the mistaken impression that only "unregistered" and therefore illegal denominations are targets of Soviet persecution. In fact, even the old, established Russian Orthodox Church is an object of political pressure.

Before the 1917 Revolution there were eighty thousand Orthodox churches, chapels, and monasteries. Now there are a mere eight thousand.[46] In 1959, when Khruschev's concerted attack against Christianity commenced, there were about sixteen thousand Orthodox churches in operation. Five years later only half of them remained open.[47] The flow of young men into the priesthood has likewise been choked off. In 1955 about 1,500 were studying theology at any given time, and this produced about 400 ordinands annually. This supply of clergy was cut down to 155 per year by 1960.[48]

A special report printed in *Christianity Today* during

1963 revealed especially severe persecution of Orthodox believers in the Byclorussia and Western Ukraine regions. Churches and monasteries were closed down. Children were forcibly removed from religious instruction of any sort and young boys were forbidden to act as acolytes. A refinement of Soviet strategy was outlined in an inside report: "In order to exterminate the Orthodox faith and to speed up the closing of churches, the government is secretly training its godless Communists as priests. They [the government] appoint them as heads of churches and cathedrals and make them bishops and priests."[49]

Some of the actions taken against Christians are almost humorous. One GUM governmental department store in Moscow was discovered to have criminally received and sold ornamental crosses. In 1960, a man was jailed because he received a shipment of a thousand icons and twenty-five hundred crosses.[50] Archbishop Job of Kazan was publicly tried and sentenced to three years in prison for illegally trafficking in candles.

Direct persecution against the Orthodox Church, however, does not seriously limit its influence. In fact, it strengthens the resolve of faithful worshipers. According to Timothy Ware, the Orthodox Oxford don, about 10 percent of the Russian population worships weekly. This respectable percentage far outstrips the average in most western European lands.[51]

A far more serious threat to the integrity of Russian Orthodox Christianity is the subtle strategy of coercion and infiltration. As early as 1922, the collaborating "Council of the Living Church" urged "that every honorable Christian should take his place among these warriors [i.e., Communist revolutionaries] for humanitarian truth and use all means to realize in life the grand principles of the October Revolution"[52]

By the late sixties Communist control of the Orthodox hierarchy was virtually complete. Speaking in New York during 1973, Patriarch Pimen of Moscow defended Communist overlords. "The social evils so typical for the life of many people today just cannot occur within our [Soviet] social structure," he claimed.[53]

At the Central Committee meeting of the World Council of Churches in August 1976, a portfolio of violations against religious rights in Russia was presented. These violations were condemned in the light of the Helsinki agreement initialled by Russian politicians in 1973. When confronted with the catalog of persecution, the Russian delegate Bugvskiy dismissed them with a casual comment and a claim that they were "anti-Communist propaganda." The official hands of the World Council of Churches were tied by the fact that one of the copresidents of the Council was Nikodim, a Kremlin appointee.[54]

Also in 1976 a warning came from Seraphim, administrator of the Moscow diocese and Metropolitan of Krutizy and Kilomna. He ordered priests to suspend discussion of political and social questions and to desist from discussing church finance. Actually, this was an attempt to gag the clergymen and thwart the sending of protest documents to Western churchmen.[55]

In 1973 a young art historian with impeccable Communist credentials wrote an essay criticizing the World Council of Churches for its silence on human rights in Russia. In his paper entitled "The Moral Pre-requisites of Christian Unity," Yevgeni Barabanov condemned the World Council of Churches for playing politics, or to use his word, "politicisation." According to him, the Geneva organization follows a policy in which "expediency is sacrificed for moral integrity, and the peace which is produced is no peace."[56]

CHRISTIAN COURAGE

It was Chrysostom, the fourth-century bishop of Constantinople, who said, "It behoves thee not to complain, if thou endurest hardness, but to complain, if thou doest not endure hardness." Certainly the trials of Russian Christians have rather produced strength than weakness.

One of the most dramatic effects of persecution in Russia is the worldwide fame it has given to articulate dissidents. In his famous Lenten Letter of 1972, Alexander Solzhenitsyn spoke out against the taming of the Orthodox Church: "A church dictatorially directed by atheists is a spectacle that has not been seen for 2,000 years." Within days this courageous protest against Soviet power politics was flashed around the world.[57]

In 1974 Solzhenitsyn was expelled from Russia because of his flagrant criticism of the government. Ironically, this served to undergird the cause of Christian dissidents. The families of prisoners received hundreds of thousands of dollars from the royalties of Solzhenitsyn's *Gulag Archipelago*.[58]

Another influential protester against persecution in Russia was the Nobel Prize Winner Andrei Sakharov, a humanist. In 1974 he directed a protest to the World Council of Churches meeting in Amsterdam: "Freedom of conscience is an individual part of freedom as a whole," Sakharov said. "Honest people throughout the world should defend the victims of religious persecutions wherever these take place—in tiny Albania or in the vast Soviet Union."[59]

Throughout the dismal sixties and seventies, as persecution increased, so did Christian commitment. In fact, an American delegation sent by the National Council of Churches discovered in 1962 that many Russian Orthodox Churches were crowded with worshipers. According to the Americans' report, "religious feeling continued strong among the populace and... the atheistic drive sponsored by the Communist party was making little headway."[60]

One of the most virulent atheistic journals in Russia is *Science and Religion*, whose aim is to debunk the Christian church. Still the admission was inserted in 1976 that "religion is like a nail: if you hit it on the head it will go deeper." The solution suggested by scientific atheism was "We must surround religion, squeeze it from the bottom and pull it up." A scientific approach to life could uproot religion, the journal optimistically proclaimed. (Hope springs eternal in the atheists' materialistic heart!)[61]

A few weeks after the printing of the above story the Orthodox Easter was celebrated in Russia. According to a news service report, "Russian Christians in their thousands packed churches in Moscow until the small hours... to celebrate Easter, ignoring official Press attacks."[62]

Even funeral services are turned into triumphant church services. When a Russian pastor died in the Ukraine in 1975, a special funeral service was scheduled. The congregation numbered two thousand, and thirty pastors took part. The entire open-air service went on nonstop for six hours.[63]

Strangely enough, this religious renaissance is mainly a movement among the young. Among Russians in their twenties and thirties there is a persistent interest in Christianity, despite the militantly atheistic character of the education they have received. The religious awakening among young people, according to Michael Bourdeaux, an English expert on religion and communism, "can be seen above all in the mood of the young intelligentsia."[64]

A letter written by an outspoken Orthodox layman, Anatoly Levitin, reached the West in 1970. Young people had been left hungry by the dry crusts of atheism and were turning to Christianity. The more simple peasants were becoming Baptists, and those "capable of deep mythical experience" went to Orthodoxy. In Moscow it happened frequently that the sons of Communists and even Security Police sought baptism.[65]

Another confirmation of that report came from Michael Bourdeaux. He likened the influx of young people into the Orthodox Church to a "small but significant trickle." On the other hand, the Baptists were receiving young converts in a measure amounting "to something like a flood."[66]

Orthodox theological seminaries are a good thermometer of religious interest. At the 1974 graduation exercises of the

seminary at Zagorsk, Archbishop Vladimir of Dmitrov mentioned the level of applications. Three-quarters of all who
applied had to be turned down because of lack of space.[67]
Trevor Beeson confirmed this state of affairs by reporting that
"recent increases in the student intake" at theological colleges
guaranteed a steady flow of clergymen.[68] One only hopes that
these young clergymen will not succumb to the soft option of
collaborating with the Communist regime.

Bereft of formal seminaries, the Reformed Baptist pastors
train young men by the apprenticeship method. Informally,
the older men pass on pastoral and theological knowledge to
the young. Special study groups help budding preachers develop skills in speaking.[69]

Another indicator of spiritual life in Soviet Russia is the
popular interest in the Bible. When in 1966 an edition of a
hundred thousand children's Bible story books was printed,
the entire stock was sold within hours.[70]

So keen is the interest for the Bible that some Christians
actually write out copies of the Scriptures by hand. From the
West there come radio programs in which the Bible is read in
Russian at dictation speed. If a copy of the Bible is procured
from some outside source, it is often torn into thirty or forty
parts so that many can have a small portion.[71]

Since the Russian Revolution of 1917, fewer than one
million Bibles have been printed. The deplorable inadequacy
of this supply is seen when one considers that there are 30
million Orthodox and 3 million nonconformist Christians.
Since 1969 a team of Orthodox scholars has been at work
producing a translation of the New Testament, but this project will take some time to complete. It is small wonder that
customs officers often earn a handsome profit when they sell
confiscated Bibles on the black market.[72]

Mission societies in Western countries attempt to smug-
gle or send Bibles into the Soviet Union. However, their
success is modest. Peter Dyneka, founder of the Slavic Gospel
Association, admitted, "Despite all the creative and persistent
ways that were tried to carry Bibles beyond the border, the

trickle getting through did not even begin to meet the demands of 250 million people in the Soviet Union."[73]

The Blood of the Martyrs

In Soviet Russia the age-old axiom of Tertullian is being
proved every day: "The blood of the martyrs is the seed of the
Church." Persecution has only served to arouse greater interest in the message of the Bible and the life of the church.

A Lithuanian Communist journal recently took notice of
the movement among youth in that Catholic republic: "We
must not be lulled into complacency by the fact that atheism is
winning the battle against religion." Even after eleven years
in Soviet schools, many young people are still loyal to Christianity.[74]

In a *New York Times* report from 1974 it was reported
that Christians outnumber Communists in Russia by two to
one. Even nonbelievers are drawn into the celebration of
Christian festivals, such as Christmas and Easter. *Pravda* put
it this way: "The dying off of religion under socialism is not an
automatic process."[75]

Just as Christianity survived Roman persecution, so contemporary Christians in Russia have an endurance that is
made firm in the fire of suffering. Their spontaneous witness
to the reality of Christ is irresistible to even the most hard-
ened Communist. In his masterful study of Eastern Europe,
Trevor Beeson concluded, "It has become clear that obedience to God in a Communist-ruled society has a dynamic
quality, and one which cannot leave a society unaffected."[76]

9

Christians in the Soviet Empire

In the cold-war climate of the fifties and sixties, the Soviet Union constantly condemned Western nations for their supposed "colonialistic" activities. A special subject for Soviet censure was the involvement of the United States in Vietnam. Communists claimed that the United States propped up the corrupt Thieu regime while the Russian "Robin Hoods" gave aid to the Viet Cong "liberation" forces. Cold-war rhetoric invariably linked capitalism with colonialism, and communism with liberation.

After the United States beat a hasty retreat from Vietnam, the focus of foreign policy shifted to Africa. Again the Communists backed so-called "liberation" movements against minority white governments in Rhodesia, South Africa, and Angola. In the Angolan civil war, Cuban soldiers supported the Angolan "freedom fighters." Former United States ambassador to the United Nations Daniel P. Moynihan called the Cubans "Gurkhas of the Russian empire."[1]

During the early spring of 1977 the Russian president Nikolai Podgorny visited southern Africa. He urged nationalists to persist in their battle against white supremacy, that is against *Western white supremacy*. President Podgorny regarded "the liquidation of the last vestiges of colonialism and racism . . . to be one of the most important international tasks."[2]

146

Actually, since 1917 more than one-third of the world has fallen under Communist control. Throughout Eastern Europe the Russians have woven a tight net of political control. Militarily they call this the Warsaw Pact. Its economic counterpart is Comecon.

Any attempt by constituent countries to break out of the Marxist mold is quickly quashed. For instance, when Stalin died in March 1953, the Soviet satellites hoped for greater freedom. It was the East Germans who tested the water by revolting in June. Their attempts were cut short as Russian tanks rolled into Berlin.[3]

Three years later the Hungarians tried to break out of the Russian orbit. During the autumn of 1956 Hungarians protested against Soviet control. The result was a moderate government under Imre Nagy, but public opinion soon called for reforms far beyond those intended. The Soviets feared a rebirth of Fascism and sent in the soldiers. Before the affair ended, seven thousand Russian troops and thirty thousand Hungarians lay dead. Russia had reestablished control of another of its satellites, but in so doing it had created a legacy of bitterness among Hungarians.[4]

A third exhibition of Soviet strength came in 1968. During the "Prague Spring," Alexander Dubcek set up a creatively progressive government in Czechoslovakia. Fearing yet another crack in the Communist monolith, the Soviets again opted for force. On August 18, 1968, Russian armored columns snaked through the streets of Prague. Rather than taking up arms, the people of Prague simply offered passive resistance. By March 1969 Dubcek had been replaced, and his reforms were annulled. Secretary Leonid Brezhnev declared his own "Doctrine of Limited Sovereignty." In other words, the solidarity of the Soviet bloc always outweighs any quest for national identity.[5]

Just as the Soviets keep a tight rein on political, economic, or social aspirations, so they also enforce atheism and resist religious liberty. Throughout the Warsaw Pact lands there is only limited freedom for Christian worship. Although military might is seldom employed to enforce atheism, the pressure is nonetheless real.

RUMANIAN REVIVAL

In 1962 the atheistic Rumanian weekly, *The Agitator*, heralded the success of the propaganda program. In the province of Bukovina, eighteen thousand atheistic lectures had been given in one year. More than a hundred thousand workers had come to hear Christianity denounced. The "House of the Atheist," a center for antireligious propaganda, said, "The practice of our best agitators shows that relaxed, friendly talk with a man on this theme is the best way to his heart and reason."[6]

In fact, this aggressively atheistic program of lectures has been coupled with a systematic stripping away of Christians' rights. After 1954 the right of meeting was severely restricted. Local pastors could no longer be paid by their congregations. It was forbidden to baptize publicly. The teaching of children and the production of Christian literature were completely outlawed.[7]

Formerly the officially recognized church in Rumania, the Orthodox Church came under governmental attack in 1958. Patriarch Justinian was jailed, and many monks were reduced to a lay state. Two years later the authorities arrested fifteen hundred Orthodox monks and nuns in one sweeping purge.[8]

It was the Orthodox monasteries that suffered most. Despite pressure, these conservatories of the Orthodox faith had been "flourishing and increasing in number." In 1959 all nuns under the age of forty and all monks under fifty were required to take up "more socially useful work."[9]

Meanwhile, Orthodox churches continued during the early sixties to attract large congregations. Furthermore, parish priests were busily engaged in officiating at domestic ceremonies, viz., the baptism of infants at home.[10]

Since then, progressive freedoms have been won by Rumanian Orthodox Christians. This can be seen in the number of churches still operating. In 1960 the *Europa Year Book* reported that three hundred churches were open in Bucharest, in contrast with fifty-five in Moscow, thirty-nine in Sophia, and twelve in Belgrade.[11]

One reason for a relative degree of freedom in Rumania has been the government's attempt to forge trade and diplomatic links with the West. This milder approach toward the church has actually produced an increase in recorded church membership. When the Rumanian Orthodox Church in 1961 joined the World Council of Churches, its official membership stood at 13 million. Twelve years later 16.6 million claimed membership in that church.[12] The main emphasis in Orthodox worship is sacramental. Since sacraments are celebrated according to a fixed liturgy, there is less cause for conflict than there would be in a Protestant preaching service.[13]

While the Orthodox Church shows signs of strength, it is the Baptists whose numbers are burgeoning despite official opposition.[14] Between 1968 and 1971 the government closed down the Baptist Seminary in Bucharest. When it first reopened, there were still serious problems. Only twelve resident students were enrolled in 1973.[15]

Writing under the alias "Andre Morea," a Rumanian Christian produced a revealing report on Eastern European Christianity. Observing Christian life, this anonymous Rumanian traveled frequently across borders within Eastern Europe. One small-town mayor lamented, "These evangelicals are an absolute plague. They go around the countryside organizing meetings where they talk to people about repentance, speak against the state and twist men's minds."[16]

In November 1975 a new Baptist chapel was opened in Bosca. Six days later the government had reduced it to rubble. Christians met among the ruins to demonstrate their defiance of the government's bullying tactics.[17]

From the Bucharest Baptist Seminary a protest letter against the paucity of professors was smuggled to England. All twenty students signed the petition requesting the return of two professors who had been dismissed. These professors were Josif Ton, who had studied at Oxford, and Petru Belicov, former director of the Seminary.[18]

The persistent pressure on Rumanian Baptists has served, however, to strengthen their will to survive. In 1968 they received permission to print a new hymnal, the first since 1941. Furthermore, leaders of the 120,000 Rumanian Baptists were permitted to attend Baptist World Alliance meetings in Liberia.[19]

When British Baptist clergyman David Russell visited Rumania in 1973, he returned with an enthusiastic report. According to Russell, "Baptists in Rumania are increasing despite the restrictions of a Communist State." On average, ninety thousand Baptists worship regularly in four hundred churches.[20]

In 1976 *Christianity Today* carried a report on Baptist survival in Rumania. Special emphasis was given to the work of Pastor Olah in Ordea. In one year his church had grown from six hundred to fifteen hundred. Baptists had gained freedoms to hold services and conduct baptisms. A new edition of a hundred thousand Bibles was being printed in Bucharest.[21]

Reporting to the twenty-seventh Congress of the Rumanian Baptist Union, the former general secretary, Joachim Tunea, claimed, "There has never been so much understanding, freedom and cooperation from the authorities in Rumania as today." Virtually every congregation has doubled in size since World War II. Buildings are crowded with worshipers. New congregations are springing up and buildings are being erected.[22]

A fitting summary of the situation was penned by Josif Ton: "We believers have a place within the socialist state.

God chose us to follow Him from *within socialism*. Evangelical Christians are increasing rapidly despite opposition. God has set the Christian within socialism and given him a mission to socialist society."[23] This mission has cost Ton imprisonment and suffering.

GERMAN DEMOCRATIC REPUBLIC: SOVIET SHOWPIECE

"East Europe's most prosperous state is also the land of Bach, Handel, Luther, and Goethe," begins Trevor Beeson's report. Then he portrays the political bosses' dilemma concerning the German Democratic Republic: "Abroad the policy is one of detente and peaceful coexistence. The more that policy succeeds the more vigilance is thought to be needed at home to keep the nation free of ideological ferment."[24]

From 1961 on, Khruschev's attack on Christianity reached its grasping tentacles into East Germany. At the outset of the German Protestant "Kirchentag" (Church Day) in 1961, all rallies outside church walls were strictly forbidden. Only one East German bishop was permitted to cross into the West to attend the Protestant conference.[25] That same month the "wall of shame" was swiftly erected to thwart the flow of refugees from the "workers' paradise."

In 1968 a revised penal code officially disestablished the Lutheran Church in East Germany. President Walter Ulbricht decreed that the East German Lutherans should no longer have official ties with their brethren in the West. A completely separate ecclesiastical structure was set up to serve the Communist sector, and thus the final link to the West was cut off.[26]

That same year a new constitution was promulgated by party bosses. It declared the rights of free worship and tolerance for Christians. They were even offered the option of being conscientious objectors to duty along the barbed-wire barrier. Still it was painfully obvious that Christians were practically without rights. None could enter a university, and occupational advancement was blocked for believers.[27]

As East Germany entered the seventies, church attendance had dwindled to a pitiful average of 5 percent of the church members. According to pastors' reports, most were elderly people who had been Christians before the successive waves of Nazism and Communism inundated their native land.[28]

Fearing for their families and themselves, many pastors fled from Eastern German parishes. By 1976 half of the Lutheran churches were without pastors. Seminary enrollments had slumped from 751 in 1958 to 585 in two years.[29]

This problem was highlighted at a "Kirchentag" (Church Day) in Rostock during June 1976. Bishop Werner Krusche decried the fact that churches were allotted no room in modern state-built apartment complexes. "If we cannot meet," reasoned the bishop, "what use are all the assurances of religious freedom?" Furthermore, he admitted that clergymen are "fewer and poorer," and they have no respect in the community.[30]

As in most socialistic states, it is the young people who feel most keenly the sting of persecution. In 1961 *Christianity Today* reported that "the practical de-Christianization of East Germany is picking up steam." More than 80 percent of the parents submitted their children to the socialistic "name giving" rather than Christian baptism. Over 88 percent of the young people attended "Jugendweihe" rather than confirmation.[31] One reason for this was the refusal of school authorities to accept pupils who boycotted socialistic ceremonies. Students who refused to sign the atheist oath or to cease attending worship were automatically excluded from selection for university places.[32]

The historian Richard Pierard cataloged the complaints of East German Christians in 1969. Religious teaching in the schools was suspended. Restrictions on the repair of church buildings were strengthened. Pastors were jailed on the flimsiest charges. Christians found it impossible to gain entrance into certain professions and virtually all higher education.[33]

In the face of this seemingly successful socialistic crusade, Christianity has survived. In 1974 a report reaching the West indicated that 55 percent of all East Germans still had their names on a church roll. In 1973 more than 316,000 Scripture portions had been circulated in the German Democratic Republic. Most of the country's theological seminaries remained evangelical, a trophy to the refining effect of persecution.[34]

The Evangelical Alliance continues to conduct its annual conference at Blankenburg in East Germany. About four thousand attended the eightieth annual conference in 1974. William Gilbert attended as representative of the West German Evangelical Alliance. He recorded his delight at "the spiritual life and courage to confess Christ which was being shown by Christians in Eastern Europe." Delegates to the convention came from East Germany, Czechoslovakia, Poland, Hungary, and Rumania.[35]

A rather macabre testimony to the seriousness of East German Christians occurred in 1976, when the forty-seven-year-old Lutheran pastor Oscar Brüsewitz saturated his clothing with gasoline and set a match to himself. According to one Western report, the death of the pastor showed anew "the tensions that pervade society and the testing strains to which many are exposed." The suicide victim carried a placard accusing the Communist authorities of oppressing young Christians and blocking pastors from emigrating. The political powers sought to write off Brüsewitz as being mentally unstable, but the victim's colleagues claimed that the poor man had accurately portrayed the pressures under which pastors labor.[36]

Despite the oppression under which Christians suffer, their lot in East Germany is in some ways better than in other Communist countries. For instance, 28 percent of the people there possess a Bible. By contrast, in Soviet Russia only one percent can procure even a portion of Scripture.[37]

In 1977 East German authorities relaxed restrictions

against the construction of church buildings. Work was immediately begun on forty new places of worship. This reversal of policy left Christians slightly perplexed, but very thankful.[38] Much of the money used to build churches comes from the West. A Catholic lawyer from East Germany negotiates with East Berlin authorities for the release of political prisoners. In turn the Protestant Church in West Germany hands over millions of American dollars. As a by-product, some funds are channeled into the building of churches behind the Berlin Wall.[39]

Just as economic prosperity has made East Germany a prize display of Soviet Communism, so also the Marxists boast about the degree of religious freedom allowed. Still the concrete wall that separates East from West hides a good deal of misery and repression. It also effectively blocks those who want to seek freedom in the West.

CZECHOSLOVAKIA: SOVIET SACRIFICIAL LAMB

The year 1968 is a watershed in the history of Czechoslovakia. Before that date there were sincere, if naive, attempts by Czech Christians to achieve a peaceful coexistence with the Communists. Afterward the illusion was shattered.

In 1961 the Czech professor Josef Hromadka organized his Christian Peace Conference. After studying in Aberdeen, he had taught from 1920 to 1939 at Prague, and during World War II he lectured at Princeton in Christian ethics. It was 1947 before he could return to Prague.

Already before 1940, Hromadka had expressed approval of the Communist revolution in Russia. Marxism was, in his words, "the church of the future." In 1958 he was awarded the Lenin Peace Prize for promoting dialogue between Christians and Communists.[40]

At the first meeting of the Christian Peace Conference at Prague in 1961, more than a thousand people participated. There was even a delegation from Red China. In summarizing the results, Trevor Beeson concluded, "In the context of post-Stalinist hopes, everything relating to peace was debated more openly than was customary in Prague, though still within strictly circumscribed limits."[41]

The Christian Peace Conference, however, lost all credibility in 1968. When the Russian forces moved in, the conference demurred to denounce the invasion. To multiply the insult, Metropolitan Nikodim, a Kremlin puppet, was named president of the Christian Peace Conference.[42]

Against the background of previously peaceful relations, the so-called "Prague Spring" developed in 1968. Alexander Dubcek had emerged as leader of a moderate government. Parents were allowed to register their children for religious education. Lutherans in Bratislava were encouraged to petition for the right of regular radio broadcasts. Some of the 350 deposed Lutheran pastors began to trickle back to their pulpits. Church magazines were licensed for publication. "Censorship was abolished and the churches were given freedom of which, since the Communists came to power, they had only dreamed," exclaimed Beeson.[43]

Politically, Dubcek granted even more astounding liberties. Free speech and a free press were advocated. A secret ballot was promised—a totally unique idea in Eastern Europe. Emigration of dissidents was to be allowed. Dubcek was designing a new concept in Communist government.[44]

Spring hope turned to winter freeze, however, when the Russians rolled their tanks into Prague on August 18, 1968. Dubcek was soon deposed. Freedoms were suspended. The Christian Peace Conference stood silently by, as did the World Council of Churches. Professor Hromadka was deeply disillusioned with the Soviet performance, and a year later he died of shame.[45]

In commenting on Czech Christianity since 1968, the American Roman Catholic bishops' conference was very critical. They described the Czech regime as "one of the most repressive in eastern Europe in regard to the exercise of human rights." The ban on women joining religious orders was especially deplored. This restriction effectively cut off twenty-two Catholic convents in Czechoslovakia.[46]

The breadth of Communist repression was documented in *Sparks*, an organ of the Slavic Gospel Association. Pastors are constantly in danger of losing their license to preach. Bibles and theological books are scarce. When young people are faithful to Christian principles and worship, they are expelled from school. During one year, a concerted crusade was staged to increase the percentage of atheists among children from 13 percent to 25 percent of the young population.[47]

The comprehensive program of persecution has predictably strengthened the Christians. As early as 1966, one Czech pastor described this to British Bible teacher Richard Bennett. With a thankful heart, the Eastern European minister said, "Communism has purged our Church. Not a pastor ascends the pulpit steps on Sunday, who is not true to the Word."[48]

When the European Baptist Confederation met in 1969, more than one thousand delegates came from Eastern Europe. Six hundred of these were Czechs. Looking back over the year since Russia invaded their country, Billy Graham told the Czech Baptists: "You are a triumphant Church, and the whole world is watching you."[49]

Since the invasion, baptisms have jumped in number by 50 percent. Christian weddings and funerals also show a marked increase. The government propaganda machine has stepped up production of anti-Christian broadcasts and literature. One propaganda pitch warned, "Your attitudes will inevitably become anti-communist if you cling to the church and support it."[50]

The Russian rape of Czechoslovakia in 1968 and its aftermath showed up forever the bankruptcy of Soviet ideology. Despite multiplying measures against Czech Christians, their numbers and faithfulness grows. As always, persecution strengthens the fortitude of the faithful, and thus it produces a result exactly opposite to the original intention.

YUGOSLAVIA: RELATIVE FREEDOM

"We don't consider ourselves behind the Iron Curtain," claimed the young Baptist leader in Zagreb, Branco Loverec. "We have no limitations, no problems."[51]

Yugoslavia has been a maverick within the Communist camp ever since World War II. Under Josip Broz Tito a more liberal, nationalistic form of socialism has developed. Realizing the folly of depending too much on Eastern European trading partners, Yugoslavia has cultivated strong economic ties with both Western Europe and the United States.

Only 5 percent of all Yugoslavians are card-carrying Communists. On the other hand, a vast majority profess allegiance to Christianity. In the eastern half of the country, 85 percent belong to the Orthodox Church, while in the western half 90 percent are Catholics. There is a strong Muslim population in the south. Protestants—mostly Baptists, Pentecostals, and Brethren—comprise a further 5 percent of the population.[52]

In 1968 *Christianity Today* reported that there was freedom to publish and distribute Bibles and other literature. Permission to build churches was also readily available. Even 70 percent of the army officers questioned claimed religious interests.[53]

The popular interest in religion made it possible for Billy Graham to conduct a massive rally in Zagreb in 1967. On a field owned by the Catholic Church and loaned to Graham, ten thousand gathered to hear him preach.[54]

One of the most significant signs of spiritual life in Yugoslavia has been the formation of theological training centers. In 1973 the Assemblies of God announced the establishment of a Bible college at Zagreb. Eighteen enrolled in the first year. The small school is led by Peter Kusmic, who was educated at Wheaton Graduate School of Theology, Wheaton, Illinois.[55]

At the end of 1974 *World Vision* magazine carried a survey of trends in Eastern Europe. At that time it gave special mention to the Yugoslavian Baptist Seminary at Novi Sad. In its twentieth year of operation the seminary had an enrollment of seventy students. This gave much hope for the future. First, there was ample liberty to maintain a seminary program. Second, young men were coming forward to volunteer for the ministry. Third, this augured well for the future existence and growth of the denomination.[56]

An exciting innovation in theological education appeared in 1976. It is a combined Baptist and Lutheran theological college, which arose out of talks at the International Congress on World Evangelization in Lausanne in 1974.[57] Many keen young men had been traveling to Germany for training by both Baptists and Lutherans. Inevitably some stayed and thus impoverished the Yugoslavian church. To preserve this pool of manpower for the church, Baptist Josip Horak and Lutheran Vlado Deutsch joined hands in 1976 to open a seminary at Zagreb. There were fifty-eight students in the first year, and the Orthodox and Catholic Churches were represented among the first students. At the opening of the seminary there was also official government representation, as well as spokesmen for the Orthodox and Catholic communions. In reporting on the event, World Vision president Stanley Mooneyham characterized the faculty as "stoutly Evangelical in their theology."[58]

Despite the unusual degree of liberty accorded Christians in Yugoslavia, certain pressures are brought to bear against them. When a public-opinion poll turned up a large percentage of nominal Christians in 1968, one Belgrade newspaper called for intensifying atheistic propaganda to persuade the people.[59]

Individual congregations have also been the objects of discrimination. In 1971 one Belgrade Baptist church was placed under a compulsory purchase order to provide space for a governmental housing scheme. A payment of $50,000 was promised. However, no land was subsequently granted to replace the expropriated church. In fact, practically no building of churches has been allowed since 1945.[60]

In 1975 reports reached Western Europe of an increase of repression of Christianity in Yugoslavia. Governmental leaders branded organized religion as "a dangerous domestic enemy." Strict new laws were expected that would suppress the public celebration of Christian holidays such as Christmas. Religious functions outside church buildings would be curbed. A socialist ceremony was expected to replace the elaborate, popular Christian funeral services. Any distribution of tracts would be summarily punished.[61]

Although there has been an unusual degree of freedom for Yugoslavian Christians, there are limits. As Tito grows older, internal security becomes more difficult. The fragile cohesion between the constituent republics in Yugoslavia could dissolve. Also, the chilling precedent of Prague 1968 hovers over any desire to assert independence from Communist neighbors. The future of Christian life in Yugoslavia depends to a large degree on the government that succeeds Tito.

BULGARIA'S CHOKED CHURCH

Speaking to a conference on "Christianity in Eastern Europe" in 1972, the noted "Bible smuggler" Brother Andrew mentioned Bulgaria. According to him, the only expatriate workers allowed into Bulgaria were Russian refugees. No Westerners could penetrate that land.[62]

The Orthodox Church is officially accepted in Bulgaria. According to Ernst Benz, in 1960 about 6 million Bulgarians of the 8.76 million citizens claimed nominal connections with the Orthodox Church.[63] Predictably, most of these were peasants. In fact, a recent survey showed a much lower level of faith among higher social strata. Among private farmers 72 percent claim to be Christians. Peasants working in governmental communes are only about 47 percent Christian. Among the intelligentsia this statistic slumped to 13 percent.[64]

Visitors to Bulgaria observe a respectable proportion of public worshipers in Orthodox churches. In 1966 there were 3,700 Orthodox churches still open in Bulgaria, but they were served by only 1,785 priests. Still, in the large cities there are often well-attended services. A tourist from the West attended Easter worship in 1973 at the Cathedral of St. Alexander in Nevsky, and reported that there were several hundred young people present.[65]

For Protestant churches, however, the picture is not quite so encouraging. Baptists, Congregationalists, and other groups have formed an association. This has provided governmental recognition, but there are also many rigid restrictions placed upon them.[66]

In 1976 the Bulgarian authorities announced plans to close down the remaining eight Protestant churches. One pastor, Stephan Bankov, told that his church had been shut down along with fifty-six others in 1964. Subsequently he assumed pastoral care for fifty underground Bible study groups. From 1966 to 1969, Bankov distributed four thousand Bibles and thirteen thousand New Testaments among his clandestine congregations.[67]

The Eastern European Bible smuggler who wrote under the pen name of Andre Morea pointed out a peculiar problem in Bulgaria: There are many "official Christians" who function as spies within Christian churches. On the orders of Communist party bosses their members often join Christian churches. Some even undergo believers' baptism. Once inside, they act as a direct channel of information on Christian activities to the party hierarchy.[68]

Compared with less-restricted Eastern European lands, Bulgaria is a virtual concentration camp. Christianity can exist only in underground cells and strictly controlled associations. Now only 17 percent of the populace, as practicing members, profess any connection with Christianity. In fact, active Christians are reckoned to comprise only 2 percent of the entire Bulgarian population. There are 40 Protestant pastors to serve a population of 8.76 million, and the danger of government spies makes these pastors mistrustful of one another.[69]

ALBANIA: "THE FIRST ATHEISTIC STATE"

Summarizing the situation in Albania, Trevor Beeson wrote, "From almost every point of view—political, social, economic, and religious—Albania is the bleakest place in Europe."[70] In 1967 the government in Tirana declared Albania to be "the first atheistic state in the world."

Since then it has ruthlessly pursued a policy of religious repression. In 1966 all relations between the government and the churches were suspended. At a stroke, 2,169 places of worship were closed and all worship was outlawed. Since then, churches have been transformed into dance halls, gymnasia, offices, etc. Scutari Cathedral, for instance, serves as a sports palace.[71]

In 1973 a woman prisoner requested to have her infant baptized. Accordingly, a seventy-year-old priest carried out the clandestine ceremony. When it was discovered, the old man, who had long since retired from parish ministries, was summarily shot for "subversive activities designed to overthrow the state."[72]

Where religion still exists, it is strictly a private affair. All religious training of children is forbidden. No social work may be undertaken by the churches. Many church leaders have been executed. Still a few are faithful to the Lord. Recently, sixteen couples were married in a secret ceremony at the ruins of an old church. The brides even wore white gowns, a practice prohibited in the "first atheistic state."[73]

Late in 1975 Albanian radio took up the subject of religion. It was discussed in the context of criticism against Soviet Russia. (Albania holds to the Chinese brand of communism and denounces the post-Stalinist communism of the Soviet Union.) Albanian radio declared that Russia was using religion to oppress and exploit the working classes. In an emotive charge, the spokesman said, "The poisoned roots of religion are spreading out more and more in the Soviet Union." He continued, "Medieval relics that spread reactionism and obscurantism are awakening to new life."[74]

A final touch to the secularization of society in Albania

occurred in 1976. A special law was announced banning the use of names found to be "unsuitable from a political, ideological, or moral viewpoint." This applied especially to Christian names that reminded the citizens of the Bible.[75]

Since the Communist takeover of Albania in 1946, all signs of Christianity have been systematically purged from the land. A culture once rich in Roman Catholic and Orthodox tradition is now strictly socialistic. In order to maintain the "purity" of the country, most connections with the outside world are cut off. Albania is becoming what it has declared itself to be—"the first atheistic state in the world."

DETENTE AND HUMAN RIGHTS

During the seventies Russia sought to relax relations with the West for economic reasons. Willy Brandt, the West German chancellor, spoke of his *Ostpolitik*, his positive policy toward the Eastern European nations. The United States, under the influence of Secretary of State Henry Kissinger, adhered to a doctrine of "detente." Concerted efforts were made to establish friendly relations with the Kremlin.

In 1973 a summit of European heads of state met in Helsinki. Their aim was to produce a climate of relative security. All attempts were made to eradicate the remnants of the cold war. Part of the Helsinki Declaration included assurances of human rights, including the right of religious freedom. Although the Soviets and their satellites signed the Declaration, persecution continued unabated after 1973 and it was found throughout Eastern Europe.

Two events served to awaken the West to the plight of persecuted minorities in the Soviet States. Both occurred in 1974. The Baptist minister Georgi Vins was thrown into a Siberian prison camp for preaching the gospel. His story was flashed around the world, and ultimately his autobiography was published in the West. Christians by the thousands marched to Russian embassies demanding his release.

The other event was the exile of the Russian writer Alexander Solzhenitsyn from the Soviet Union. His *Gulag Archipelago* chronicled the repression of religious practice since the Russian revolution in 1917. When he came to the West, Solzhenitsyn became a conscience to the lethargic citizens of free countries. He wrote the epitaph for flirtations with Russia when he said, "I think there is no such thing as detente.... Detente becomes self-deception—that's what it's all about."[76]

10

Church of England: Revival or Ruin

In describing religious life in Britain, the Anglican bishop of Truro in Cornwall was remarkably frank: "A majority of people in this country are neither practising Christians nor draw upon a capital of Christian moral standards."[1]

Just as secularization has eroded the spiritual stamina of continental Protestantism, so many Britons have become increasingly enamored of the humanistic approach to life. In his *Daily Telegraph* column, Paul Johnson claimed that Britain was rapidly evolving into a "nation of agnostics." The secular spirit had spread more speedily in England than in any other industrial nation, he asserted. Then Johnson drew this startling conclusion: "It seems to me at least arguable that the almost complete de-Christianisation of the British working class has been a potent element in the breakdown of industrial discipline and our relative economic decline."[2]

When the House of Lords debated the issue of pornography in March 1976, several "Lords spiritual," i.e., bishops, joined in. The Bishop of Wakefield, Eric Treacy, seemed almost to have fallen into the quagmire of despair. "We have arrived at a point at which we have to ask ourselves, How long can we continue to call ourselves a civilized nation?" he lamented.[3]

A transatlantic confirmation of the dilemma of English church life comes from the pen of the astute missions expert, Herbert Kane. He reckoned that English church life was at its lowest ebb since the pre-Wesley days of the eighteenth century. "Even so," Kane reminded the reader, "England is much better off than the Lutheran countries." Indeed, there is a larger remnant of real believers in Britain than in any other European nation.[4]

When one contemplates the situation in Britain, he is tempted to agree with the late dean of St. Paul's Cathedral, W. R. Matthews. According to him, the world is "living on a volcano, not on a rock." In England the spiritual situation is seething, and one awaits with anxiety the outcome of the revolution in religion.[5]

IS FAITH REDUNDANT?

Each year dozens of churches close in Britain. They are consigned to a list of "redundant" churches. Appropriate uses are found for them only with great difficulty. For many, faith is as "redundant" as the closing churches.

Archbishop Michael Ramsey was quoted as saying, "Let African and Asian missionaries come to England to help to convert the post-Christian heathenism in our country."[6] Writing in the evangelical Anglican magazine, *The Churchman*, Talbot Mahon concluded, "Prosperity and righteousness do not go hand in hand. As material standards climb higher, moral standards decline."[7]

One of the first and most obvious symptoms of religious decline is seen in attendance at worship. According to Trevor Beeson's authoritative survey, church attenders in Russia outnumber those in Britain by a large percentage.[8] According to the same writer, in 1968 only 6 percent of all Anglicans worshiped weekly. Allowing for the large number of infants and infirm old people who cannot attend, this still is a rather appalling statistic.[9] Easter and Christmas communicants fell off by about 50 percent during the period of 1956 to 1970.[10] It was sobering when Ronald Williams, bishop of Leicester, lamented in 1973: "Honest observers must admit that religious activities play a smaller part in the life of the *Church* than they previously did."[11] In other words, the substratum of spiritual truth has been eroded, leaving only a vague residue of social activism.

As previously mentioned, this poverty of worshipers has produced an excess of church buildings. In 1969 there were seven "redundant" churches in England. Five years later that number had swollen to 170.[12] More than five hundred parishes have been closed during the sixties and seventies. During the first half of the seventies, the number of parish priests declined by twenty-five hundred.[13]

The secular trend of society in Britain has become increasingly apparent in the educational system. In 1975 the Birmingham education authority came up with a new syllabus for religious education. Its emphasis had been "broadened" to include not only traditional Christian teaching, but also "non-religious stances of living," viz., communism and humanism.[14] Non-Christian religions were also recommended for inclusion in the syllabus by a government study group. The rationale was that a growing Asian minority in Britain made it necessary to include their religious traditions in the educational process. Consequently, it was argued that Islam, Hinduism, Sikhism, and Buddhism should be taught as alternative religions.[15]

Of the Birmingham syllabus, Neil Scrimshaw, a Conservative education spokesman on the city council said, "This syllabus places a loaded revolver in the hands of Communist teachers who wish to conduct propaganda in the classroom."[16]

Both in the pulpit and in the classroom a thickening fog of ambiguity has fallen. Socialism has downgraded Scripture as the source of authority. Christianity has largely been consigned to the "idol shelf" beside numerous religious and non-religious philosophies. Meanwhile, the Church of England has declined in size and influence throughout the land.

THE TRIUMPH OF HUMANISM

As interest in organized religion wanes, one also notices a progressively humanistic outlook among many British theologians. Daniel Jenkins exposed the heart of the problem when he wrote, "The chief reason why British churches are weak today is that they do not believe enough in the Christian God whom they profess to serve."[17]

Many would characterize the sixties and seventies as the "Age of Robinson" in British theology. In 1963 the Bishop of Woolwich, John A. T. Robinson, stirred up an ecclesiastical hornet's nest with his *Honest to God*. The basic humanism of Robinson emerges in a later book, when he wrote, "I would expect instinctively to find myself closer to some humanists I know than to many Christians I know."[18]

In *Honest to God* Robinson attempted to redefine Christianity in such a way that it would become palatable to modern man. He drew a close connection between the "non-Christian secularist view of Jesus" and that held by "liberal Christianity." Robinson then went on to define his own view of Christ. Jesus was not and never claimed to be God. Furthermore, his disciples never regarded him as divine.[19]

The spiritual character of Christ, said Robinson, is summarized in the statement "Jesus is 'the man for others.' " He is completely at one with "the Ground of his being," i.e., with God. Because Jesus lived his life for other people, he expressed perfectly the love of God. This was the essence of his unity with God. (The biblical concepts of God's holiness and justice are totally absent from Robinson's writing about Christ.)[20]

In regard to prayer, Robinson was equally "this-worldly." People are supposed to "give themselves to people." This is not a religious act. Nevertheless, to "open oneself to another *unconditionally* in love is to be with him in the presence of God, and that is the heart of intercession."[21]

When he speaks of morality, Robinson appears to advocate so-called "situation ethics." "Nothing can of itself always be labelled 'wrong,' " he wrote. There can never be "packaged" moral judgments. People are far more important than moral standards.[22] With a naivete found frequently among humanistic theologians, Robinson assumed that all will be well if man is set free to "do what comes naturally." He never seems to consider realistically that man may be less than perfect or perfectable. His is the enlightenment view of man, that is, man can live a perfect life if only he has a good environment.

Robinson left his mark on the crusade for free sexual expression. As chairman of the Sexual Law Reform Society, he had the audacity to argue in 1972 that the age of consent for sexual acts should be lowered to fourteen.[23]

In November 1976 Robinson made the headlines again. In his book *Can We Trust the New Testament?* he argued for an early dating of the New Testament documents. He defended the viewpoint that most of the New Testament books were written between A.D. 40 and 60.

Since he had taken a more conservative viewpoint of dating, one would expect a correspondingly conservative approach to the reliability of these writings. However, he dismissed the docrine of inerrancy and verbal inspiration by calling it "Fundamentalism of the Fearful." Then he noted that neither the Roman Catholics (who traditionally upheld inspiration) nor the evangelicals still cling to this position. Robinson simply wrote off this viewpoint as being no longer current.[24] A serious study of Robinson's latest book on the New Testament reveals his continuing humanistic bias. While admitting the probable earlier dating of the books, he nevertheless argued against any serious acceptance of the authority of the Scriptures.

While deprecating any "fundamentalism," Robinson seems to identify himself with a viewpoint he labeled "Conservatism of the Committed." He speaks of a strong conservative "undertow" in the Church of England. This group has largely rejected the destructive biblical criticism of the nineteenth and twentieth centuries.[25]

It is important, in Robinson's view, that we regard the New Testament as "a portrait, not a photograph" of Jesus Christ. Jesus is alive in the faith of his followers. His ascension described his ascendancy over human affairs. It is this self-styled committed conservatism that Robinson defends: "It exhibits that self-rectifying balance and solidarity which has enabled English scholarship, as well as religion, to weather the extremes of Continental radicalism and Transatlantic [American] fashion."[26]

Another valuable contribution to understanding British theological thought is the Cambridge compendium, *Objections to Christian Belief*. When discussing the Trinity, J. S. Bezzant wrote, "As the human mind cannot conceive such an actuality it can reasonably be said that nothing can justify the assertion of its actual existence." He summoned this doctrine before the tribunal of human reason only to condemn it.[27]

The Cambridge compendium similarly dismissed the authority of the Bible. "Modern theologians who are not Roman Catholics or biblical fundamentalists reject the notion of Divine revelation as consisting in the conveyance of propositional truths," the dons wrote. They felt that the relationship of biblical revelation to historical fact was minimal and not essential to faith.[28]

In the view of the Cambridge contributors, Christianity was explicable only in human terms. Any notion of divine intervention in human history was mythological. They were essentially in agreement with Rudolf Bultmann, who attempted to rescue a minimal kernel of truth from the husk of myth.

One of the most articulate spokesmen of contemporary theology was William Barclay, a Scottish professor. Throughout the sixties and seventies he became famous as a radio and television lecturer. His homey and devotional approach to religion often disguised the heresy he was teaching.

Calling himself a "liberal evangelical," Barclay vested evangelical words with liberal meanings. As he saw it, "Miracles were often not so much stories of what Jesus did, but symbols of what he still can do."[29] For instance, he treated the story of Christ stilling the storm in this way: "It is not important whether Christ stilled a real storm on the Sea of Galilee," Barclay declared. "What is significant is that he stills the storm of anxiety in my breast." The historical reality of

Christ's words and deeds are thus drowned in a sea of pietistic interpretation.

In many ways the humanistic theological thought that was observed among Continental Protestants has also gained a foothold in British academic institutions. Nevertheless, the innate good sense and reserved character of most British theologians have prevented them from running to some of the extremes of German theology. Even John Robinson warned against "Continental radicalism."

Despite the relatively moderate views of the British thinkers, their theology has still served to undercut the proclamation of the preachers. Once confidence in the Scriptures has been weakened, preaching soon flies off into realms of speculation. As an old farmer once said, "My horse does not understand agriculture, but he does know the difference between oats and nails." So the people in the pew can discern between the authoritative preaching of the Word of God and the speculations of an articulate speaker.

CAUTIOUS ECUMENISM

While humanism has gained ground in theological faculties and pulpits, ecumenism has also become a concern in church circles. Michael Ramsey steered the Anglican ship as Archbishop of Canterbury from 1961 to 1974. Upon his retirement, *Time* magazine carried a report emphasizing his role as "a determined ecumenist."[30] Surely he set the tone in making serious approaches to both the Roman Catholic Church and the Methodists.

Despite the prevailing ecumenical winds from Geneva and Rome, Ramsey had to contend with considerable skepticism. A survey of clergymen in 1973 revealed that most ecumenical enthusiasts were among the older clergy. They were, however, unable to fan a spark of interest among younger ministers. Even A. J. Van Der Bent, librarian of the World Council of Churches in Geneva, was compelled to concede failure of the World Council to "produce any dramatic move towards unity."[31]

In 1962 the Catholic archbishop of Liverpool, John Heenan, lamented the lack of progress in ecumenism. His efforts to forge links with the Anglicans had been less successful than those of his Dutch and French colleagues. The reason for Anglican reticence to negotiate with Catholics was, in Heenan's words, "a long tradition of mistrust."[32]

By the end of the Second Vatican Council, however, the tide had begun to turn. In 1963 Heenan had become head of English Catholics as Archbishop of Westminster. In that capacity Cardinal Heenan applied himself ceaselessly to ecumenical dialogue with Anglicans.[33]

Soon after the conclusion of the Vatican Council a plan was set in motion to bring the Archbishop of Canterbury to Rome. In March 1966 Ramsey made the journey and met with Pope Paul VI. The pope greeted the archbishop with these words: "By your coming, you rebuild a bridge, a bridge which for centuries has lain fallen between the Church of Rome and Canterbury."[34]

In the joint declaration issued after Pope Paul and Archbishop Ramsey had met, the encounter was praised as a "new stage in the development of fraternal relations." A serious dialogue was to be initiated between the two churches, and basic issues such as those regarding Scripture, tradition, and liturgy would be discussed. Both sides were keenly aware that "serious obstacles stand in the way of a restoration of complete communion of faith and sacramental life."[35]

Anglican evangelicals were mistrustful of this ecumenical initiative. Canon Thomas Livermore spoke of the persistent differences between Catholic dogma and biblical truth. "Nothing can be done until they are resolved," he insisted.[36] John Stott welcomed the idea of "serious dialogue" between Rome and Canterbury, but he lamented that these discussions would be based on "the Gospels and on the ancient common traditions" instead of on the Scriptures alone.[37]

Shortly after the archbishop's visit to Rome, an

Anglican-Roman Catholic International Commission was set up to debate these issues. In 1971 they had agreed on a statement concerning the Lord's Table. It was not a repetition of Christ's sacrifice, but rather a celebration of his real presence. The Catholic dogma of transsubstantiation (the teaching that the elements are transformed into Christ's body and blood) was relegated to a footnote.[38]

In 1973 a "Common Catechism" was published. It first appeared in German, and an English version came out two years later. This document revealed an unusual degree of unity concerning the basic doctrines of the Christian faith. However, some of the persistent problems remained, viz., papal infallibility and mariology.[39]

In 1976 the Commission issued a joint statement on "Authority in the Church." Contrary to Reformation teaching, it concluded that authority was vested in Scriptures, the Church Fathers, and Canons of the Councils. All doctrinal matters were to be measured by Scripture and tradition. Rome was recognized as having "universal primacy" over the Christian church.[40]

It appears that the Anglicans had sacrificed more doctrines than the Catholics in their ecumenical dialogue. Whether the subject was communion or authority, the compromise that was agreed on favored the Catholic teaching. Concessions by the Catholics were usually insignificant or only academic.

The second major ecumenical development of the sixties and seventies was the discussion between Anglicans and Methodists. In 1962 two phases of development toward unity were foreseen. A first stage would bring intercommunion and the second would produce organic unity. Methodist lay class leaders would continue to function, but they would not be permitted to administer the sacraments of the Lord's Table and baptism. Relationships between Methodists and nonepiscopal (i.e., bishopless) churches would be jeopardized. A blue-ribbon panel of Methodist theologians decried the projected union as a move "from a Church committed to the evangelical faith into a heterogeneous body permitting, and even encouraging, unevangelical doctrines and practices."[41]

Despite these doubts concerning the evangelical nature of the church, Methodists seemed eager to rejoin the Anglican Church. It was almost as though they felt their forefathers had been mistaken in leaving the Church of England. In 1965 the Methodist Conference approved preliminary proposals for unity. However, the whole plan was scuttled in 1972 when the vote was lost in the General Synod of the Church of England. The House of Bishops approved the plan by a large 85 percent majority. However, the clergy could muster only 65.52 percent support, and the laity had 62.82 percent. Since a vote of three-fourths was required in all three houses, the motion was lost.[42]

Undaunted by this defeat, ecumenical enthusiasts set up the Church's Unity Commission to explore ways of uniting the Church of England, the Roman Catholic Church, and the Free Churches. It was hoped that ultimately there would be joint parishes where all these denominations could use a single building. There would be inter-communion across all the borders, and the ordination of all ministers would be respected.[43]

Early in 1976 this commission issued "Ten Propositions for Church Unity." These contained most of the elements expected. There was to be recognition of baptism by all participating churches. Full intercommunion would be accepted across the boundaries of various churches. Furthermore, the ordination of clergymen would qualify them to officiate in the various cooperating churches. These propositions were essentially to be a basis for discussion, and the major emphasis was placed on church order rather than doctrine.[44] However, one cannot but fear that a realization of these proposals would seriously weaken the worship and doctrinal distinctives of the constituent churches. (Historical evidence for this is seen in the result of the union of the Congregational and Presbyterian Churches in England in 1972.)

In studying the ecumenical advance during the decades

under study, one notes a diminishing emphasis on Scripture. The source of authority is sought either in tradition or in the consensus of participating clergymen. A belief in Scripture is often regarded as a remnant of the religious past.

ANGLICAN EVANGELICALS: A REDEMPTIVE REMNANT

A dominant figure in Anglican evangelicalism during this period was the Archbishop of Canterbury, Donald Coggan. His career took him through teaching posts in Canada and Britain before he became Bishop of Bradford in 1956. In 1961 he was elevated to the archbishopric of York.[45] He was essentially a scholar, who once said in an interview, "I would like to have been Erasmus. Think of the thrill of entering into new learning."[46]

Nevertheless, Coggan took to the administrative challenges of the episcopacy with relish. In fact, he even brought a firm of efficiency experts to study the structure and management of the York archdiocese.[47]

Early in 1974 it was learned that Michael Ramsey would retire on his seventieth birthday during that November. Speculation concerning a successor became rife. In fact, Ladbrokes, the bookmakers, started to take bets on the naming of the next Archbishop of Canterbury. From the start Coggan was the front runner.

In May 1974 the appointment of Coggan was announced. At 64, he was regarded by many as a "caretaker" archbishop. This did not disturb the softspoken and seriously spiritual man. He remarked on more than one occasion: "'Caretaker' is a splendid title.... The New Testament says, 'Take care of the Church of God.'"[48]

His accession created vacancies throughout the Church of England, and Archbishop Coggan filled most of these posts with evangelicals. Stuart Blanch was moved to York, and in his first statement he struck an evangelical chord: "It is the faith and message of the Church that are important."[49]

John V. Taylor was moved from the Church Missionary Society to the diocese of Winchester as bishop. Bishop Taylor is both a zealous advocate of social action and an articulate promoter of evangelism. In the diocesan paper he wrote, "Many people might be ready to join not a club, but a new missionary movement, which is what the church ought to be."[50]

David Sheppard moved from an inner city ministry as Suffragan Bishop of Woolwich in London to the equally challenging diocese of Liverpool. Bishop Sheppard had been a famous cricketer during his youth and he established himself as an evangelical with a social conscience during his years of leadership at the Mayflower Center in London's Canning Town.[51]

As the first evangelical Archbishop of Canterbury since John Bird Sumner in 1848, Coggan faced a significant challenge. He immediately called for a return to the spiritual foundations upon which Britain had traditionally rested. When his appointment was announced, Dr. Coggan said, "Britain will have a healthy society only when it starts living by some rules again. . . . There is a lot to be said for the Ten Commandments."[52]

The archbishop took a bold initiative late in 1975 when together with Archbishop Blanch he issued the "Call to the Nation." The Queen referred to this summons to spiritual standards when she opened the General Synod session in November 1975. She saw the "Call to the Nation" as "an example in challenging us all to a fresh understanding of our duties and responsibilities."[53]

Many Britons from various church backgrounds hailed the spiritual leadership given by the archbishops. By February 1976 more than twenty-five thousand written responses to the challenge had been received.[54]

Not all churchmen were so enthusiastic, however. The left-leaning Bishop of Southwark, Mervyn Stockwood, criticized the "Call to the Nation" in a signed article published in the Communist *Morning Star*. Stockwood accused the archbishops of "trying to brainwash the people into accepting cuts in living standards."[55]

This criticism of Archbishop Coggan was, however, unfounded. He never shrank from social issues. In his Easter message of 1976 he urged Christians to actively combat "dirt in the media, far too high an abortion rate, cheapening of sex, lack of reverence for life."[56]

As a Member of the House of Lords, he led the debate in favor of establishing the office of Minister for the Family. His points were well made. Marriage provides economic, social, and psychological support not found anywhere else. Divorce and sexual promiscuity weaken not only the home but also society.[57]

Sometimes his sense of responsibility to the church at large runs counter to the viewpoints of most evangelicals. For example, he has been a supporter of the ordination of women.[58] Another red flag to most evangelicals is his enthusiasm for ecumenical dialogue with the Catholic Church. In 1977 Coggan undertook a tour to meet Eastern Orthodox leaders and the pope. This was hailed by the press as a new height in cordial relations between Canterbury and Rome. However, the difference between the documents issued after the first meeting of Ramsey and Pope Paul in 1966 and those issued after the second meeting in 1977 showed that there had been a compromise of many Reformation principles. For example, the Catholic emphasis on the Eucharist had eroded the Reformation primacy of preaching. Although the Catholic Church had modified its view of the papacy slightly, the Church of England had largely agreed to accept the pope's primacy in any eventual united church. Thus Archbishop Coggan's pursuance of this relationship was unacceptable to many evangelicals.[59]

Despite these shadows, Archbishop Coggan has maintained the evangelical standard in a courageous way. At the World Council of Churches Assembly in Nairobi he declared, "Do not think only of liberation in terms of 'freedom from temporary shackles'... man's greatest curse from which he needs liberation is sin and death."[60]

The appointment of Coggan to Canterbury only emphasized a rising tide of evangelicalism in the Church of England. In 1967 Anglican evangelicals met at the University of Keele in the Midlands for their first Congress. They established themselves as a vocal minority within the Church of England and they exploded the myth that their secession from the church "was both probable and imminent."[61] Gordon Landreth, chief executive of the Evangelical Alliance, points to 1967 as the time when Anglican evangelicals became "involved in church life as an aggressive group pulling its own weight."[62]

The documents of the Keele Congress were edited by James Packer and published under the title *Guidelines: Anglican Evangelicals Face the Future*. There was a call for active participation in shaping modern society according to Christian principles. Worship should be opened up to innovations, and evangelism should become primarily the concern of the local parish. Sir Norman Anderson challenged the delegates to wrestle with such crucial issues as Christian philanthropy in a socialized state, abortion, and euthanasia.[63] The subjects discussed were less important, however, than the impetus the evangelicals gained at Keele.

Another public exhibition of evangelical strength came in 1972 when several thousand rallied to the "Festival of Light." Popular Britons such as singer Cliff Richard, broadcaster and writer Malcolm Muggeridge, and antipornography peer Lord Longford led a massive public rally against moral pollution. This gave birth to a movement that never again quite reached the level of initial interest, but it still had an on-going presence throughout the seventies.[64]

A second Evangelical Congress was convened in April 1977 at Nottingham. More than two thousand attended this gathering, many of them under forty years of age. Led by John Stott, the popular preacher and rector emeritus of All

Souls Church in London, three preparatory books had been sent out. Under the general title *Obeying Christ in a Changing World*, the books dealt in three volumes with theological foundations, the nature of the church, and attitudes toward contemporary issues.[65]

Although there was some "nit-picking" discussion of the documents and their wording, there was also some real progress. The congress brought out a strong statement on baptism, opposing the indiscriminate baptism of infants. Only believers' children should be accorded that rite.[66] The congress rejoiced in the knowledge that now one-half of all ordinands for the Church of England are evangelicals. All of the evangelical theological training colleges are comfortably filled.[67]

When Morgan Derham, a British evangelical leader, was interviewed in 1976 by *Eternity* magazine, he heavily emphasized the importance of Anglican evangelicalism. He mentioned many of the well-known leaders, such as John Stott, Stuart Blanch, and David Sheppard. Then Derham concluded strongly, "I think it's a fair generalization to say that the interesting developments in the British church life at the moment are in the evangelical Anglican churches."[68]

The General Synod: Religious Democracy?

In 1970 a new era in the history of the Church of England dawned when Queen Elizabeth opened the first session of the General Synod. This "Parliament of the Church" was composed of 545 members sitting in three houses: 43 bishops and archbishops, 251 clergymen, and 251 laymen.[69]

The Dean of Westminster hailed the body as "a truer style of Christian association than we had before." With a bit of good-natured pleasantry, the moderator of the Church of Scotland congratulated the "southern sister in approximating at last to the presbyterian model" of church government.[70]

Several issues occupied the General Synod during its first five-year term. Demanding a greater voice in the appointment of bishops, the church insisted that it must have more influence on the selection of its leaders. Trevor Huddleston, bishop of Stepney, criticized the prevailing system of royal appointments in this caustic statement: "It is equivalent to St. Paul being appointed by Caesar on the advice of Pontius Pilate."[71] In the end, the General Synod won a concession whereby a commission with church representation selects two acceptable candidates. These are then passed on to the prime minister who makes his recommendation to the queen for appointment. The church thus gains a role in the process, and the queen remains head of the church.[72]

A similar issue was the matter of General Synod control of the worship of the church. Archbishop Ramsey championed the "Worship and Doctrine Measure," which was designed to give the Church of England control over its own liturgy without seeking parliamentary approval for changes. Under this bill the church, on its own, could revise the Prayer Book. One Conservative member of Parliament criticized the measure as "arrogance and presumption," for taking away parliamentary control of liturgy. Another from the same party expressed fear that the church would fall under control of "trendy clergymen who wanted to replace the traditional liturgy with lots of your modern rubbish." Still the Parliament agreed to give the General Synod control over the church's liturgy. Perhaps this was, as another parliamentarian said, "the first step towards disestablishing the Church of England."[73]

Other matters debated by the General Synod arose out of the social context of the seventies. The church's ban on remarrying divorcees came up for discussion. Several pleaded for charity in "picking up the people after the marriage has been declared dead." Many Anglicans had been forced to seek second marriages in Methodist churches because of their own church's restrictions. When a resolution to allow the remarriage of divorced people was brought before the General Synod, it lost by a vote of 363 to 130.[74]

Yet another contemporary issue was the matter of ordaining women to the Anglican ministry. Archbishop Coggan had openly declared his sympathy for this, although he felt the time was not yet ripe. As other overseas Episcopal churches began to ordain women, the pressure on the Church of England mounted. A poll of the forty-three Anglican dioceses revealed strong grass-roots support for ordaining women. The General Synod declared in a resolution that there were "no fundamental objections to women's ordination." Still the Church of England hesitated. The reason was ecumenical. Both the Russian Orthodox Church and the Roman Catholic Church announced that the ordination of women would damage ecumenical relations between them and the Church of England. [75]

The General Synod has indeed changed the complexion of the Church of England. It has created a vehicle for governing the church in a democratic way. Thus the consensus of clerical and lay viewpoints can be brought to bear in steering the ship of the church.

A CANDLE IS LIT

In 1960 the future of the Church of England looked bleak. The revival movements of the forties and fifties had begun to wane, and the secular spirit of postwar Europe was spreading its paralysis to the British church. Only the emergence of a strong evangelical party has saved the Church of England from the degeneration suffered by its European neighbors.

John Stott could say after the Keele Congress of 1967: "During the last twenty years, Evangelical Anglicans have grown in number, scholarship, cohesion and confidence." Stott himself had played a significant role in leading that party out into the light of responsible churchmanship. [76]

By 1973 a groundswell of revival had begun to permeate the parishes. *Christianity Today* news editor Ed Plowman was in London for the Billy Graham–sponsored youth event, "Spree '73." Afterwards Plowman reported that there was a "quiet spiritual awakening going on among youth inside of churches all over Britain."[77]

The future of evangelicalism within the Church of England seems bright. More young men are coming forward for ordination than ever before. There are scarcely enough traditionally evangelical parishes to absorb all the men who are taking holy orders. In the words of Gordon Landreth, in the last few years evangelicals "have become so influential that the mainstream of the Church of England cannot ignore them."[78]

11

English Free Churches:
Is Dissent Dying?

Since the days of Cromwell, England has had an illustrious history of religious dissent. The story is sprinkled with such great personages as Wesley, Whitefield, and Spurgeon. According to the census of 1851, more Britons worshiped weekly in non-Anglican than in Anglican services.[1]

By the end of the Victorian Era in 1901, however, Nonconformist churches had begun to decline drastically. Prosperous members were drawn from Baptist, Methodist, and Congregational pews into the established Anglican Church. Nonconformists had won the freedom to study at universities and sit in Parliament.[2]

The growth of rationalistic liberal theology in the early part of this century also powerfully affected the Free Churches. Once the biblical basis of their preaching became eroded by destructive criticism, the very reason for the Free Churches' existence was called into question. They were no longer bulwarks of biblical preaching. Their theological colleges one by one slipped the moorings of biblical doctrine. Gilbert Kirby, principal of London Bible College, diagnosed the malady of the Free Churches when he lamented "their lack of theological colleges which have a strong biblical basis."[3]

As the spiritual virility of the Free Churches faded, so did their distinctive role in British society. No longer were they working class centers of spiritual and social fellowship.

(One recalls that the trade union movement sprang up in Nonconformist soil.) One observer noted that there appeared to be a "decline in need for dissent."[4] These churches ceased to represent a viable, attractive alternative to Anglicanism.

Serious students of the British church scene are agreed on their assessment. The twentieth century has been disastrous for the traditional Free Church denominations, viz., Baptists, Methodists, and Congregationalists. Gilbert Kirby concluded, "Probably the free churches have suffered to an even greater extent than the Church of England."[5] It is significant that Kirby writes from the vantage point of a Congregational minister and former executive secretary of the Evangelical Alliance.

Another Congregationalist is Daniel Jenkins. In his book *The British: Their Identity and Their Religion* he further documents the failure of Free Churches. There had been a "steady numerical decline over the last two or three generations." On the other hand, Jenkins concluded, "Free Churches are much weaker than they were, but they are far from being at death's door."[6] It is the cause and symptoms of this decline that are dealt with in this study. During the sixties and seventies events snowballed to illustrate the plight of British Free Churches.

SPIRITUAL AND NUMERICAL DECLINE

At the concluding session of the British Baptist Union assembly in Nottingham during April 1977, the delegates directed their attention to the subject of decline. Douglas Mc-Bain, an outspoken evangelical from Streatham in south London, proposed the appointment of a commission "to study the spiritual and statistical decline" among Baptists. Denominational authorities protested the accusations of spiritual slippage, but they were overruled by the floor and a committee was named.[7]

Across the board, Free Churches have lost members at

an alarming rate. During 1975, the British Free Churches lost a total of 53,000 members, and the Methodists led the loss with an exodus of 44,000.[8] Between 1917 and 1967 aggregate membership of the Free Churches fell from 2.15 million to 1.55 million, a massive 28 percent.[9]

Inevitably, so large a decrease in membership renders many church buildings superfluous. In 1970 the Methodists reported that they were closing churches at the rate of four per week.[10] This was reechoed by the Methodist Lord Soper when he spoke on the British Broadcasting Corporation of the probable demise of all religious organizations within a century. According to Soper, who is both peer and parson, "We are facing a serious decline in organized religion. I very much doubt that many of the existing organizations will survive for very long."[11]

If Lord Soper was concerned, the Baptists had equal cause for anxiety. The offical organ of the Baptists, the *Baptist Times*, lamented in 1971 that the "annual fall in membership has occurred with depressing regularity ever since the outbreak of World War I."[12] Having reached their peak in 1930, the Baptists lost 14 percent during the period of 1966 to 1976.[13] In fact, during 1976 death and defection produced a net loss in Baptist churches of 5,268 members.[14]

Actually, the fall in numbers mirrors the diminishing spiritual vitality of many Free Church denominations. A most dramatic example of this occurred in 1971. At the Baptist assembly meetings a paper was presented by Michael Taylor, principal of the Baptist theological college at Manchester. His topic was "How Much of a Man was Jesus?" The gist of his remarks was this: "I believe that in the man Jesus we encounter God. I believe that God was active in Jesus." Then Taylor took an extremely controversial stand by saying: "It will not quite do to say categorically that Jesus is God."[15] Many evangelicals were incensed.

The governing council of the Baptist Union met during the next November to still the storm that had raged through the denomination. Although they reaffirmed their belief in the deity of Christ, they stopped short of censuring Taylor. Several churches summarily withdrew from the Baptist Union, and forty ministers removed their names from the list of accredited clergymen.[16]

One layman from Wimbledon wrote to the editor of the *Baptist Times*: "It would seem that the principal of the Northern Baptist College is in a state of paralysed uncertainty about the person of Jesus Christ." Then the concerned correspondent added that, were Jesus not divine, the doctrinal basis of the Baptist Union would be totally invalid.[17]

In the autumn of 1971 several evangelical Baptists met in the Baptist Central Hall in London, having invited David Pawson from Guildford to refute Taylor's claims. Pawson, an articulate Baptist minister, took as his title: "How Much of a God was Jesus?" The Guildford pastor referred to the confession of Thomas when he said, "As long as I mean no more and no less than Thomas meant by the word, God, it is valid for me to say 'Jesus is God.'"[18] In summarizing Pawson's main point, the *Baptist Times* hit upon these statements: "Experience of Jesus today puts him firmly on the Divine side of reality. He is still Creater rather than creature."[19] At the conclusion of Pawson's address most of his hearers stood to express their conviction that Jesus Christ was "their Lord and their God."[20]

The Baptists are not the only ones who have suffered the inroads of critical theology. The Methodists also have had to contend with unbiblical theology. In 1964 at the Methodist Conference meetings, their president, Frederic Greeves, brought up the case of the Rev. Walter Gill. For two successive years Gill had declined to sign the doctrinal statement of the Methodists. His main objection was the virgin birth of Christ, which he relegated to the realm of mythology, stating that it was "worthless as history." Consequently Gill was stricken from the roll of Methodist ministers.[21]

In 1966 the Eleventh World Methodist Conference took place in London. A prophetic word was delivered by the Norwegian bishop Odd Hagen, president of the World Council. In an age of ecumenism, doctrinal ambiguity was an ever-present threat. Therefore Bishop Hagen warned, "We shall be willing to compromise or yield regarding details and 'opinions,' as Wesley said. But I am sure that the spirit of Methodism will not allow us to give up central New Testament teaching."[22]

At the same conference, Albert Outler from the United States, warned his fellow Methodists not to lightly presume that "supernaturalism has had it; modern man is radically secular." Evangelical interests were still inexplicably alive. "Billy Graham has made at least as much of a dent on modern London ['the swinging city'] as the Bishop of Woolwich [J. A. T. Robinson]." Despite the advances of liberal biblical criticism, there was still discernable in Methodism a fidelity to the fundamentals of Christianity.[23]

Both the Baptist and Methodist controversies highlight the problem in British Free Church circles. Essential biblical doctrines have been brought into question by theological teachers. Consequently the preaching in churches has been diluted. The biblical basis that was unchallenged until this century has largely been lost, leaving the Free Churches (like many Anglicans) adrift in a sea of speculative, humanistic philosophy.

ECUMENISM: POOLING THEIR POVERTY

The ultimate ecumenical dream was given publicity in 1976, when the *Church of England Newspaper* floated the idea of one all-embracing "United Free Church." For many Free Churchmen, this dream is far more appealing than unity with the established Church of England. Furthermore, the Free Churches would have fewer problems with the questions of intercommunion, ordination of ministers, and even baptism. (To many Baptists, believer's baptism has long since turned into a mere initiation rite.)[24]

During the sixties and seventies ecumenical history was

made by combining the Congregational and Presbyterian Churches in England in 1972. The resulting denomination was christened the United Reformed Church, and its thirst for mergers was stimulated to such a degree that it committed itself "wherever possible and with all speed to seek further mergers."[25]

The significance of the United Reformed Church was further explained by editors of the *Baptist Times*. The new denomination combined different theological heritages and it also united two forms of church government: congregational and synodical. The resulting church has become mainly synodical.[26]

Negotiations leading to the merger of the Presbyterians and Congregationalists took almost a decade. Beginning in May 1963 with the forming of a joint committee the ultimate merger was consummated in May 1971. Eighty-nine percent of the Congregationalists approved the union, and 79.3 percent of the Presbyterians concurred.[27]

The *Scheme of Union* laid down in detail both the nature of the proposed united church and also the steps to be taken in accomplishing the merger. In a preamble, the negotiating committee explained, "We see the union as the contribution that can be made by us to that necessary re-shaping of the structure and life of the Church here for Mission today." In other words, a united church should stimulate more interest in the Christian message.[28]

Just as mass production often forces parts together with a heavy hammer, so reluctant participants were quickly coerced into place. The Congregationalists protested an eldership. This was overruled in the interest of unity.[29]

Some disgruntled churches inevitably withdrew from the new body. Congregationalists were regarded as not belonging unless they made a congregational decision to join. On the other hand, Presbyterians were presumed to have joined unless the local church voted to stay out. Dissenting churches of both denominations retained their church property.[30]

In the actual service of union, heavy emphasis was placed

on the presumed glory of unity for its own sake. The sin of
fragmentation was confessed, and the resolution to unite was
exalted. They rejoiced that the participating congregations
"see their union as a part of what God is doing to make his
people one."[31]

Attendance at the United Reformed Church persisted in
its downward trend, and over one hundred congregations
were still without a minister in 1976.[32] Nevertheless, the
United Reformed Church was regarded as a model of ecumenical success. Meanwhile, the Methodists and Anglicans suffered a setback during the sixties and seventies.

In 1963 an innovative plan was introduced to unite the
Methodists and the Anglicans. The merger would proceed in
two stages. First, there would be a period of intercommunion
between the two churches. Then, organic union would be
achieved after the "warm-up" period.[33]

A group of evangelical scholars lodged their protest
against this plan. They feared the primacy of Scripture would
be compromised. Episcopacy, the government by bishops,
would be forced on the Methodists, and these scholars found
no biblical precedent for bishops in the Anglican sense. Finally, they feared that the concept of minister would be replaced with that of a priest—a human mediator between God
and man. This violated the universal priesthood propounded
by the Reformation and espoused by Wesley.[34] Throughout
Methodism it was the evangelicals who protested most loudly
against the projected merger.[35]

At the World Methodist Conference in London during
1966, much was made of the pending union. The successful
union of Methodists with Evangelical United Brethren in
Germany during 1963 was hailed as a model for the
Anglican-Methodist merger. Already on the local, grass-roots
level Anglicans and Methodists were meeting for ecumenical
services, and the organic unity of the two was almost accepted
as a foregone conclusion.[36]

Beyond the Anglican-Methodist talks there was an indication that conversations had commenced already between the

Methodists and Roman Catholics. Addressing the conference, Cardinal Heenan indicated that he desired talks with the Methodists, Baptists, Congregationalists, and Anglicans. Another ecumenical enthusiast, the American Methodist Bishop Fred Pierce Corson, declared proudly that John Wesley was "the first truly ecumenical leader in Protestantism." It fell to Harold Roberts, principal of Richmond College, to sound a solemn warning note. He admonished his fellow Methodists not to sidestep the important issues of mariology, the Catholic priesthood, and mixed marriages.[37]

The Methodists rushed headlong down the ecumenical path. In 1969 they readily approved plans to unite with the Anglicans, and evangelical voices were drowned out in the roar of enthusiasm. In 1971 the president of the Methodists, Rupert Davies, warned, "If Anglicans reject the present Anglican-Methodist Scheme of Unity, as 'the one viable scheme,' Methodists will not have the stomach to go through the weary business again."[38]

Perhaps Davies was prophetic. When the Anglican-Methodist scheme for union came up before the General Synod in May 1972, it was defeated. Although the requisite three-quarters vote was gained in the House of Bishops, it was soundly defeated in the Houses of Clergy and Laity.[39] The Anglican ecumenicist Archbishop Michael Ramsey was close to tears as he saw his most cherished plan dashed to defeat.[40]

Die-hard ecumenical clergymen quickly established a broader-based movement to bring together the Free Churches, the Church of England, and the Roman Catholic Church. This committee was christened the Churches Unity Commission. It aimed at a time when all Christian churches in a community could share one building. They would have intercommunion and joint confirmations. Their clergymen would be free to minister without restriction across old denominational boundaries.[41]

After fifteen months of deliberation, the Churches Unity Commission in January 1976 issued "Ten Propositions on Church Unity." These contained provision for intercommunion, recognition of baptism by participating churches, and the acceptance of ordained ministers from all involved denominations.[42]

Initial debate centered around the question of Free Church ordination. The Ten Propositions contained provision for "episcopal, presbyteral and lay roles" in ordination. This has been interpreted to mean that some form of episcopacy would be recognized in all churches. The framers of the Propositions made mention of Free Church moderators and Baptist secretaries as filling the role of bishop.[43]

At the 1977 assembly of the Baptist Union, reports concerning the Ten Propositions had been received from 962 out of 1,749 Baptist Churches (55 percent). More than two-thirds of the responding churches favored a "covenant of mutual recognition" in contrast to "a united church." Many Baptists declared their openness to learn and, presumably, to change their views on such matters as infant baptism, the nature of the church, and the role of tradition.[44]

Initial reports indicate an enthusiastic response to the Ten Propositions from other major Free Churches. Both the United Reformed Church and the Methodists expressed approval. Although these denominations were engaged in their own merger talks, they declared their desire not to endanger the work of the Churches Unity Commission.[45] While the United Reformed Church approved the Ten Propositions, the staunch Congregationalists resisted them. At the merger of Presbyterians and Congregationalists, a sizeable number of conservative Congregationalists withdrew to form their own denomination. It is this largely Evangelical Congregational Federation that roundly rejected the Ten Propositions.[46]

When Anglican evangelicals met in Congress at Nottingham in 1977, they too expressed their interest in the Ten Propositions. They welcomed the goals of the Ten Propositions and "the whole project of multilateral talks from which they spring." They likewise affirmed the "actual corporate reunion of the Christian denominations in England." However, they somewhat naively sounded a word of caution, declaring that this unity should have as its foundation a common acceptance of the authority of Scripture.[47]

When it comes to Free Church ecumenism, however, the recognized organ of that movement is the Free Church Federal Council. Beginning before the turn of the century, this Council has gained prestige as a coordinating agency for Free Church activities. In his address to the annual Congress in 1970, Baptist leader E.A. Payne pointed out the distinctive role of the Free Church Federal Council. It buried the "traditional differences" between the participating bodies. Together the Free Churches presented a united front in new towns and urban housing developments. A united voice was sounded in matters of legislation and social action.[48]

In 1976 the noted Methodist church historian Gordon Rupp addressed the Free Church Congress. His topic, rooted in history, was "Reformations and Renewals." After briefly tracing the history of religious renewal and reformation in Britain, he turned to analysis of the present-day church. To the delight of his hearers, Rupp proclaimed himself to be "an unrepentant ecumaniac who believes that ecumenism is the grand instrument for the renewal of the Church in our time."[49]

The actions of the Free Church Federal Council mirror contemporary social issues. For instance, in their report for 1965 they urged on the British Broadcasting Corporation "vigilance against undesirable tendencies" in television broadcasting. There was also an appeal for the continuation of private secondary education when the government was pushing for state-controlled comprehensive education. Again, there was an appeal for the strengthening of laws against drunken driving.[50]

In the face of a rising tide of non-Christian, Asian immigrants into Britain, the Free Church Federal Council took a more "trendy" view of religious education. Immigrants should be instructed in their own religious tradition as a part of religious education. Humanism should be offered as an alternative to Christianity in educating the children. School assemblies should be stripped of their "semireligious" character.[51] The task of religious education should be committed mainly to the churches, who would be urged to "give greater importance to Christian education."[52]

Throughout the Free Church movement in Britain there has been an enthusiastic participation in the ecumenical movement. Many individual Christians feel that this movement is an honest attempt to unify true believers across denominational lines. Some religious leaders share this simple, and apparently spiritual, goal.

Others are more outspokenly skeptical. One such skeptic is Sir Fred Catherwood, advisor on industry to several British governments and a keen Christian. In his view, the ecumenical movement is "a hasty cobbling together of unlikely allies in a desperate attempt to retain some footing for official religion against the powerful tides of secularism." When he suggested this to the moderator of the Methodist Church, Sir Fred received this startling reply: "The problem, quite frankly, is money. We can't afford to keep all our churches, so we have to merge."[53]

Perhaps the Free Church's urgent desire for unity is more a desperate attempt at survival than it is a sign of strength. At any rate, the Free Churches have certainly blazed new trails of ecumenism in England during the past two decades.

INDIVIDUALISTIC EVANGELICALS

In the ecumenical atmosphere that prevails among British Free Churches, the evangelicals have adopted a position of protest. Daniel Jenkins referred to this when he wrote that evangelical Baptists were building alliances with other evangelical minorities in Free Church denominations. This would create "a new kind of dissenting churchmanship."[54] He remarked in another place that the evangelical Baptists have more in common with evangelical Anglicans than with liberal Baptists.[55]

As a whole, evangelicals seem to seek friendships across denominational lines rather than within the strict confines of their churches. For this reason the Evangelical Alliance has gained considerable strength since World War II. More than seven hundred churches and many individuals are aligned with the alliance. It has sponsored both mass evangelistic crusades with Billy Graham and efforts aimed at stimulating evangelism within the local church context. An example of the latter was the POWER program. During 1975 it aimed to activate local Christians in evangelism, but it was received with less than universal acclaim.[56]

When the Evangelical Alliance sponsored a National Assembly of Evangelicals in 1976, more than five hundred delegates traveled to the University of Salford for the event. Several key speakers represented both European and Third World Evangelicalism. Carlos Ortiz, a fiery Pentecostal preacher from Argentina, seemed to have most successfully kindled the ardor of the participants. He called for a gospel free from cultural trappings and firmly linked to social reform.[57]

Although it is not nearly so large as the Evangelical Alliance, there is yet another evangelical association that must be mentioned. This is the British Evangelical Council. About 1964 the prophetic preacher of Westminster Chapel, Martyn Lloyd-Jones, turned his interest to church affiliations. He called on Anglican and Baptist evangelicals to leave their theologically mixed denominations. They should form a separate Evangelical church. John Stott and many less-well-known leaders respectfully disagreed. They made a case for the practice of staying in the denomination to win it for scriptural principles.[58]

Actually, Lloyd-Jones had already thrown his weight behind the British Evangelical Council. It had been formed in 1952 by committed evangelicals "to discover and experience that true ecumenicity which the Scriptures certainly teach."[59] It had four aims. First, it intended to advance the Christian faith in Britain by a fellowship of biblical churches. Second, it sought to awaken Christians to the insidious departures of liberal theologians from the biblical faith. Third, full opposition would be exerted against atheistic trends in society and the decline in moral standards. Finally, the evangelical viewpoint would be more accurately represented before governmental bodies.[60]

Predictably, one of the foremost spokesmen of this movement was Sir Fred Catherwood. At the annual Leicester conference of Reformed clergymen in 1975, Sir Fred warned about involvement in politics. The danger was a subservience of spiritual to political aims. "Politics is the art of the possible," he remarked, "while Christian values are absolute."[61]

Another main target for British Evangelical Council criticism was the ecumenical movement. In a booklet entitled *Ecumenicity*, the author pleaded for biblical unity based on a firm doctrinal basis. He expressed the Council's "opposition to the development of that form of unscriptural ecumenicity represented by the World Council of Churches."[62]

Not content to castigate Geneva, the British Evangelical Council also attacked the Evangelical Alliance. The Alliance had set up a commission on church unity. Furthermore, it was comprised of members representing doctrinally mixed denominations, viz., Anglicanism, Methodism, and the Baptists. "In effect it had bolstered up the unscriptural status quo," the anonymous author concluded.[63]

In all probability, most of these anonymous pamphlets were written by the general secretary of the British Evangelical Council, Roland Lamb. He warned British evangelicals of the danger that many hitherto reliable scholars were departing from their traditional position. They were abandoning the adherence to "belief in Scripture as being the inspired, infallible and inerrant Word of God."[64]

Members of the British Evangelical Council put a practical face on their theological views. Since ministers were being urged to withdraw from theologically mixed denominations, there must be some provision for supporting these exiles. Members of the Council established a fund to provide financial support and also housing for clergymen who surrendered their churches by holding to their convictions.[65]

The British Evangelical Council rests mainly on a Reformed theological position, similar to that of Martyn Lloyd-Jones. The Council opposes much of traditional evangelistic efforts, especially any sort of public invitation to accept Christ. Such a proclamation is called "man-centered evangelism . . . characterized by preaching a God who is love, without declaring His holiness, His wisdom, His sovereignty, His laws." The result of such evangelism, the Council declares, is a class of Christians who follow a gospel of "easy-believism."[66]

In 1975 when the Billy Graham Evangelistic Association sponsored a youth festival at Brussels, called "Eurofest," the British Evangelical Council issued a condemnation. They protested that Arminians were included as speakers, too much emphasis was placed on religious entertainment, and young people were trained in the Bible outside the local church context. In addition, it was too costly to put on such a festival.[67]

Although its doctrinal purity is admirable, the British Evangelical Council still is too small to exert much positive influence on British churches. Like many other evangelical efforts, it is mainly composed of individuals who share its doctrinal foundation and fellowship without influencing the British church at large.

Another approach to evangelical action is through the fellowships that exist within most Free Churches. The Baptist Revival Fellowship led in 1972 to the formation of an Association of Evangelical Baptists. Recently, however, this group has been wracked by dissension over the charismatic issue.[68]

Evangelicals within the former Presbyterian and Congregationalist denominations expressed their opposition to liberal trends by abstaining from membership in the United Reformed Church. The result was an Evangelical Fellowship of Congregational Churches, which has remained true to traditional evangelicalism.[69]

Realizing that Methodism was also abandoning the doctrines of Wesley, many evangelicals in that fellowship sought to express their fidelity to the Scriptures. With its center at Cliff College, an association grew up under the name of Conservative Evangelicals in Methodism.[70]

As it is throughout the world, evangelicals tend to go their individual ways. They seek personal guidance from the Lord and play down the need for fellowship with others of like faith. So in England there is a multiplication of evangelical associations representing various theological, denominational, and cultural heritages. Despite this diversity, the size of the evangelical minority gives cause for optimism concerning the future of Free Churches in Britain.

Fellowship of Independent Evangelical Churches

During the 1920s, E. J. Poole-Connor formed an association of churches that had withdrawn from the denominations because of doctrinal conflict. Originally this group bore the unwieldy name Fellowship of Undenominational and Unattached Churches and Missions. It was theologically broad enough to embrace both Calvinistic churches and those holding to a Wesleyan Arminianism. With regard to the sacraments, the association maintained a deliberately vague position.[71]

After World War II this association streamlined its name to Fellowship of Independent Evangelical Churches. Throughout Britain "Evangelical Free Churches" sprang up, and most identified themselves with the Fellowship. In addition, many older churches joined the association. One such church was Westminster Chapel, of which Martyn Lloyd-Jones was rector. As the nature of the Fellowship changed, so did its doctrinal basis. It became much more Calvinistic in its outlook.

When Sir Fred Catherwood became president of the Fellowship of Independent Evangelical Churches in 1977, he highlighted the aims of that group. Its creed was now "Reformed and evangelical." Despite the association, high priority was placed on the autonomy of the local congregation.[72] In many ways this epitomizes the theological and ecclesiastical flavor of British evangelicalism. It also holds out a major hope for the survival of the Free Church movement in this day of ecumenical compulsion and theological ambiguity.

12

The Enigmatic Orthodox Church

To most western observers, the Orthodox Church is a riddle. Although Christianity first took root in eastern Europe, its history has been distorted by prolonged Islamic influence. Having been cut off from European Christianity, it has also cultivated a form of worship strange to Western eyes and ears.

Nevertheless, the Orthodox Church commands the allegiance of more than 150 million members. In Greece, for instance, 90 percent of the nation's 9 million citizens are on Orthodox Church rolls.[1] Under the overall primacy of the Ecumenical Patriarch of Constantinople (Istanbul), more than one-sixth of all nominal Christians follow the Orthodox faith.[2]

Present-day Orthodox Christianity rests on a rich historical foundation. During the first four centuries after Christ, major theological issues were debated and settled at councils held in eastern Europe, Asia Minor, and North Africa. The cities of the primary patriarchs of Christianity included Rome, Constantinople, Alexandria, Antioch, and Jerusalem. All of these except Rome are now heavily influenced by the Orthodox Church.

As the Byzantine Empire flourished during the millennium after Constantine (died 337), both culture and Christianity took on an Eastern tint. Referring to the Orthodox sacred art, the icon, Byzantium has been called the "icon of the heavenly Jerusalem." Church and state were wed in the marriage of "caesaropapism," the church actually ruled over the state as the divine Bridegroom rules his bride, the church.

For many centuries, Rome was eclipsed by the glory of Byzantium, and economic and political estrangement accompanied the religious separation. A final break came at the Great Schism of 1054. The Orthodox Church refused to submit to papal control. Furthermore, it rejected the Roman teaching that the Holy Spirit is sent by both the Father and Son. (This teaching was enshrined in the famous "filioque" clause in the Nicene Creed [A.D. 325]: "The Holy Spirit... proceedeth from the Father *and the Son*.") Another circumstance contributing to the rupture between Rome and Constantinople was the marriage of Orthodox priests in contrast to the celibacy of Roman priests.[3] Because of these and many other issues, Roman and Byzantine bishops excommunicated each other and the churches were acrimoniously separated.

Today the Orthodox Church differs genuinely from Western Catholicism and Protestantism. The central point of difference concerns the doctrine of the Trinity. In the Orthodox teaching, God the Father is seen to be primarily transcendent. Man is not totally depraved, as Augustine and Calvin saw him, so he can attain fellowship with God through unaided human effort. Jesus is seen as both human and divine, and his glory is the primary attribute emphasized. The Holy Spirit sanctifies the believer to an extreme degree. In fact, the believer ultimately becomes divine.

In worship the liturgy is all-important. Prayers are said to the saints, and prayers are made for the dead. The worshiper stands throughout the entire service. Heavy stress is placed on the beautiful and valuable religious engravings known as "icons." The Orthodox Church retains seven sacraments: baptism, charismation (confirmation), marriage, eucharist, repentance/confession, holy orders, and the anointing of the sick.[4]

Orthodox worshipers tend to be more faithful in church attendance than their Western counterparts. According to a 1963 survey, 31 percent worshiped weekly. A further 32 percent attended services two or three times a month. Only 3 percent were estranged from the church.[5]

It is the peasants who maintain singular obedience to the Orthodox Church. In the introduction to his book, Rinvolucri pointed out this phenomenon: "The unquestioning faith of people in Greek villages is something remarked on by all observers."[6] When *Time* magazine featured the Orthodox Church in 1963, Patriarch Theodosius VI of Antioch substantiated reports of faithfulness: "Our church is healthier today than it has been for the last 1000 years."[7] Nevertheless, change has also made incursions into the age-old fabric of Orthodoxy.

ORTHODOXY FACES CHANGE

Wherever one goes in Greece, he can see black-garbed priests. Although they are still extremely influential among the peasant population, respect for them among sophisticated urban dwellers is declining. The clergy are both financially and educationally impoverished. Consequently, many regard them as an anachronistic symbol of a forgotten age.[8]

When he wrote his definitive report for *America*, George Maloney discovered that 59 percent of the priests in Greece had finished only sixth grade. The remaining clergymen had achieved either university entrance level or basic degree status. Since World War II, fourteen seminaries have been opened to train priests, and the theological faculties at Athens and Salonika have been upgraded.[9]

In 1967 Orthodox priests in Greece were generally earning from $32.70 to $63.23 per month, according to the *New York Times*.[10] In severe cases, the income dropped to $17 per month. The resulting poverty produced a pitiful priesthood. Furthermore, there was a minimum age of thirty for ordination, and this precluded many men of ability and ambition. Under no circumstances could they ever aspire to own a car or any other symbol of emerging Greek affluence.[11]

Traditionally many Orthodox people of a mystical bent have entered monasteries. In 1913 the primary Orthodox monastery on Mount Athos had 7,970 monks, but fifty years later that number had plummeted to 1,588. As male monasticism has declined, however, more women have taken the vows. In 1969 nuns took over the declining monastery of Evangelistria. The decadent building was refurbished and a new wing added by local donations. Now the convent is a flourishing place of pilgrimage.[12]

A further blow to the flagging clergy came in 1976. Most theological students at Athens and Salonika hope to earn a living wage by teaching religion in the schools. In 1976 the government cut in half the number of teaching priests. Reaction was a violent demonstration.[13]

At best, the role of the priest in Greece is a rather pathetic one. Those who cannot teach are condemned to poverty beyond the norm of Christian sacrifice. The *Christian Century* writer who reported on the Orthodox Church observed, "There is little anti-clericalism; the people neither reject nor despise the clergy, rather they endure them. But to the church itself, and to the Orthodox faith, they are unshakably loyal."[14]

A low level of clerical education leaves a leadership vacuum in the church, and laymen have filled it. Decisions by the ruling Holy Synod in Greece are measured, not by the canons of Scripture or the tradition of the church, but by the probable acceptance of them among laymen.[15]

Lay influence has been harnessed by religious societies committed to a renewal of the faith. The most significant of these has been the Zoe (Life) movement, founded by Archimandrite Eusebius in 1911. Its magazine, *Zoe*, now has about 200,000 subscribers. Heavy emphasis is placed on Bible study and frequent communion.[16] To encourage laymen, Zoe maintains a series of religious societies catering to scientists, teachers, workers, and students. Some have been specifically formed to meet the needs of women.[17] According to Rinvolucri, who studied for three years in Greece, the aim of Zoe is "to rouse people from a merely formal and outward Christianity to an active, personally committed faith."[18]

In pursuit of this laudable object, Zoe members often show extreme zeal. They plead for a radical reduction in the length of the liturgical service. Congregational singing in the style of the Protestant and post-Conciliar Catholic churches is to be introduced. Spurning the obsolete traditional translation of the Bible, Zoe has commissioned a modern language version. Consequently the bishops often opposed the movement, fearing that it will produce a schismatic "church within the church."[19]

When a new superior of the Zoe movement was elected in 1960 by a democratic ballot, fifty conservative members walked out. They formed a new movement called Soter (Savior). Soter takes a strongly traditional line and finds its main enemy in the emerging ecumenical movement among Orthodox Churchmen. In 1964 the Soter movement attacked the Catholic Church in a book bearing the emotive title *The Misbeliefs of Papism*. Papal infallibility was the main object of criticism.[20]

An optimistic picture of Soter was presented by the lay theologian Panagiotis Bratsiotis. Obviously a conservative, Bratsiotis praised the Soter movement, saying that "in the seven years since its establishment the new confraternity *Soter* has made great progress and has contributed to spreading the Word of God even further afield."[21]

Another movement has been formed with official approval of the Holy Synod. It is Apostolike Diakonia (Apostolic Deacons) and its headquarters is the monastery of Petraki. It propagates traditional Orthodox doctrines through circulating sermons, Sunday school materials, and other literature. It also maintains a student hostel and has set up a Center for the Social Education of Greek Women. By taking the initiative, the Holy Synod hopes to avoid the danger of an exclusive splinter group within the church as a whole.[22]

In the future the Orthodox Church will undoubtedly change. Bratsiotis lists a dozen changes that he anticipates, but these can be summarized in a shorter list. First, he expects a deeper emphasis on personal piety and Bible knowledge. (Perhaps this reflects developments in Catholicism since Vatican II.) Second, laymen will take a stronger role within the church. Third, this will produce an emerging social conscience and a commitment to missionary expansion. Fourth, the various Orthodox churches can be expected to seek a deeper level of unity.[23] Change is in the air, even in the hidebound home of Orthodoxy.

MARRIAGE OF CHURCH AND STATE

From the first the Orthodox Church has been inextricably linked to the Greek nationality. During four centuries of Turkish domination (from about 1453 until 1821) Hellenistic national consciousness was bound up with the Orthodox faith. As the *America* writer Raymond Etteldorf put it, "The Orthodox Church was more than a symbol and a rallying point for the oppressed Greek people; it was the Greek nation."[24]

When nationalism boiled up into insurrection in 1572, it was Archbishop Macarios Melissinos who led the movement. This religious leadership of Greek nationalists persisted until independence was achieved in 1821. Then the church willingly submitted to the overlordship of the state in its affairs. Bishops were appointed by the king. Parishes were mapped out by the government. Monasteries were expropriated for governmental purposes.[25]

It is against this background that one must understand current trends in state-church relations. When the colonels seized power in 1967, they immediately placed their man in the primate's palace. He was Ieronymos Kotsonis, known officially as Ieronymos. After a long tenure as professor of canon law at Salonika, Ieronymos became chaplain to the royal family in 1949. It was from that office that he was picked by the junta in 1967. The king considered Ieronymos's collusion with the colonels to be treachery.[26]

The junta leader George Papadopoulos relied heavily on Ieronymos to keep the ordinary people in line. Obligingly the archbishop excused political imprisonment: "This is an extraordinary period in which nothing can be done." Forming his own hand-picked Holy Synod, Ieronymos soon filled ecclesiastical offices with "yes men." The archbishop also excluded outside influence by ignoring the commands of the Ecumenical Patriarch of Istanbul, Athenagoras.[27]

When outside forces criticized the right-wing junta, it was Ieronymos who came to the colonels' defence. The World Council of Churches attacked the perversions of power that were occurring in Greece. Their rebuke was issued within six months of the April coup. Ieronymos's answer to the ecumenical office was the threat of withdrawal. If they did not cease criticizing the colonels, the Greek Orthodox Church would resign from the World Council of Churches. Obediently, the Genevan headquarters assumed a position of silence.[28]

By the end of 1967 Papadopoulos had forced the king to flee from Greece. The next year he promulgated a new constitution, and in 1969 he restored minimal freedoms: the inviolability of citizens' homes, freedom of association, and freedom of assembly. Even so, the accusations of torture and repression recurred. In 1973 university students rioted in protest against the lack of academic freedom, and a conspiracy of naval officers was unmasked. Papadopoulos responded by setting out a new constitution and creating a republic, of which he was president.[29]

Although democracy was supposedly reestablished, the oppression continued. In 1974 Amnesty International issued a report documenting the decay of Greek society. According to Amnesty, the junta in its harshness had "surpassed all limits of savagery." One foreign visitor said concerning martial law in Greece: "It's too bad to last, but I can't see how it's going to change." To all of this oppression and corruption Ieronymos gave his tacit and sometimes explicit approval.[30]

In the spring of 1973 Ieronymos disappeared from public view. He was reported to have suffered "psychological depression." From his retreat the archbishop submitted his resignation to the Holy Synod. In desperation Ieronymos admitted

that he had lied. In 1968 he had claimed that the Ecumenical
Patriarch had approved changes in the Greek church charter.
This was untrue, he confessed; the Ecumenical Patriarch had
not given his assent.[31] Still the Holy Synod ordered Ieronymos to stay on. Small wonder, for Ieronymos had appointed
the members of the Holy Synod and they owed their position
and power to him.

By May 1973, however, the government intervened.
Ieronymos had become an embarrassment to Papadopoulos
and the colonels. When two bishops requested the dissolution
of the Holy Synod and the dismissal of Ieronymos, the government agreed. In the new Synod, supporters of Ieronymos
were outnumbered by a ratio of ten to three.[32]

A new primate was appointed in early 1974. His name is
Seraphim. After serving from 1949 until 1958 as Metropolitan
of Arta, Seraphim was appointed to be Metropolitan of Ioan-
nina. From there Holy Synod chose him in January 1974 to
replace Ieronymos. Seraphim had been a wartime resistance
fighter and comrade of President Phaidon Gizikis, who replaced the disgraced Papadopoulos.[33] Seraphim vowed to
bring unity to the Greek church, which had been so rent by
dissension and political intrigue.[34]

By early 1975 the turmoil of revolutionary change
seemed to have passed, and Constantine Karamanlis had become prime minister. He was recalled from France, where
the colonels had driven him into exile. As vestiges of the
military regime faded, so did their ecclesiastical puppets.
Twenty bishops followed the expelled Ieronymos into obliv-
ion. Eleven of the deposed bishops had the impertinence to
protest to the Council of Europe that the Greek government
had unfairly dismissed them. To paraphrase a biblical axiom:
"He who lives by political patronage will also die by political
purge."[35]

Throughout the era of the colonels the church and the
state had walked hand in hand. Under Karamanlis there has
arisen agitation for the separation of religion and politics. Ac-

cording to Karamanlis, "the old statement 'the Kingdom of Greece is the Eastern Orthodox religion' is anachronistic." Despite impressive parliamentary opposition, the prime minister is advocating a constitution that grants complete freedom of religion. In this he is supported by the socialists.[36]

It is the Pan-Hellenic Socialistic Movement (PASOK) under Andrea Papandreou that leads the fight for divorcing the Orthodox Church from Greek government. They charge the church with being "fat and lazy." Furthermore, they call for an end of religious consecration of officeholders. The unholy alliance that persisted throughout the seven years of the military junta is remembered with regret. However, PASOK has only twelve of the three hundred seats in the Greek legislature, and their radical approach to the Orthodox Church is unlikely to prevail.[37]

In the hearts of the Greek people the church holds a particularly prominent place. Though they criticize the abuses of the clergy and the conspiracy between Ieronymos and the colonels, the common man is loyal to the Orthodox Church. "A Greek will speak against the clergy," one reporter concluded, "but never against the Orthodox faith."[38] Thus it is a safe assumption that an annulment of the church-state marriage in Greece is still a long way off.

UNEASY ECUMENISM

According to Robert Evans, the veteran missionary observer of Europe, "the Greek Orthodox Church is not ecumenical in the least."[39] This assessment is confirmed by Rinvolucri who lived in Greece and studied the Orthodox Church over a three-year period: "The ecumenically inclined priests are a tiny minority in Greece and not more than a dozen or two of these have actively taken part in ecumenical work."[40]

Ecumenical relations began first among the various Orthodox Churches, of which there are fourteen in Europe. In 1960 Alexius, the Patriarch of Moscow, visited Athens at the invitation of the Archbishop of Athens. Alexius expressed his desire for a greater unity among all the Eastern Orthodox Churches.[41]

About that time the Ecumenical Patriarch Athenagoras I called for a Pan-Orthodox Conference in Rhodes. This meeting was the first general council of Orthodox churches in thirty years, and it took place during September and October 1961 on the island of Rhodes. Eighty delegates came from a dozen countries. This was hailed as the "most fully representative" conference of modern times. On the agenda were several items: a common confession of faith, a new Bible translation, birth control, remarriage of divorcees, and admission of the Russian Orthodox Church into the World Council of Churches.[42]

The representative from Moscow, Nikodim, was a regular gadfly to the delegates. He insisted that the Ecumenical Patriarch of Constantinople (Istanbul) relinquish his claim of primacy and place all prelates on equal footing. The Russian fought for an ecclesiastical "classless society." There was also a plea by Nikodim that political issues, especially disarmament, be discussed in future. Much of Nikodim's sarcasm was directed at Athenagoras, who had been an American citizen for fourteen years.[43]

When a second Pan-Orthodox Conference was convened at Rhodes in 1963, the Greek Orthodox Church protested. Speaking for the Greeks, Patriarch Chrysostomos of Argolis said, "The Church of Greece hopes that Patriarch Athenagoras will be convinced that it was one of his biggest mistakes to have initiated the forthcoming Rhodes Pan-Orthodox Conference." Spurning any dialogue with the postconciliar Catholic Church, the Greek prelates emphasized that "in subjects like religion it is not possible to bargain and retreat."[44] Nevertheless, Athenagoras insisted on pursuing talks with Rome, and the Greeks grudgingly sent three bishops to the second Rhodes conference.[45]

In 1968 Athenagoras announced the formation of a Pan-Orthodox Commission to prepare for a "Great Synod." The purpose was primarily ecumenical, namely the "renewal of the church and the establishment of the unity of all Christian churches."[46] Bratsiotis concluded that the Pan-Orthodox conferences at Rhodes had demonstrated the unity of the Orthodox Church and the strength of the "primacy of the ecumenical patriarch."[47]

The first stage of ecumenism was to be a restoration of unity among Orthodox communions, and the second phase was the search for unity with Roman Catholicism. Pope John XXIII sought unity with Orthodoxy under a "common and solid creed." Pope Paul persisted by issuing the call to the Ecumenical Patriarch: "Come! Let fall the barriers that separate us!"[48]

Chrysostomos, who had become primate of Greece, was horrified. Orthodox churches could never accept the infallibility of the pope. Neither could they submit to the "centralist and absolutist" rule of the bishops.[49] When the Ecumenical Patriarch announced that he would meet the pope in Jerusalem during 1964, the Greek Holy Synod passed a resolution condemning the meeting in advance.[50] Chrysostomos referred to "the abominable ecumenism."[51]

During January 1964 Athenagoras and Paul VI met in Jerusalem, the first meeting between pope and patriarch since 1439. Athenagoras was jubilant. "The ice is broken," he said. "Soon a new era will begin in the history of Christendom."[52] Pope Paul was equally enthusiastic. "Who knows where the love of Christ may lead us?" the Pope conjectured. "Like the arches in your Gothic churches we may gradually come together and be one."[53] Chrysostomos sat in Greece and fumed, "The Pope is going, allegedly, to kneel at the Saviour's Sepulcher." Then he thrust the dagger into Athenagoras's side: "But you are going there to kneel before the Pope and bury Orthodoxy."[54]

The joint communique issued by Paul and Athenagoras spoke of the meeting as "a fraternal gesture, inspired by the charity of Christ."[55] By December 1965 the breach had been all but healed. At that time, the mutual decrees of excommunication were lifted. A joint statement declared regret for past offensive words, annulment of excommunication, and a deploring of the hostility that had driven a wedge between the churches.[56] Both churches accepted the holy orders and the sacraments of the other church. Mixed marriages between the two were likewise approved.[57]

When Ieronymos came to the primacy of Greece, he reversed the trend of opposition to ecumenism. He supported wholeheartedly the Ecumenical Patriarch in his strivings toward unity with Rome. However, Ieronymos did ask the Catholics to stop "propaganda and proselytism" aimed at winning Greeks for Catholicism. He likewise expressed his skepticism about papal infallibility.[58]

During July 1967 Pope Paul traveled to Istanbul. There he held a special ecumenical service in the cathedral of St. George. He also visited the sites of ancient churches at Smyrna and Ephesus. Athenagoras hailed the pope, "Axios" ("worthy")![59] In October 1967 Athenagoras went to Rome and conducted a similar service in St. Peter's. The Ecumenical Patriarch maintained the momentum by asserting, "What unites us is much more than what separates us."[60]

The ecumenical atmosphere began to have practical results during the late sixties. When Pope Paul VI issued his controversial encyclical on birth control in 1968, Athenagoras supported him. He claimed that conservative elements had forced the pope to take that stand. Furthermore, the Ecumenical Patriarch preferred evolution (slow change) rather than revolution (violent change) in church affairs.[61]

In 1969 Athenagoras suggested that all Christians celebrate Easter on the second Sunday in April. This would stop the rather absurd, but historically significant, controversy that had raged since 1573—the year the Roman Church took up the Gregorian Calendar instead of the Julian calendar.[62]

Practical ecumenism came to Russia in 1970. The Orthodox Church was authorized to administer the sacraments to Roman Catholics. This would alleviate the pressure on Russian Catholics, who had but one church to serve a community of ten thousand Catholics in Moscow. The Vatican called this a "significant ecumenical step." From Greece came a predictably conservative response. The Russian Orthodox hierarchy was criticized for its "unilateral haste of action." Such a momentous step would require Pan-Orthodox approval, according to the Greek Holy Synod.[63]

When Athenagoras died in 1972, he was replaced by Dimitrios I. The pope immediately sent a letter assuring the new Ecumenical Patriarch that he "would always find the Bishop of Rome to be an affectionate brother." Cardinal Willebrands, head of the Secretariat for Christian Unity, persisted in his visits to various Orthodox leaders.[64] Willebrands even visited Ieronymos in Athens and was warmly received by the Greeks.[65]

The whole complexion of ecumenical relations with the Greek Church was transformed, however, when Ieronymos was replaced by Seraphim in 1974. The Pope had appointed a bishop to rule the Uniate Catholics in Greece, and this angered Seraphim. Accusing the pope of perpetuating an "ecclesiastical scandal" within the Greek Orthodox Church, Seraphim said, "I personally interrupt all contacts with the Vatican."[66]

Besides traveling the bumpy road to ecumenism with Rome, the Ecumenical Patriarch also cultivated relations with some Protestant churchmen. In 1962 Anglican archbishop Michael Ramsey visited Athenagoras in Istanbul. Like Pope Paul, Ramsey spoke of "healing of the division between East and West."[67] Later in that same year, Ramsey traveled to Moscow to meet Archbishop Alexius. Archbishop Ramsey praised the "heroism of the Russian Orthodox Church in existing in spite of 'intense anti-God propaganda.'"[68]

During the sixties several Orthodox Churches joined the World Council of Churches. The Russians persisted in their attempts to turn the Council into a platform for political propaganda. Increasingly, the Orthodox delegates gained positions of influence on World Council of Churches commissions and even the central committee. The caustic critic of the World

Council of Churches, Peter Beyerhaus from Tübingen, hailed
Orthodox participation in the affairs of the ecumenical movement. He found their contribution at the Nairobi Assembly of
1975 to be a fresh breeze of theological sincerity.[69]

Ecumenism did indeed infect the Orthodox churches
during the sixties and seventies. A remarkable degree of unity
with Rome was achieved in the wake of Vatican II. The World
Council of Churches warmly received the Orthodox churches
into its membership, while the latter sought to maintain their
theological integrity. Still, skeptical Greeks stood by, refusing
to plunge into the stream of twentieth-century church unity
talks and action.

HAS ORTHODOXY CHANGED?

The short answer to the question "Has Orthodoxy
changed?" must be yes. Despite the unfortunate links between the Greek Church and the brutally repressive military
junta, it has survived. After the stress of revolutionary pressures was lifted, the church returned to its previous state of
influence. Still it bears, however, the scars of centuries of
political compromise.

Among the clergy there is a greater openness toward the
larger Christian community. This is seen in the striving
among some priests for both higher educational standards and
also more contact with academics and clerics outside their
own church.

Another sign of change is the activity of laymen. Through
the associations Zoe, Soter, and Apostolike Diakonia, the laity
is grasping a greater share in the propagation and shaping of
modern Orthodoxy. This lay involvement is largely a modern
phenomenon.

Finally, change is most clearly seen in the field of
ecumenism. A high degree of unity has been achieved with
Rome. Since the sixties, the Orthodox churches have become
full participants in the World Council of Churches. Through

frequent contacts with Protestant leaders, such as the Anglican archbishops, Orthodoxy is broadening both its basis of unity and its influence in other parts of Christendom.

Over the period of the sixties and seventies hovers the immense shadow of Athenagoras, the Ecumenical Patriarch of Istanbul. In announcing the "Great Synod" in 1968, he summarized his eminently successful dual purpose: the "renewal of the church and the establishment of the unity of all Christian churches."[70]

13

How Much Has Changed?

"Serious decline in organized religion" has been prophesied by British Methodist Lord Donald Soper. Eminent American church historian Kenneth Scott Latourette concurred when he spoke of "de-Christianization of a predominantly Christian population." Both label the sixties and seventies an age of sweeping secularism. In their opinion, very little could be done to stop the deterioration.

This survey of contemporary European Christianity has to some degree confirmed Soper's and Latourette's analyses. Indeed the traditional, religious structures are being riddled with dry rot. However, to regard this as an unbroken picture of gloom is to oversimplify the situation. It seems that four major statements must be made by way of summary.

1. European theological thought has become progressively humanistic

In studying contemporary trends in theological writing, there seems to be some justification for regarding secularism as triumphant. Erlangen's Walter Künneth was right when he said, "Contemporary theology is characterized by a high degree of confusion."

At the outset of the sixties, Rudolf Bultmann reigned supreme over Germanic theology, just as German scholarship rules the world theological scene. To Bultmann, Jesus was a mere myth. One could deduce from the biblical documents only a bare minimum of fact. The Scriptures had to be interpreted by the standard of human experience, i.e., "existentialism" in the school of Martin Heidegger.

When Bultmann passed from the scene, the next generation became predictably reactionary. Ernst Fuchs, Ernst Käsemann, and Gerhard Ebeling asserted that there was indeed a "historical Jesus." Albert Schweitzer had not been barking up the wrong fairy-tale tree when in 1906 he wrote his *Quest of the Historical Jesus*. Despite their insistence that Jesus was a historical person, none of Bultmann's disciples seriously accepted the inerrancy of Scripture. To them the Bible was a fallible, human book that reported on the remarkable life of Jesus. While he did exist in history, his miracles were exaggerated beyond the bounds of fact.

This strain of theological thought also emerged across the English Channel. John A. T. Robinson released his bombshell, *Honest To God*, in 1963. Within the first year this little paperback ran to nine printings. The German translation was titled *Gott ist Anders*, ("God is different"), and this embodied the gist of Robinson's thesis. God is not the transcendent, holy, personal Deity portrayed in the Bible. He has been created by man in his own finite, fallible image.

In the post-Bultmann era the "Theology of Hope" also emerged as a dominant force. Jürgen Moltmann and Wolfhart Pannenberg became the primary representatives of this school of thought. In the thinking of these men, history becomes a vehicle of revelation eclipsing the biblical picture of God. Moltmann sees salvation as a process occurring within history and he describes it in political terms. Redemption is release from socio-political oppression by the means of revolution.

It is this political picture of salvation that has been embraced by the World Council of Churches. In the disastrous conference on "Salvation Today" at Bangkok in 1973, the Council totally overthrew the biblical doctrine of salvation. The only definition of redemption was henceforth to be political. Man was to be "saved" from exploitation by others, and

the ecumenical movement would financially back any movement serving that end.

If one were to restrict his vision to theological developments, pessimism would be inescapable. The basis of authority was shifted from the rock of divine revelation to the sands
of human reason. Salvation was reinterpreted to fit the revolutionary movements of the day. God was whittled down to
human dimensions.

2. *Roman Catholics have become open to the Bible*

The second conclusion pertains to the multitude of
Roman Catholics—252 million in Europe. After the Second
Vatican Council (1962–65), Catholics were urged to read the
Scriptures assiduously. As the documents put it, "Ignorance
of the Scriptures is ignorance of Christ."

The faithful Catholics were urged to become "steeped in
the spirit of the Scriptures." Almost immediately there
emerged a ravenous hunger for the Word of God. The hierarchy instructed their flocks to read proper translations rather
than paraphrases, which are popular among Protestants. Consequently, Bibles began to sell throughout Catholic Europe.
One Italian publisher sold the Scriptures in installments from
supermarket stands. Within a few months he had distributed
over a million copies. Orders of nuns were formed to bring
Bibles to the people, and they too showed remarkable success.

Along with the renewed interest in the Scriptures came a
new openness to Protestants. No longer looked upon as heretics, they were regarded as "separated brethren." The long-
pre-Reformation years of common history had left Protestants
and Catholics with a solid basis of creedal unity. Furthermore, Protestant sacraments imitated Catholic rites.
Consequently, these also undergirded the spirit of rap-
prochement.

Dialogue was designed to reinforce the relationship between Catholics and Protestants. It occurred on the highest
level as Protestant leaders beat a path to the Vatican, and the
pope made a momentous visit to the headquarters of the

World Council of Churches in Geneva. The result of serious discussions was the publication in 1975 of a "Common Catechism" embodying the doctrinal beliefs shared by Catholics and Protestants. Two years later there also appeared a statement on "Authority in the Church." This agreed communique was written to smooth the way for ultimate unity between Catholics and Protestants.

A further revolutionary development in Roman Catholicism was the appearance in 1967 of the Catholic Renewal Movement. Under the popular leadership of Joseph Cardinal Suenens, the charismatic Catholics have become extremely vocal. They have been aided by post–Vatican II developments, because they emphasize both the Bible and relations with non-Catholics. On Pentecost Sunday 1975 more than twenty-five thousand of these Pentecostal Catholics packed St. Peter's Basilica in Rome for a special service. Pope Paul greeted them with a mixture of enthusiasm and caution. While he applauded their spiritual sincerity and life, he warned them to stay within the doctrinal framework of the Catholic Church.

It is estimated that there are only about 600,000 charismatic Catholics among the 252 million "faithful" in Europe. They are very obvious because of their flamboyant style of worship and their bold ecumenical moves. Each year many of them travel to the United States for a summer conference at the University of Notre Dame. Still they remain true to the mass, reverential toward Mary, and sincere in their veneration of the Eucharist and the saints.

Change has come to Rome since 1965, and many Roman Catholics have become responsive to the gospel. Indeed, a significant number profess evangelical conversion. It remains to be seen whether most or some of them will turn their back on the Roman system of sacramental salvation and align themselves with biblical churches.

3. Communist repression has produced spiritual virility

As the sixties dawned, Khruschev initiated a horrifying era of persecution against Christians. It has been reliably estimated that he closed about ten thousand churches between 1953 and 1964. Hundreds of Christians were jailed for their faith, and the exile of Alexander Solzhenitzyn served to underscore the truth of those estimates. Solzhenitzyn's *Gulag Archipelago* traced this grisly tradition of persecution against Christians right back to 1917. Further substantiation came from reports by Amnesty International and the British Centre for the Study of Christianity and Communism at Keston College.

Through the publicizing of one Reformed Baptist pastor and his plight, this violation of religious rights has become almost universally known. During much of the sixties and seventies the Reformed Baptist pastor Georgi Vins was shut up in Siberian prison camps. His story leaked out when an autobiography was smuggled to the West and published under the title *Three Generations of Suffering*. Still the Soviet authorities persisted in their inhumane activities, and even the complaints of President Carter were rudely rebuffed.

Another Communist country to gain wide publicity was Poland. There the majority of the population (almost 90 percent) are on Catholic church rolls. Each week about 80 percent go to mass, and more than 90 percent of the children are confirmed. The strength of Polish Catholicism is rooted in the leadership of Stefan Cardinal Wyszynski.

Although Catholicism in Poland has a firm grip of the people, the Communists are not letting the populace go by default. Every effort is made to fortify the communistic control of the educational process. The church is thwarted in many efforts to maintain its position. Most of all, the Communist authorities play the waiting game, looking to the time when the tough old cardinal passes from the scene. Then a puppet can become prelate, and communism will rule with greater ease. For now, though, a thousand years of Catholicism carries much more weight with the Poles than does three decades of communism.

Another example of Christian virility in the face of Communist control is Rumania. From the "House of the Atheist," lecturers crisscross the country trying to convince skeptical workers of the validity of Marxism. In some years they reach a hundred thousand hearers with these talks.

When dealing with Christian ministers, however, the government often takes off the kid gloves. Josif Ton returned to Rumania after studying at Oxford and assumed responsibility for a Baptist Church. First his library was confiscated by the authorities. Then he was expelled from a teaching post at the Baptist Seminary in Bucharest. Finally, he and a colleague were arrested on suspicion of treason. A conviction could mean the death penalty.

This blatant brutality against Baptists in Rumania has stirred revival fires. Since 1972, an astounding 20,000 believers have been baptized each year. This boosts the membership of Baptist churches there to 160,000, an increase of one-third since 1968.

It can be trite to quote Tertullian in illustrating Christianity under communism. The second-century church father could not have realized how often his words would prove true when he said, "The blood of the martyrs is the seed of the Church." From the Arctic to the Adriatic, faithful Christians are proving this axiom at the cost of their lives.

4. Evangelical minorities are growing throughout Europe.

The sixties started with a series of Billy Graham crusades throughout Western Europe. These evangelistic efforts made timid evangelicals aware that they were not alone. Not only was there a sizeable evangelical minority in America, but in Europe too there had emerged a body of believers who were true to the Bible and zealous in evangelism.

Between 1966 and 1974 there were several congresses that further consolidated the European evangelicals into a force for spiritual change. Worldwide conferences met in 1966 at Berlin and eight years later in Lausanne. Besides these, there were European conferences for evangelists at Amsterdam (1971), children's workers in Lausanne (1972), young people at Brussels (1975), and theologians in Heverlee, Belgium (1976). All served to strengthen the sinews of unity between evangelical leaders throughout Europe.

In Germany evangelicals banded together in 1966 to form the *Kein anderes Evangelium* ("No Other Gospel") movement. An opening rally drew twenty thousand to Dortmund, as committed Christians spoke out against the dilution of biblical Christianity by professors and pastors. By 1975, the "No Other Gospel" movement was able to mobilize a force of forty thousand Christians in support of evangelical Christianity.

In France there also grew up a significant body of believers. They cooperated in 1967 to establish a theological seminary at Vaux-sur-Seine. There instruction is offered on a university level by men who are thoroughly committed to biblical beliefs. Throughout the sixties and seventies French evangelicals forged new links among themselves. In the wake of the International Congress on World Evangelization in 1974, French evangelicals decided to launch a nationwide evangelistic thrust. It has been called "Impact '78," and the leaders hope to enlist large segments of the Christian population in this movement. There are only about 40,000 believers among 52 million Frenchmen, but the evangelicals are intent on reaching their contemporaries with the gospel.

It is in England that the evangelicals have shown themselves to be most virile. When evangelical Anglicans met at Keele University in 1967, they were a relatively small and fragmented minority. That congress drew one thousand delegates, and together they shed the sheltered image of evangelical withdrawal from society. They committed themselves to penetrate both the Church of England and society with their evangelical message. No more would they hide away in a protective shell, lest they come under attack by the dreadful dragons of liberal theology. In the words of John Stott, titular head of Anglican Evangelicals: "Something happened at Keele: Excitement grew!"

During the ensuing decade Anglican evangelicalism burgeoned. Anglican theological colleges (Oak Hill, St. John's

Nottingham, and Trinity Bristol) filled with zealous young ordinands who had been recently converted. In 1974, the evangelically inclined Donald Coggan was elevated to the archbishopric of Canterbury. He in turn named evangelicals to key bishoprics. Stuart Blanch was moved to York, David Sheppard took over Liverpool, and John Taylor went to Winchester.

Ten years after Keele another Congress took place, this one was held at Nottingham. At that Congress two thousand delegates took part. Anglican evangelicals committed themselves to aggressive evangelism and social action. They also regarded unity talks with Rome as a desirable goal, an aim not acclaimed by all evangelicals.

No corner of continental Christianity has been untouched by change during the sixties and seventies. Theologically, the change has been for the worse. Rationalism has by and large supplanted the Scriptures as the source of authority.

Negative change has also been seen in Communistic eastern Europe. Throughout the Soviet empire, Christians have fallen under increasing oppression. The prayer and pleas of Christians in the West have helped to release some, but most still languish under the heel of dictatorship.

Within the Roman Catholic Church there is genuine change. No doubt the average Catholic is more open now to the message of the Bible than he was in 1960. Both Vatican II and the charismatic movement have contributed to this. However, this change is to some degree superficial, and the basic balance between Catholics and Protestants remains unchanged.

It is the growth of evangelicalism in Europe that is most encouraging. An older generation of leaders has passed away, leaving an optimistic corps of dedicated young men and women. They believe that Jesus Christ has committed to them the task of evangelizing their post-Christian continent.

Notes

NOTES ON CHAPTER 1

[1]*Time*, April 8, 1966.

[2]Ibid., April 12, 1968.

[3]Francis A. Schaeffer, *Death in the City* (London: Inter-Varsity, 1969), pp. 12–13.

[4]A. L. Rowse, "Striding through English History," *Sunday Telegraph*, London, February 15, 1976.

[5]Fred Brown, *Secular Evangelism* (London: SCM, 1970), p. 17.

[6]Norman Goodall, ed., *The Uppsala Report 1968* (Geneva: World Council of Churches, 1968), pp. 79–80.

[7]Robert L. Richard, S. J., *Secularization Today* (London: Burns and Oates, 1967), p. 151.

[8]Robert P. Evans, "The Missionary Situation in Europe," *Christianity Today*, July 20, 1962.

[9]Jan van Capelleveen, "Europe in a Changing Mood," *Christianity Today*, January 20, 1967.

[10]Harvey Cox, *The Secular City* (London: SCM, 1965), pp. 60–61.

[11]Francis A. Schaeffer, *The Church at the End of the Twentieth Century* (London: Norfolk, 1971), p. 98.

[12]J. D. Douglas, ed., *Let the Earth Hear His Voice* (Minneapolis: World Wide, 1975), p. 152.

[13]Horst Marquardt, "Swifter than Reuter's Pigeons," *International Christian Broadcaster's Bulletin*, First Quarter, 1975.

[14]*Christianity Today*, July 20, 1962.

[15]Werner Bürklin and Bram Krol, "Denmark-Report," Unpublished Report for Youth for Christ International, 1973. (A late report indicates that because of the protest of evangelical believers in Germany the film will not be produced.)

[16]*Time*, August 12, 1966.

[17]British Broadcasting Corporation, Radio 4, November 11, 1972.

[18]*Daily Telegraph*, London, September 30, 1974.

[19]Ibid., November 3, 1972.

[20]Bernard Hollowood, "Austerity Holidays at Home," *Daily Telegraph*, London, August 16, 1975.

[21]*Daily Telegraph*, London, April 24, 1975.

[22]Rudolf Weckerling, ed., *Jenseits vom Nullpunkt?* (Stuttgart: Kreuz, 1972), pp. 23–24.

[23]John England, "Where God is losing out to Mammon," *Sunday Telegraph*, London, January 4, 1976.

[24]*Newsweek*, January 5, 1970.

[25]*Moody Monthly*, November 1974.

[26]*Daily Telegraph*, London, July 10, 1975.

[27]Flora Lewis, "Urban Europeans Worry About the Quality of Life," *New York Times*, March 27, 1975.

[28]*Sunday Telegraph*, London, September 15, 1974.

[29]Fact Sheets on Sweden. "Drug Abuse" (Stockholm: Swedish Institute, 1973).

[30]*Bunte*, March 1, 1967.

[31]*Moody Monthly*, July-August 1973.

[32]*Evangelism Today*, March 1975.

[33]Stuart Harris, *Eyes on Europe* (Chicago: Moody, 1970), p. 15.

[34]Ernst Wilhelm Benz, "Secularization," *Encyclopaedia Britannica* (Macropaedia), (1974), 4:530.

[35]Joachim Kahl, *Das Elend des Christentums* (Hamburg: Rowohlt, 1968), p. 91. English ed., *The Misery of Christianity* (Harmondsworth: Penguin, 1971).

[36]George M. Winston, "Religious Situation Affects Outreach in Europe," *Evangelical Missions Quarterly*, January, 1974, p. 97.

[37]Klaus Bockmuhl, "Theology as Servant," *Christianity Today*, February 27, 1976.

[38]Manfred Kober, "Theology in Germany," *Reformation Review*, April 1969.

[39]Ibid.

[40]Francis A. Schaeffer, *The Church Before the Watching World* (London: Inter-Varsity, 1972), p. 17.

[41]Rudolf Bultmann, *Jesus Christ and Mythology* (London: SCM, 1960), p. 16.

[42]Rudolf Bultmann, *Theology of the New Testament* (London: SCM, 1952), 1:295, 305.

[43]Bultmann, *Jesus Christ and Mythology*, p. 35.

[44]Ibid., p. 57.

[45]Ernst Käsemann, *New Testament Questions of Today* (London: SCM, 1969), p. 37.

[46]Bultmann, *Jesus Christ and Mythology*, p. 80.

[47]*Alliance Witness*, November 10, 1965.

[48]*Christianity Today*, September 25, 1964.

[49]Kahl, *Das Elend des Christentums*, p. 113.

[50]Käsemann, *New Testament Questions*, p. 11

[51]John Macquarrie, *Twentieth-Century Religious Thought* (London: SCM, 1971), p. 380.

[52]Gerhard Ebeling, *Word and Faith* (London: SCM, 1963), p. 205.

[53]Ibid., p. 303.

[54]Daniel Fuller, *Easter Faith and History* (London: Tyndale, 1965), p. 117.

[55]Käsemann, *New Testament Questions*, p. 25.

[56]Ernst Fuchs, *Studies of the Historical Jesus* (London: SCM, 1964), pp. 30–31.

[57]Otto Rodenberg, *Um die Wahrheit der Heiligen Schrift* (Wuppertal: R. Brockhaus, 1962), p. 12.

[58]*Time*, March 8, 1976.

[59]Wolfhart Pannenberg, *Jesus—God and Man* (London: SCM, 1968), pp. 100–101.

[60]Clark H. Pinnock, "The Tombstone That Trembled," *Christianity Today*, April 12, 1968.

[61]Pannenberg, *Jesus, God and Man*, p. 84.

[62]Wolfhart Pannenberg, *Basic Questions in Theology* (London: SCM, 1970–73), 1:13.

[63]Jürgen Moltmann, *Theology of Hope* (London: SCM, 1967), p. 25.

[64]Weckerling, *Jenseits vom Nullpunkt?* p. 148.

[65]Moltmann, *Theology of Hope*, p. 25.

[66]Carl F. H. Henry, *Frontiers in Modern Theology* (Chicago: Moody, 1964), p. 92.

[67]Schaeffer, *Church Before the Watching World*, p. 34.

NOTES ON CHAPTER 2

[1]Gilbert W. Kirby, "Evangelical Alliance," *The New International Dictionary of the Christian Church*, eds. J.D. Douglas (Grand Rapids: Zondervan, 1974), p. 359.

[2]Arthur P. Johnston, "The Unanswered Prayer of Edinburgh," *Christianity Today*, November 22, 1974.

[3]James Taylor, "Edinburgh Missionary Conference," *New International Dictionary of the Christian Church*, p. 329.

[4]Gerald H. Anderson, ed., *The Theology of the Christian Mission* (New York: McGraw Hill, 1961), p. 7.

[5]W.A. Visser't Hooft, ed., *The First Assembly of the World Council of Churches* (London: SCM, 1969), p. 70.

[6]Robin E. Nixon, *The Churchman*, Editorial, July-September, 1975.

[7]W.A. Visser't Hooft, *The New Delhi Report* (London: SCM, 1962), pp. 56–58.

[8]Peter Beyerhaus, *Missions: Which Way?* (Grand Rapids: Zondervan, 1971), p. 14.

[9]Visser't Hooft, *New Delhi Report*, p. 65.

[10]Ibid., p. 67.

[11]Robert B. Ives, "New Delhi Assembly (1961)," *New International Dictionary of the Christian Church*, p. 701.

[12]Visser't Hooft, *New Delhi Report*, p. 93.

[13]Ibid., p. 86.

[14]Ibid., pp. 107–8.

[15]Arthur H. Matthews, "The WCC: Words in the Wilderness," *Christianity Today*, January 2, 1976.

[16]Beyerhaus, *Missions: Which Way?* p. 37.

[17]Norman Goodall, ed., *The Uppsala Report 1968* (Geneva: World Council of Churches, 1968), p. 91.

[18]Ibid., p. 31.

[19]Ibid., pp. 62–66.

[20]Ibid., p. 48.

[21]Ibid., p. 72.

[22]Ibid., pp. 169–70.

[23]Robert B. Ives, "*Uppsala Assembly (1968),*" *New International Dictionary of the Christian Church,* p. 1003.

[24]Goodall, *Uppsala Report,* p. 26.

[25]Beyerhaus, *Missions: Which Way?* p. 46.

[26]Peter Beyerhaus, *Bangkok '73: The Beginning or End of World Mission?* (Grand Rapids: Zondervan, 1974), p. 12.

[27]Ibid., p. 137–38.

[28]Ibid., p. 163.

[29]Ibid., p. 163.

[30]Ibid., p. 135.

[31]Ibid., pp. 21, 27.

[32]Ibid., pp. 179–80.

[33]David Johnson, ed., *Uppsala to Nairobi* (London: SPCK, 1975), p. 82.

[34]Stephen Neill, "Some Realism in the Ecumenical Illusion," *The Churchman,* July-September, 1975.

[35]Ibid., pp. 226–28.

[36]*Moody Monthly,* Editorial, February 1976.

[37]Ecumenical Press Service, November 27, 1975.

[38]Harold Lindsell, "Nairobi: Crisis in Credibility," *Christianity Today,* January 2, 1976.

[39]*Daily Telegraph,* London, September 29, 1975.

[40]Ibid., December 15, 1975.

[41]Lindsell, "Nairobi: Crisis in Credibility."

[42]*Time,* December 22, 1975.

[43]Lindsell, "Nairobi: Crisis in Credibility."

[44]Ecumenical Press Service, December 1, 1975.

[45]*Time,* December 22, 1975.

[46]Ecumenical Press Service, December 9, 1975.

[47]Lindsell, "Nairobi: Crisis in Credibility."

[48]*Daily Telegraph,* London, December 20, 1975.

[49]N.T. Wright, "Universalism and the World-Wide Community," *The Churchman,* July-September 1975.

[50]Beyerhaus, *Bangkok '73,* p. 144.

[51]*Daily Telegraph,* London, March 15, 1976.

[52]*Christianity Today,* October 9, 1970.

[53]Edward Norman, "How Marx's Sirens Lure the Church," *Daily Telegraph,* London, April 14, 1976.

[54]G.C. Berkouwer, *The Providence of God* (Grand Rapids: Eerdmans, 1972), p. 20.

NOTES ON CHAPTER 3

[1]*Christianity Today,* January 16, 1961.

[2]Gilbert W. Kirby, ed., *Evangelism Alert* (London: World Wide, 1972), p. 127.

[3]Stephen Neill, "Some Realism in the Ecumenical Illusion," *The Churchman,* July-September 1975.

[4]*Eternity*, November 1976.

[5]Carl F. H. Henry and Stanley W. Mooneyham, eds., *One Race, One Gospel, One Task* (Minneapolis: World Wide, 1967), 1:19.

[6]Ibid., 1:34.

[7]Kirby, *Evangelism Alert*, p. 8.

[8]*Moody Monthly*, March 1975.

[9]*Christianity Today*, December 20, 1974.

[10]J. D. Douglas, ed., *Let the Earth Hear His Voice* (Minneapolis: World Wide, 1975), p. 34.

[11]*Crusade*, September, 1974; *Time*, August 5, 1974.

[12]*Time*, August 5, 1974.

[13]*Christianity Today*, August 29, 1975.

[14]Ibid., January 1, 1976.

[15]*Der Feste Grund*, November 1976.

[16]*Christianity Today*, October 24, 1960.

[17]Billy Graham Evangelistic Association, Official Statistics.

[18]Hartmut Stratmann, *Kein anderes Evangelium: Geist und Geschichte der neuen Bekenntnisbewegung* (Hamburg: Furche-Verlag H. Rennebach, 1970), p. 66.

[19]Ibid., pp. 68–69.

[20]Rudolf Weckerling, ed., *Jenseits vom Nullpunkt?* (Stuttgart: Kreuz, 1972), p. 35.

[21]*Christianity Today*, July 21, 1967.

[22]Ibid., July 17, 1975.

[23]Peter Beyerhaus, *Missions: Which Way?* (Grand Rapids: Zondervan, 1971), pp. 113–120.

[24]*Greater Europe Report*, July-August 1974, September-October 1974.

[25]*Christianity Today*, July 16, 1976.

[26]Samuel Külling, *Das Übel an der Wurzel Erfassen* (Bettingen: Privately Published, 1966), pp. 10–11.

[27]Ibid., pp. 15–17.

[28]Festschrift zur Eröffnung der Freien Evangelisch-Theologischen Akademie Basel. (Basel, 1970), p. 16.

[29]Edward B. Fiske, "Fundamentalist Conducts a Spiritual Haven in the Alps," *New York Times*, September 10, 1973.

[30]Wayne Christianson, "Dutch TV Treat," *Moody Monthly*, December 1974.

[31]Interview with Björn Donobauer, member of the organizing committee.

[32]Greater Europe Mission Archives, Wheaton, Illinois.

[33]Bill Yoder, "The Nineteenth-Century Revivals in Finland and Their Abiding Influence," Unpublished Research Paper, Wheaton Graduate School of Theology, n.d., p. 27.

[34]Ibid., pp. 21–22.

[35]Vela-Pekka Toivianen, "Characteristics of the People's Bible Society," Unpublished Paper, Copenhagen, February 3, 1976.

[36]Robert P. Evans, "Billy Graham in Europe," Unpublished Manuscript.

[37]*The Branch* (Inter-Varsity Christian Fellowship), January 10, 1974.

[38]*Christianity Today*, June 4, 1965.

[39]Ibid.

[40]*Idea*, Autumn 1974.

[41]*Christianity Today*, June 21, 1963.

[42]*Annuaire Evangelique* (Grenoble: Defi, 1973), p. 15.

[43]Interview with David Barnes and Robert P. Evans, Paris, May 7, 1976.

[44]*Newsletter of the World Presbyterian Mission*, April 1976.

[45]*Christianity Today*, April 23, 1976; *La France Évangeliqué 1977* (Amneville: Federation Evangelique de France, 1976), p. 238.

[46]William H. Boerop, "A Missionary Survey of Belgium," Unpublished M.A. thesis, Columbia, S.C., 1965, pp. 35, 82.

[47]W. T. Stunt, et al., *Turning the World Upside Down*, 2nd ed. (Bath: Echoes of Service, 1972), p. 314.

[48]*Christianity Today*, April 10, 1964.

[49]Ibid., December 20, 1974. *World Vision*, July-August 1973.

[50]James W. Reapsome, "Wherefore So Many Christians?" *Greater Europe Report*, July-August 1973.

[51]*Christianity Today*, December 20, 1974.

[52]Ibid., December 6, 1973.

[53]Ibid., November 21, 1975.

[54]*The Church Around the World*, July 1976.

[55]Evans, "Billy Graham in Europe."

[56]Ibid.

NOTES ON CHAPTER 4

[1]*Eternity*, December, 1976.

[2]Kurt Hutten, *Was glauben die Sekten?* (Stuttgart: Quell-Verlag, 1965), pp. 17–18.

[3]Ibid.

[4]Kurt Hutten, *Seher, Grübler, Enthusiasten*, (Stuttgart: Quell-Verlag, 1966), p. 113.

[5]*Yearbook of the Jehovah's Witnesses 1975* (New York: Watchtower Bible and Tract Society, 1974), pp. 257-58.

[6]*Yearbook of the Jehovah's Witnesses 1973* (New York: Watchtower Bible and Tract Society, 1972), pp. 137-41.

[7]Joachim Heldt, *Gott in Deutschland* (Hamburg: Nannen, 1963), p. 134.

[8]Hutten, *Seher, Grübler, Enthusiasten*, p. 113.

[9]*Yearbook of the Jehovah's Witnesses 1973*, pp. 10-11.

[10]Ronald Fisher, "The why and how of reaching Jehovah's Witnesses," *Evangelical Missions Quarterly*, October 1976.

[11]Ibid.

[12]*Yearbook of the Jehovah's Witnesses 1975*, p. 17.

[13]Dale G. Vought, *Protestants in Modern Spain*. (South Pasadena: William Carey Library, 1973), p. 101.

[14]*Floodtide*, Fall, 1973.

[15]*Yearbook of the Jehovah's Witnesses 1975*, p. 17.

[16]Hutten, *Seher, Grübler, Enthusiasten*, p. 105.

[17]Trevor Beeson, *Discretion and Valour* (London: Fontana, 1974), p. 92.

[18]Hutten, *Seher, Grübler, Enthusiasten*, p. 596.

[19]*Christianity Today*, May 7, 1976.

[20]*Fortune*, April 1964; Hutten, *Seher, Grübler, Enthusiasten*, p. 597.

[21]Hutten, *Seher, Grübler, Enthusiasten*, p. 597.

[22]*Daily Telegraph*, London, June 19, 1976.

[23]Hutten, *Seher, Grübler, Enthusiasten*, p. 598.

[24]*St. Petersburg Times*, Crossroads, August 7, 1976.

[25]Interview with Duane Olson, Copenhagen, December 17, 1976.

[26]Dale G. Vought, *Protestants in Modern Spain*, p. 103.

[27]Letter from Walter Frank, Wheaton, Illinois. November 5, 1968.

[28]*Dublin Sunday Press*, January 4, 1976.

[29]*Crusade*, January 1976.

[30]*Daily Telegraph*, London, August 16, 1972.

[31]*New York Times*, August 13, 1972.

[32]Ibid., January 19, 1973.

[33]*Time*, February 18, 1974; *Christianity Today*, February 15, 1974.

[34]*Plain Truth*, April 1976.

[35]Russell L. Chandler, "The Armstrong Battle of Britain," *Christianity Today*, February 13, 1976.

[36]Hutten, *Seher, Grübler, Enthusiasten*, p. 641.

[37]Beeson, *Discretion and Valour*, p. 172.

[38]Daniel Jenkins, *The British: Their Identity and Religion* (London: SCM, 1975), p. 117.

[39]M. C. Burrell, *Divine Light Mission* (London: Church Book Room, n.d.), pp. 3–4.

[40]Ibid. p. 5.

[41]Ibid. pp. 6–9.

[42]Ibid. pp. 9–10.

[43]*International Herald Tribune*, Paris, April 2, 1975.

[44]*Time*, April 28, 1975.

[45]*Chicago Daily News*, February 7–8, 1976.

[46]*Daily Telegraph*, London, May 5, 1976, June 2, 1976; *Time*, June 14, 1976.

[47]Robert P. Evans, Lecture at Wheaton, Illinois, June 22, 1976.

[48]Ibid.

[49]*Daily Telegraph*, May 3, 1976.

[50]*Crusade*, July 1971.

[51]*Back to Godhead*, March/April 1976.

[52]Ibid.

[53]Ibid.

[54]*Christianity Today*. February 28, 1975.

[55]*Back to Godhead*, March/April 1976.

[56]*Bournemouth Evening Echo*, March 19, 1975.

[57]Jack Forem, *Transcendental Meditation: Maharishi Mahesh Yogi and the Science of Creative Intelligence* (New York: Dutton, 1974) p. 10.

[58]Ibid.

[59]Ibid., p. 217.

[60]Patrick Sookhedo, "Up the Guru's Garden Path," *Crusade*, July 1975.

[61]*Idea*, February 24, 1975.

[62]*Time*, October 13, 1975.

[63]*Christianity Today*, March 26, 1976.

[64]Factsheet on Germany," Greater Europe Mission, 1966.

[65]Peter Mayer, *Dass Sie Los Sein Sollen* (Beatenberg: Bibelschule Beatenberg, 1974) p. 11.

[66]Ibid. p. 71.

[67]Heinrich Kemner, *Weg und Ziel: Aus Meinem Leben*, quoted in Peter Mayer, *Dass Sie Los Sein Sollen*, p. 12.

[68]Ibid. p. 40.

[69]*Daily Telegraph*, London, April 24, 1975.

[70]*Wall Street Journal*, December 10, 1974.

[71]*Daily Telegraph*, London, April 24, 1975.

[72]John Wesley White, *Re-Entry* (Minneapolis: World Wide, 1971), p. 90.

[73]"This Week," Independent Television, London, April 24, 1975.

[74]Interview with Heinz Strupler, Walzenhausen, Switzerland, April 10–18, 1975.

[75]*New York Times*, December 18, 1975.

[76]*Church Around the World*, April, 1975; Alice Mathews, "Phobia-Filled France," *The Christian Reader*, February/March 1968.

[77]Frank Orna-Ornstein, *France . . . Forgotten Mission Field* (Watford: European Missionary Fellowship, 1972), p. 130.

NOTES ON CHAPTER 5

[1]Peter Hebblethwaite, *The Runaway Church* (London: Collins, 1975), p. 10.

[2]Karl Barth, *Ad Limina Apostolorum: An Appraisal of Vatican II* (Richmond, Va.: John Knox, 1968), pp. 69–70.

[3]Ibid., p. 62.

[4]Ibid., pp. 70–76.

[5]Hebblethwaite, *Runaway Church*, p. 228.

[6]Lawrence Elliott, *I Will Be Called John: A Biography of Pope John XXIII* (London: Collins, 1974), p. 275.

[7]Edward Schillebeeckx, *The Mission of the Church* (New York: Seabury, 1973), p. 25.

[8]Elliott, *I Will Be Called John*, pp. 281–82.

[9]Ibid., p. 284.

[10]Ibid., pp. 279–80.

[11]Ibid., pp. 287–89.

[12]Fritz Leist, *Der Gefangene des Vatikans* (Munich: Koesel, 1971), pp. 285–86.

[13]Elliott, *I Will Be Called John*, p. 290.

[14]*Collier's Encyclopedia: 1962 Yearbook*, s. v. "John XXIII."

[15]Elliott, *I Will Be Called John*, pp. 298–99.

[16]John Allen Moore, ed., *Baptist Witness in Catholic Europe* (Rome: Baptist Publishing House, 1973), p. 93.

[17]Eliott, *I Will Be Called John*. p. 290.

[18]*Present Truth*, June, 1972.

[19]Austin Flannery, ed., *Vatican Council II: The Conciliar and Post-Conciliar Documents* (Dublin: Dominican, 1975), p. 467.

[20]Ibid., pp. 483–85.

[21]Ibid., p. 488.

[22]Ibid., pp. 474–78.

[23]Ibid., pp. 469–70.

[24]Schillebeeckx, *Mission of the Church*, p. 22.

[25]Hans Küng, *That the World May Believe* (Hastings, New York: Sheed and Ward, 1963), pp. 18–20.

[26]John L. McKenzie, *The Roman Catholic Church* (New York: Holt, Rinehart and Winston, 1969), pp. 121–22.

[27]Barth, *Ad Limina Apostolorum*, pp. 67–68.

[28]Ernst Fischer, *Kirche und Kirchen nach dem Vaticanum II* (Munich: Christian Kaiser, 1967), p. 89.

[29]W. T. Stunt, et al., *Turning the World Upside Down*, 2nd ed. (Bath: Echoes of Service, 1972), p. 315.

[30]Moore, *Baptist Witness*, pp. 96, 123–24, 150.

[31]Richard P. McBrien, *Has the Church Surrendered?* (Denville, New Jersey: Dimension, 1974), pp. 100–102.

[32]*Minneapolis Tribune*, October 24, 1976.

[33]*New York Times*, March 3, 31, 1975.

[34]*Daily Telegraph*, London, January 20, 31, 1977; "Authority in the Church," London, Catholic Truth Society and SPCK, 1977.

[35]Barth, *Ad Limina Apostolorum*, pp. 47–48, 54.

[36]Flannery, *Vatican Council II*, p. 762.

[37]Ibid., p. 764.

[38]Ibid., p. 755.

[39]Ibid., p. 268.

[40]Royal Peck, "New Stride by the Big Boot," *The Christian Reader*, February–March 1968.

[41]Moore, *Baptist Witness*, p. 136.

[42]*The Gospel Message* (Gospel Missionary Union), Winter 1973.

[43]Stunt, *Turning the World Upside Down*, p. 361.

[44]*World Vision*, October 1975.

[45]Hans Küng, *Infallible? An Enquiry* (London: Collins, 1971), p. 62.

[46]Flannery, *Vatican Council II*, p. 566.

[47]Ibid., p. 379.

[48]Leist, *Der Gefangene des Vatikans*, p. 316.

[49]David F. Wells, *Revolution in Rome*, p. 95.

[50]Hebblethwaite, *Runaway Church*, pp. 94–95.

[51]Ibid., pp. 209–10.

[52]H. M. Carson, *Dawn or Twilight?* (Leicester: Inter-Varsity, 1976), p. 52.

[53]Flannery, *Vatican Council II*, p. 892.

[54]*New York Times*, February 28, 1975.

[55]*Daily Telegraph*, London, January 31, 1977; *Chicago Tribune*, January 28, 1977.

[56]*Time*, February 2, 1977.

[57]*Daily Telegraph*, London, March 22, 1974.

[58]*Christianity Today*, June 9, 1967.

[59]Carson, *Dawn or Twilight?* p. 10.

[60]Ibid., pp. 100–13.

[61]*Sunday Telegraph*, London, January 4, 1976.

[62]Moore, *Baptist Witness*, p. 38.

[63]*New York Times*, June 23, 1973.

[64]*Time*, April 4, 1974; *Christianity Today*, February 1, 1974.

[65]*Together*, Paris, November 1973.

[66]*Erstes Deutsches Fernsehen*, May 5, 1968.

[67]Kay Withers, "Callouses of Power," *Chicago Tribune*, May 26, 1974.

[68]*New York Times*, November 12, 1973.

[69]British Broadcasting Corporation, August 28, 1975.

[70]Herbert J. Kane, *Understanding Christian Missions* (Grand Rapids: Baker, 1974), pp. 237–38.

[71]*Christian Times*, November 10, 1968.

[72]*Chicago Tribune*, May 26, 1974; *Time*, January 31, 1977.

[73]Moore, *Baptist Witness*, p. 195.

[74]*The Wall Street Journal*, July 28, 1976.

[75]*Newsweek*, January 5, 1970.

[76]*Christianity Today*, November 11, 1974.

[77]*International Herald Tribune*, October 14, 1976.

[78]*Daily Telegraph*, London, January 20, 31, 1977.

Notes on Chapter 6

[1]John McKenzie, *The Roman Catholic Church* (New York: Holt, Rinehart and Winston, 1969), p. xi.

[2]*News Letter of the International Catholic Priests' Association*, Polegate, East Sussex, Winter, 1975.

[3]Donald S. Connery, *The Irish* (London: Arrow, 1972), p. 42.

[4]David F. Wells, *Revolution in Rome*, p. 36.

[5]Karl Rahner, *The Priesthood* (New York: Seabury, 1973), p. 136.

[6]*Chicago Tribune*, May 26, 1974.

[7]*Christianity Today*, October 9, 1970.

[8]Fritz Leist, *Der Gefangene des Vatikans* (Munich: Koesel, 1971), p. 351.

[9]Francis A. Schaeffer, *The Church Before the Watching World* (London: Inter-Varsity, 1972), p. 56.

[10]*Daily Telegraph*, London, February 17, 1977.

[11]Hans Küng, *Infallible? An Enquiry* (London: Collins, 1971), pp. 144-45, 179.

[12]*Time*, July 9, 1973.

[13]*Christianity Today*, May 7, 1971; H. M. Carson, *Dawn or Twilight?* (Leicester: Inter-Varsity, 1976) p. 27.

[14]*New York Times*, July 7, 1973.

[15]Peter Hebblethwaite, *The Runaway Church* (London: Collins, 1975), pp. 112, 114.

[16]*International Herald Tribune*, Paris, April 10, 1975.

[17]Hans Küng, *The Church* (London: Burns and Oates, 1967), pp. 370-71, 375-79.

[18]Carson, *Dawn or Twilight?* pp. 87-88, 96.

[19]Hans Küng, *That the World May Believe* (New York: Sheed and Ward, 1963), pp. 27-29 and 100-101.

[20]*Time*, January 3, 1977; *Daily Telegraph*, London, February 17, 1977.

[21]Carson, *Dawn or Twilight?* p. 23.

[22]Karl Rahner, *The Christian of the Future* (New York: Herder and Herder, 1967), p. 35.

[23]Ibid., pp. 55, 71, 85.

[24]Karl Rahner, *The Priesthood* (New York: Seabury, 1973), pp. 161-62, 263-64.

[25]*Stern*, Hamburg, January, 1970.

[26]Carson, *Dawn or Twilight?* p. 44.

[27]Ibid., p. 22.

[28]Wells, *Revolution in Rome*, p. 52; Edward Schillebeeckx, *God the Future of Man* (New York: Sheed and Ward, 1968); *The Problem of Eschatology* (New York: Paulist, 1969).

[29]Carson, *Dawn or Twilight?* pp. 12, 133.

[30]*New York Times*, January 29, 1973.

[31]*Time*, January 1, 1976; *Christianity Today*, January 21, 1977.

[32]John Organ, "Papacy at the Crossroads," *Sunday Telegraph*, London, January 4, 1976.

[33]*Daily Telegraph*, London, June 11, 1975.

[34]Hebblethwaite, *Runaway Church*, p. 107.

[35]*Sunday Telegraph*, London, February 29, 1976.

[36]*Daily Telegraph*, London, December 21, 1976.

[37]Interview with Stanley Mawhinney, Dublin, April 28, 1974.

[38]*Daily Telegraph*, London, March 22, 1974.

[39]Karl Barth, *Ad Limina Apostolorum: An Appraisal of Vatican II* (Richmond, Va.: John Knox, 1968), p. 60.

[40]John Allen Moore, ed., *Baptist Witness in Catholic Europe* (Rome: Baptist Publishing House, 1973), p. 107.

[41]Carson, *Dawn or Twilight?* p. 47.

[42]Wells, *Revolution in Rome*, p. 47.

[43]Hebblethwaite, *Runaway Church*, p. 19.

[44]Hans Küng, *Infallible? An Inquiry* (London: Collins, 1971), p. 37.

[45]Hebblethwaite, *Runaway Church*, pp. 74–75.

[46]Donald S. Connery, *The Irish*, pp. 161, 27.

[47]*The Beacon News*, Aurora, Illinois, July 25, 1976.

[48]*Daily Telegraph*, London, August 31, 1976.

[49]Ibid., September 1, 1976.

[50]*Christianity Today*, September 10, 1976.

[51]*The Times*, London, August 28, 1976.

[52]*Irish Times*, Dublin, September 14, 1976.

[53]Desmond Albrow, "Revolt Against the Pope," *Sunday Telegraph*, London, August 29, 1976.

[54]*Daily Telegraph*, London, February 28, 1977.

[55]Ibid., November 21, 1975, December 15, 1975.

[56]Ibid., November 20, 1975.

[57]Ibid., November 11, 1976.

[58]John W. Flanagan, *A Periscope on Teilhard de Chardin* (Polegate, Sussex: International Catholic Priests' Association, n.d.), p. 6.

[59]F. Albers, *The Hidden Schism: Or the New Catholicism* (Polegate, Sussex: International Catholic Priests' Association, n.d.), pp. 10, 20.

[60]*News Letter of the International Catholic Priests' Association*, Polegate, Sussex, Spring 1976.

[61]Ibid.

[62]Honor Tracey, "Words of Little Comfort," *Daily Telegraph*, London, November 13, 1976.

[63]*Daily Telegraph*, London, August 23, 1976.

[64]Hebblethwaite, *Runaway Church*, p. 207.

[65]Thomas Flynn, *The Charismatic Renewal and the Irish Experience* (London: Hodder and Stoughton, 1974), p. 70.

[66]John Wesley White, *Re-Entry* (Minneapolis: World Wide, 1971), p. 127.

[67]*Present Truth*, June, 1973.

[68]*Christianity Today*, June 6, 1975.

[69]Ibid., July 5, 1974.

[70]Ibid., September 26, 1975.

[71]Flynn, *Charismatic Renewal*, p. 43.

[72]Edward A. O'Connor, *The Pentecostal Movement in the Catholic Church* (Notre Dame: Ave Maria, 1974), p. 18.

[73]*Christianity Today*, July 5, 1974.

[74]*Present Truth*, February, 1974.

[75]Flynn, *Charismatic Renewal*, p. 19.

[76]O'Connor, *The Pentecostal Movement*, p. 167.

[77]*Christianity Today*, November 22, 1974.

[78]Ibid., June 20, 1975.

[79]Russell Chandler, "Charismatics Gain Pope's Approval," *Los Angeles Times*, June 8, 1975.

[80]*News Letter of the International Catholic Priests' Association.* Polegate, Sussex, Winter 1975.

[81]Edward Schillebeeckx, *The Mission of the Church* (New York: Seabury, 1973), p. 190.

[82]*Renewal*, Esher, August-September 1975.

[83]*Crusade*, London, October 1974.

[84]W. Stanford Reid, "Some Questions about the New Pentecostalism," *Christianity Today*, June 7, 1974.

[85]Carson, *Dawn or Twilight?* pp. 34–35; Simon Tugwell, *Did You Receive the Spirit?* (London: Darton, Longman and Todd, 1972), p. 99.

[86]Wells, *Revolution in Rome*, p. 100.

[87]Moore, *Baptist Witness in Catholic Europe*, p. 16.

NOTES ON CHAPTER 7

[1]Karl Marx and Friedrich Engels, *Selected Works* (Moscow: Foreign Language Publishing House, 1955), 1:56.

[2]Friedrich Engels, *Socialism, Utopian and Scientific* (London: Pathfinder, 1972), Introduction.

[3]*Daily Telegraph*, London, May 19, 1976.

[4]Peter Hebblethwaite, *The Runaway Church* (London: Collins, 1975), p. 150.

[5]Lawrence Elliott, *I Will Be Called John*, pp. 310–12.

[6]Ibid., pp. 276–77.

[7]Ibid.

[8]Hebblethwaite, *Runaway Church*, p. 164.

[9]Trevor Beeson, *Discretion and Valour* (London: Fontana, 1974), p. 324.

[10]Austin Flannery, ed., *Vatican Council II: The Conciliar and Post-Conciliar Documents* (Dublin: Dominican, 1975), pp. 1002, 1008.

[11]Hebblethwaite, *Runaway Church*, pp. 160–61.

[12]Ibid., p. 151.

[13]Ibid., pp. 165–67.

[14]*Chicago Daily News*, October 22, 1975.

[15]Hebblethwaite, *Runaway Church*, pp. 152–53.

[16]*Time*, September 2, 1974.

[17]*New York Times*, October 13, 1975.

[18]Beeson, *Discretion and Valour*, p. 162; *Time*, September 2, 1974.

[19]*The Church Around the World*, March 1976.

[20]*Christianity Today*, September 10, 1976.

[21]Beeson, *Discretion and Valour*, pp. 145–46.

[22]*New York Times*, May 13, 1973.

[23]*Time*, February 23, 1976.

[24]*Der Feste Grund*, July 1976.

[25]*U.S. News and World Report*, October 11, 1976; *New York Times*, November 2, 1976.

[26]*Daily Telegraph*, London, November 29, 1976.

[27]*International Herald Tribune*, Paris, February 14, 1977.

[28]*Time*, November 22, 1976.

[29]Hebblethwaite, *Runaway Church*, p. 92; *Time*, November 22, 1976.

[30]*New York Times*, June 9, 1975.

[31]*Sparks*, Wheaton, November, 1975.

[32]*Daily Telegraph*, London, September 20, 1975.

[33]*Sparks*, November, 1975.

[34]*Daily Telegraph*, London, Editorial, December 1, 1976.

[35]*New York Times*, September 9, 1973.

[36]*Daily Telegraph*, London, January 5, 1977.

[37]Ibid., April 14, 1976.

[38]Ibid., December 12, 1974.

[39]Beeson, *Discretion and Valour*, p. 114.

[40]Michael Bourdeaux and Kathleen Murray, *Young Christians in Russia* (London: Lakeland, 1976), pp. 122–24.

[41]*Christianity Today*, March 29, 1963.

[42]Beeson, *Discretion and Valour*, p. 116.

[43]*Times*, London, December 12, 1976; Hebblethwaite, *Runaway Church*, p. 168.

[44]Hebblethwaite, *Runaway Church*, p. 177.

[45]Beeson, *Discretion and Valour*, p. 252.

[46]Ibid., p. 247.

[47]*Time*, February 18, 1974.

[48]Hebblethwaite, *Runaway Church*, p. 149.

[49]*Der Feste Grund*, July 1976.

[50]Beeson, *Discretion and Valour*, p. 273.

[51]Ibid., p. 270.

[52]Hebblethwaite, *Runaway Church*, pp. 172–73.

[53]*Christianity Today*, February 14, 1969.

[54]*New York Times*, January 22, 1976.

[55]Hebblethwaite, *Runaway Church*, p. 156.

[56]*Christianity Today*, August 30, 1968.

[57]Beeson, *Discretion and Valour*, p. 218.

[58]Ibid., pp. 220–22.

[59]Hebblethwaite, *Runaway Church*, p. 170.

[60]Robert P. Evans, *Let Europe Hear* (Chicago: Moody, 1963), p. 63.

[61]*New York Times*, December 16, 1975.

[62]Ibid., June 17, 1973.

[63]Ibid.

[64]Julian Critchley, "How Big a Red Peril in Italy." *Daily Telegraph*, London, April 22, 1976.

[65]*Daily Telegraph*, London, January 4, 1976.

[66]*Time*, June 19, 1976.

[67]*Daily Telegraph*, London, May 19, 1976.

[68]*Christianity Today*, September 24, 1976.

[69]*Chicago Tribune*, January 22, 1977.

[70]Critchley, "Red Peril."

[71]Robert P. Evans, *Let Europe Hear*, pp. 65–66.

Notes on Chapter 8

[1]Karl Marx's gravestone, London, Highgate Cemetery.

[2]Alexander Solzhenitsyn, *The Gulag Archipelago 1918–1956* (London: Collins/Fontana, 1974), p. 326.

[3]Trevor Beeson, *Discretion and Valour* (London: Fontana, 1974), pp. 46–47.

[4]Ibid.

[5]Ibid.

[6]Xenia Howard-Johnston and Michael Bourdeaux, eds., *Aida of Leningrad* (London and Oxford: Mowbrays, 1972), p. 12.

[7]*Daily Telegraph*, London, June 23, 1976.

[8]Howard-Johnston and Bourdeaux, *Aida of Leningrad*, p. 77.

[9]Beeson, *Discretion and Valour*, pp. 43–44.

[10]Ibid., p. 66.

[11]Michael Bourdeaux, *Religious Ferment in Russia* (New York: St. Martin's, 1968), pp. 15–16.

[12]Ibid., pp. 12–14.

[13]Beeson, *Discretion and Valour*, pp. 49–50.

[14]Howard-Johnston and Bourdeaux, *Aida of Leningrad*, p. 119.

[15]Beeson, *Discretion and Valour*, pp. 49–50.

[16]William C. Fletcher, *The Russian Orthodox Church Underground* (London: Oxford University Press, 1971), p. 254.

[17]Howard-Johnston and Bourdeaux, *Aida of Leningrad*, pp. 1, 8, 11.

[18]Amnesty International, *Prisoners of Conscience in the U.S.S.R.* (London: Amnesty International Publications, 1975), pp. 26, 28.

[19]Editorial, *Daily Telegraph*, London, December 1, 1976.

[20]Howard-Johnston and Bourdeaux, *Aida of Leningrad*, p. 113; Gladys Peterson, *Zwishen Kreuz und Rotem Stern* (Wuppertal: Brockhaus, 1975), p. 19.

[21]Michael Bourdeaux and Katherine Murray, *Young Christians in Russia* (London: Lakeland, 1976), pp. 137–38.

[22]*Sparks*, Wheaton, November 1975.

[23]Bourdeaux and Murray, *Young Christians in Russia*, p. 145.

[24]Peterson, *Zwischen Kreuz und Rotem Stern*, p. 15.

[25]Ibid., p. 8.

[26]Howard-Johnston and Bourdeaux, *Aida of Leningrad*, p. 75.

[27]John Pollock, "Christian Youth in Soviet Schools," *Christianity Today*, August 28, 1964.

[28]Bourdeaux and Murray, *Young Christians in Russia*, pp. 24–25.

[29]Fletcher, *Russian Orthodox Church Underground*, p. 289.

[30]Beeson, *Discretion and Valour*, pp. 99–100.

[31]Georgi Vins, *Three Generations of Suffering* (London: Hodder and Stoughton, 1976), p. 95.

[32]Bourdeaux, *Religous Ferment in Russia*, pp. 119–21.

[33]*Christianity Today*, November 24, 1967.

[34]Howard-Johnston and Bourdeaux, *Aida of Leningrad*, pp. 17–18.

[35]*Christianity Today*, May 7, 1976.

[36]Howard-Johnston and Bourdeaux, *Aida of Leningrad*, p. 115.

[37]*Sunday Telegraph*, London, March 30, 1975.

[38]*Moody Monthly*, April 1975.

[39]Vins, *Three Generations of Suffering*, pp. 101–2.

[40]Ibid., p. 103.

[41]Ibid., pp. 66, 82.

[42]*Christianity Today*, October 22, 1976; *Moody Monthly*, April 1975.

[43]*Time*, January 27, 1975; *Church Around the World*, March 1976.

[44]*Idea*, Summer 1976.

[45]*Christian Inquirer*, January 1977.

[46]Howard-Johnston and Bourdeaux, *Aida of Leningrad*, p. 117.

[47]Fletcher, *Russian Orthodox Church Underground*, pp. 260–61.

[48]Timothy Ware, *The Orthodox Church* (Baltimore: Penguin, 1963), pp. 170–71.

[49]*Christianity Today*, December 6, 1963.

[50]Fletcher, *Russian Orthodox Church Underground*, pp. 263–64.

[51]Ware, *Orthodox Church*, p. 170.

[52]Bourdeaux and Murray, *Young Christians in Russia*, p. 58.

[53]*New York Times*, September 18, 1973.

[54]*Der Feste Grund*, December 1976.

[55]Ibid., September 1976.

[56]Bourdeaux and Murray, *Young Christians in Russia*, pp. 43–44.

[57]*Time*, April 3, 1972.

[58]*Daily Telegraph*, London, February 27, 1977.

[59]Vins, *Three Generations of Suffering*, p. 217.

[60]*New York Times*, September 14, 1962.

[61]*Sparks*, May 1976.

[62]*Daily Telegraph*, London, April 26, 1976.

[63]*Sparks*, November 1975.

[64]Bourdeaux and Murray, *Young Christians in Russia*, p. 28.

[65]*Christianity Today*, December 18, 1970.

[66]Bourdeaux and Murray, *Young Christians in Russia*, p. 73.

[67]Ibid., p. 30.

[68]Beeson, *Discretion and Valour*, p. 82.

[69]Peterson, *Zwischen Kreuz und Rotem Stern*, p. 76.

[70]*Time*, September 2, 1966.

[71]Norman B. Rohrer and Peter Dyneka, Jr., *Peter Dynamite* (Grand Rapids: Baker, 1975), pp. 166–67.

[72]*Christianity Today*, October 8, 1976.

[73]Rohrer and Dyneka, *Peter Dynamite*, p. 148.

[74]Bourdeaux and Murray, *Young Christians in Russia*, p. 14.

[75]*New York Times*, April 14, 1974.

[76]Beeson, *Discretion and Valour*, p. 25.

Notes on Chapter 9

[1]*Time*, March 20, 1977.

[2]*Daily Telegraph*, London, March 29, 1977.

[3]Colin Brown and Peter J. Mooney, *Cold War to Detente* (London: Heinemann, 1976), p. 57.

[4]Ibid., pp. 64–65.

[5]Ibid., pp. 137–39.

[6]*Christian Century*, September 19, 1962.

[7]*Sparks*, Wheaton, May 1976.

[8]Ernst Benz, *The Eastern Orthodox Church: Its Thought and Life*, trans. Richard and Clara Winston (New York: Doubleday, Anchor, 1963), p. 167.

[9]Trevor Beeson, *Discretion and Valour* (London: Fontana, 1974), p. 310.

[10]Ibid., p. 313.

[11]Timothy Ware, *The Orthodox Church* (Baltimore: Penguin, 1963), p 175.

[12]Beeson, *Discretion and Valour*, p. 302.

[13]"Sunday," British Broadcasting Corporation, Radio 4, October 10, 1976.

[14]Benz, *Eastern Orthodox Church*, p. 165.

[15]Beeson, *Discretion and Valour*, pp. 304-5.

[16]Andre Morea, *The Book They Couldn't Ban* (London: Lakeland, 1976), p. 155.

[17]*Underground Evangelism*, May 1976.

[18]*Christianity Today*, May 7, 1976.

[19]Ibid., August 30, 1968.

[20]*Daily Telegraph*, London, December 27, 1973.

[21]*Christianity Today*, October 22, 1976.

[22]*World Evangelization Information Service*, March 24, 1977.

[23]Josef Ton, "The Socialist Quest for the New Man," *Christianity Today*, March 26, 1976.

[24]Beeson, *Discretion and Valour*, p. 168.

[25]*Christianity Today*, August 28, 1961.

[26]*World Vision*, April 1968.

[27]Beeson, *Discretion and Valour*, pp. 176-77, 181.

[28]*Chicago Tribune*, March 19, 1973.

[29]*Christianity Today*, November 10, 1976.

[30]*Der Feste Grund*, August, 1976.

[31]*Christianity Today*, February 13, 1961.

[32]American Forces Network, Frankfurt, December 5, 1966.

[33]Richard V. Pierard, "New Look Over the Wall," *Eternity*, August 1969.

[34]*Church Around the World*, December 1974.

[35]*Crusade*, October 1974.

[36]*Daily Telegraph*, London, August 24, 1976, September 20, 1976; *Christianity Today*, September 10, 1976.

[37]*Church Around the World*, September 1976.

[38]Ibid., January 1977.

[39]*Christianity Today*, May 7, 1976.

[40]Beeson, *Discretion and Valour*, pp. 212-16.

[41]Ibid., p. 332.

[42]*Christianity Today*, May 7, 1976.

[43]Ibid., September 13, 1968; Beeson, *Discretion and Valour*, p. 193.

[44]*Christianity Today*, Editorial, September 13, 1968.

[45]*Christianity Today*, May 7, 1976, September 13, 1968; Beeson, *Discretion and Valour*, p. 216.

[46]*Christianity Today*, September 10, 1976.

[47]*Sparks*, February, 1976.

[48]Richard Bennett, Greater Europe Mission Annual Conference, Zeist, Netherlands, August 1966.

[49]*Christianity Today*, September 12, 1969.

[50]*World Vision*, April 1973.

[51]*Christianity Today*, September 12, 1969.

[52]Michael Johnson, Greater Europe Mission Information, June 1975.

[53]*Christianity Today*, May 10, 1968.

[54]Billy Graham Evangelistic Association, official statistics.

[55]*New York Times*, February 13, 1973; *Together* (Greater Europe Mission), March 1977.

[56]Norman B. Rohrer, "The Church and the World in 1974," *World Vision*, December 1974.

[57]*Christianity Today*, September 10, 1976.

[58]W. Stanley Mooneyham, "Yugoslavia: The Reformation Lives On," *World Vision*, January, 1977.

[59]*Christianity Today*, May 10, 1968.

[60]*World Vision*, April 1973.

[61]*New York Times*, December 22, 1975.

[62]*Renewal*, London, December 1972–January 1973.

[63]Benz, *Eastern Orthodox Church*, p. 169.

[64]Beeson, *Discretion and Valour*, p. 299.

[65]Ibid., pp. 288, 294–97.

[66]W. T. Stunt, et al., *Turning the World Upside Down*, 2nd ed. (Bath: Echoes of Service, 1972), p. 352.

[67]*National Courier*, December 2, 1975.

[68]Morea, *Book They Couldn't Ban*, p. 103.

[69]*The Church Around the World*, April 1976.

[70]Beeson, *Discretion and Valour*, p. 281.

[71]Ibid., p. 284.

[72]Ibid., p. 285.

[73]*Sparks*, November 1975.

[74]*Idea*, January 12, 1976.

[75]*Christianity Today*, March 26, 1976.

[76]*Daily Telegraph*, London, March 2, 1976.

NOTES ON CHAPTER 10

[1]*Daily Telegraph*, London, February 22, 1974.

[2]Ibid., September 13, 1975.

[3]Ibid., March 25, 1976.

[4]J. Herbert Kane, *Understanding Christian Missions* (Grand Rapids: Baker, 1974), pp. 240–41.

[5]John Wesley White, *Re-Entry* (Minneapolis: Worldwide, 1971), p. 174.

[6]Ibid., p. 121.

[7]*Christianity Today*, July 20, 1962.

[8]*Daily Telegraph*, London, September 30, 1974.

[9]Trevor Beeson, *The Church of England in Crisis* (London: David-Poynter, 1973), pp. 32–33.

[10]*Daily Telegraph*, London, April 14, 1975.

[11]Ibid., May 14, 1973.

[12]Ibid., June 10, 1974.

[13]*Christianity Today*, December 5, 1975.

[14]*Daily Telegraph*, London, March 12, 1975.

[15]Ibid., August 22, 1975.

[16]Ibid., March 13, 1975.

[17]Daniel Jenkins, *The British: Their Identity and Religion* (London: SCM, 1975), p. 181.

[18]John A. T. Robinson, *The Difference in Being a Christian Today* (London: Fontana, 1972), p. 26.

[19]John A. T. Robinson, *Honest To God* (London: SCM, 1963), pp. 66–72.

[20]Ibid., p. 76.

[21]Ibid., p. 99.

[22]Ibid., pp. 118, 120.

[23]*Daily Telegraph*, London, March 26, 1976.

[24]John A. T. Robinson, *Can We Trust the New Testament?* (London: Mowbrays, 1977), pp. 16–17.

[25]Ibid., pp. 25–26.

[26]Ibid., pp. 128, 132.

[27]D. M. MacKinnon, et al., *Objections to Christian Belief* (London: Constable, 1963,) p. 103.

[28]Ibid., p. 99.

[29]J. D. Douglas, "William Barclay: Extraordinary Communicator," *Christianity Today*, January 16, 1976.

[30]*Time*, March 25, 1974.

[31]*Daily Telegraph*, London, November 19, 1973.

[32]*New York Times*, December 1, 1962.

[33]*Daily Telegraph*, London, November 8, 1976.

[34]Peter Hebblethwaite, *The Runaway Church* (London: Collins, 1975), p. 128.

[35]Austin Flannery, ed., *Vatican Council II: The Conciliar and Post-Conciliar Documents* (Dublin: Dominican, 1975), pp. 478–80.

[36]J. D. Douglas, "Canterbury Tale, 1966," *Christianity Today*, April 15, 1966.

[37]J. I. Packer, ed., *Guidelines: Anglican Evangelicals Face the Future* (London: Falcon, 1967), p. 65.

[38]Hebblethwaite, *Runaway Church*, pp. 130–31.

[39]Ibid., p. 133.

[40]Anglican-Roman Catholic International Commission, *Authority in the Church* (London: CTS/SPCK, 1976), pp. 16–18.

[41]*Christianity Today*, March 15, 1963.

[42]Beeson, *Church of England in Crisis*, p. 10.

[43]*Daily Telegraph*, London, December 29, 1975.

[44]*Christianity Today*, February 13, 1976.

[45]*Daily Mail Yearbook* 1977, p. 119.

[46]*Sunday Telegraph Magazine*, London, September 26, 1976.

[47]*Daily Telegraph*, London, March 26, 1974.

[48]*Time*, May 27, 1974.

[49]*Daily Telegraph*, London, September 14, 1974.

[50]Ibid., February 28, 1975.

[51]David Sheppard, *Built Like a City* (London: Hodder and Stoughton, 1974).

[52]*Daily Telegraph*, London, May 15, 1974.

[53]Ibid., November 12, 1975.

[54]*Christianity Today*, February 13, 1976.

[55]*Time*, November 17, 1975.

[56]*Daily Telegraph*, London, April 19, 1976.

[57]Ibid., June 17, 1976.

[58]*Time*, May 27, 1974.

[59]*Daily Telegraph*, London, April 21, 1977.

[60]Ibid., December 8, 1975.

[61]*Christianity Today*, May 12, 1967.

[62]Gordon Landreth, "Evangelicals and the Church of England," *Global Report*, January 1976.

[63]Packer, *Guidelines*, pp. 27, 156–57, 203.

[64]*Information Service*, Summer, 1972.

[65]John R. W. Stott, ed., *Obeying Christ in a Changing World* (London: Collins, Fontana, 1977).

[66]*Sunday Telegraph*, London, April 17, 1977.

[67]"Sunday," British Broadcasting Corporation, Radio 4, April 17, 1977.

[68]*Eternity*, December, 1976.

[69]Beeson, *Church of England in Crisis*, p. 127.

[70]*Christianity Today*, December 4, 1970.

[71]*Daily Telegraph*, London, July 5, 1976.

[72]Ibid., November 13, 1976.

[73]Ibid., November 15, 1974, December 5, 1974.

[74]Ibid., November 8, 1973, November 9, 1974.

[75]Ibid., April 28, 1975, July 7, 1975; *Christianity Today*, September 24, 1976.

[76]*Christianity Today*, May 12, 1967.

[77]Ibid., September 28, 1973.

[78]Landreth, "Evangelicals in the Church of England."

NOTES ON CHAPTER 11

[1]Daniel Jenkins, *The British: Their Identity and Their Religion* (London: SCM, 1975), p. 98.

[2]Ibid.

[3]*Greater Europe Report*, January-March 1972.

[4]*Christian Century*, June 30, 1965.

[5]*Greater Europe Report*, January-March 1972.

[6]Jenkins, *The British*, pp. 112–13.

[7]"Sunday," British Broadcasting Corporation, Radio 4, April 24, 1977.

[8]*Christianity Today*, April 23, 1976.

[9]Ibid., July 31, 1967.

[10]*Daily Telegraph*, London, January 8, 1976.

[11]British Broadcasting Corporation, Radio 4, November 12, 1972.

[12]*Baptist Times*, May 6, 1971.

[13]*Lansdowne Family News*, August 1976.

[14]*Baptist Union Annual Report*, 1976, p. 11.

[15]*Baptist Times*, May 6, 1971.

[16]*British Evangelical Council Newsletter*, Summer 1972.

[17]*Baptist Times*, May 20, 1971.

[18]J. D. Pawson, *How Much of a God Was Jesus?* (London: Privately Published, 1971), p. 20.

[19]*Baptist Times*, August 19, 1971.

[20]Ibid., October 7, 1971.

[21]*Christianity Today*, July 31, 1964.

[22]Lee F. Tuttle and Max W. Woodward, eds., *Proceedings of the Eleventh World Methodist Conference* (London: Epworth, 1967), p. 217.

[23]Ibid., pp. 159–60.

[24]*Church of England Newspaper*, June 4, 1976.

[25]*British Evangelical Council Newsletter*, Spring 1972.

[26]*Baptist Times*, May 6, 1971.

[27]Colin R. Garwood, "What About This New United Reformed Church?" (Southend-on-Sea: typescript, 1971), p. 1.

[28]*Scheme of Union* (London: United Reformed Church, 1970), p. 4.

[29]Ibid., p. 5.

[30]Ibid., p. 8.

[31]Ibid.

[32]*Daily Telegraph*, London, May 4, 1976.

[33]*Christianity Today*, March 15, 1963.

[34]Ibid.

[35]Jenkins, *The British*, p. 104.

[36]Tuttle and Woodward, *Proceedings*, pp. 83–84, 98.

[37]Ibid., pp. 90, 97, 106, 178.

[38]*Baptist Times*, November 4, 1971.

[39]Trevor Beeson, *The Church of England in Crisis* (London: David-Poynter, 1973), p. 10.

[40]*Time*, March 25, 1974.

[41]*Daily Telegraph*, London, December 29, 1975.

[42]*Baptist Union Annual Report*, 1976, pp. 61–63.

[43]Ibid.; *Daily Telegraph*, London, February 8, 1977.

[44]"Ten Propositions and Our Denominational Response," Discussion Paper, Baptist Union Assembly, 1977, pp. 1–2.

[45]*Free Church Chronical*, Autumn 1976.

[46]*Daily Telegraph*, London, January 10, 1976.

[47]*The Nottingham Statement* (London: Falcon, 1977), p. 42.

[48]*Free Church Chronicle*, May/June 1970.

[49]Ibid., Summer 1976.

[50]Free Church Federal Council, Annual Report, 1965, p. 6, 16–17.

[51]*Daily Telegraph*, London, June 23, 1976.

[52]*Free Church Chronicle*, Summer 1976.

[53]*Evangelical Times*, May 1977.

[54]Jenkins, *The British*, p. 189.

[55]Ibid., p. 101.

[56]*Christianity Today*, February 1, 1974, September 10, 1976.

[57]Ibid., May 7, 1976.

[58]*Eternity*, December 1976.

[59]British Evangelical Council, *Introducing the British Evangelical Council* (St. Albans: BEC, n.d.).

[60]*British Evangelical Council Newsletter*, Summer/Autumn 1972.

[61]Ibid., Spring 1975.

[62]British Evangelical Council, *Ecumenicity* (St. Albans: BEC, n.d.).

[63]Ibid.

[64]Roland Lamb, *The State of the Church* (St. Albans: BEC, n.d.), pp. 3–4.

[65]*British Evangelical Council Newsletter*, Summer/Autumn 1972.

[66]Lamb, *State of the Church*, pp. 5–6.

[67]*British Evangelical Council Newsletter*, Summer 1975.

[68]Ibid., Spring 1976.

[69]Ibid., Summer/Autumn 1972.

[70]Lamb, *State of the Church*, p. 5.

[71]"Fellowship of Independent Evangelical Churches," in *The New International Dictionary of the Christian Church* (Grand Rapids: Zondervan, 1974), p. 372.

[72]*Evangelical Times*, May 1977.

NOTES ON CHAPTER 12

[1]George A. Maloney, "The Orthodox Church in Greece Today," *America*, March 11, 1967.

[2]Barbara L. Faulkner, "Eastern Orthodox Churches," in *The New International Dictionary of the Christian Church* (Grand Rapids: Zondervan, 1974), p. 323.

[3]Ibid., p. 324.

[4]Ibid., pp. 324–25.

[5]Mario Rinvolucri, *Anatomy of a Church: Greek Orthodoxy Today* (Bronx: Fordham University Press, 1966), p. 46.

[6]Ibid., p. 13.

[7]*Time*, July 5, 1963.

[8]*New York Times*, April 23, 1967.

[9]*America*, March 11, 1967.

[10]*New York Times*, April 23, 1967.

[11]*America*, March 11, 1967.

[12]Rinvolucri, *Anatomy of a Church*, pp. 62, 76.

[13]*Christian Century*, May 23, 1976.

[14]Ibid.

[15]Rinvolucri, *Anatomy of a Church*, pp. 119–20.

[16]*America*, March 11, 1967.

[17]Ernst Benz, *The Eastern Orthodox Church: Its Thought and Life* (New York: Doubleday, Anchor, 1963), p. 174.

[18]Rinvolucri, *Anatomy of a Church*, p. 83.

[19]Ibid., pp. 84–88.

[20]Ibid., pp. 91, 98.

[21]Panagiotis Bratsiotis, *The Greek Orthodox Church*, trans. Joseph Blenkinsopp (Notre Dame: The University Press, 1966), p. 88.

[22]Ibid., p. 89; *America*, March 11, 1967.

[23]Bratsiotis, *Greek Orthodox Church*, pp. 111–13.

[24]*America*, July 28, 1962.

[25]Ibid.

[26]*Christianity Today*, July 6, 1973.

[27]Ibid.

[28]*Christianity Today*, November 15, 1967.

[29]*New York Times*, November 26, 1973.

[30]Ibid., May 27, 1974.

[31]Ibid., April 3, 1973.

[32]*Time*, July 2, 1973.

[33]*New York Times*, January 13, 1974.

[34]*Christianity Today*, February 1, 1974; *New York Times*, January 17, 1974.

[35]*Times*, London, April 2, 1977.

[36]*Christianity Today*, March 14, 1975.

[37]*Christian Century*, January 22, 1975.

[38]Ibid.

[39]Robert P. Evans, Interview, Paris, May 6, 1976.

[40]Rinvolucri, *Anatomy of a Church*, p. 58.

[41]*New York Times*, December 27, 1960.

[42]Ibid., September 24, 1961.

[43]Ibid., September 30, October 1, 1961.

[44]Ibid., September 20, 1963.

[45]Ibid., September 22, 1963.

[46]Ibid., April 22, 1968.

[47]Bratsiotis, *Greek Orthodox Church*, p. 23.

[48]*New York Times*, April 19, 1963.

[49]Ibid., September 14, 1963.

[50]Ibid., December 18, 1963.

[51]Rinvolucri, *Anatomy of a Church*, p. 55.

[52]*Christianity Today*, January 17, 1964.

[53]*New York Times*, January 4, 1964.

[54]Ibid.

[55]Ibid., January 7, 1964.

[56]Austin Flannery, ed., *Vatican Council II: The Conciliar and Post-Conciliar Documents* (Dublin: Dominican, 1975), pp. 471–72.

[57]Ibid., pp. 449–50, 481–82.

[58]*New York Times*, March 18, 21, 1967.

[59]Ibid., July 17, 26, 1967.

[60]Ibid., October 27, 1967.

[61]Ibid., August 14, 1968.

[62]Ibid., June 12, 1969.

[63]Ibid., February 21, 1970.

[64]Ibid., July 18, 1972.

[65]Renewal, London, February-March 1972.

[66]*New York Times*, July 29, 1975.

[67]Ibid., May 4, 1962.

[68]Ibid., July 31, 1962.

[69]Peter Beyerhaus and Ulrich Betz. *Ökumene im Spiegel von Nairobi '75* (Bad Liebenzell: Liebenzeller Mission, 1976), pp. 52, 55, 138, 181.

[70]*New York Times*, April 22, 1968.

Bibliography

Barth, Karl. *Ad Limina Apostolorum: An Appraisal of Vatican II.* Translated by Keith R. Crim. Richmond, Va.: John Knox, 1968.

Beeson, Trevor. *The Church of England in Crisis.* London: Davis-Poynter, 1973.

————. *Discretion and Valour.* London: Fontana, 1974.

Benz, Ernst. *The Eastern Orthodox Church: Its Thought and Life.* New York: Doubleday, 1963.

Beyerhaus, Peter. *Bangkok '73: The Beginning or the End of World Mission?* Grand Rapids: Zondervan, 1974.

————. *Missions: Which Way? Humanization or Redemption.* Translated by Margaret Clarkson. Grand Rapids: Zondervan, 1971.

Bourdeaux, Michael. *Religious Ferment in Russia.* New York: St. Martin's, 1968.

Bourdeaux, Michael and Murray, Katharine. *Young Christians In Russia.* London: Lakeland, 1976.

Bultmann, Rudolf. *Existence and Faith.* London: Fontana, 1964.

————. *Jesus Christ and Mythology.* London: SCM, 1960.

————. *Theology of the New Testament.* London: SCM, 1952.

Carson, H. M. *Dawn or Twilight?* Leicester: Inter-Varsity, 1976.

Douglas, J. D., ed. *Let the Earth Hear His Voice.* Minneapolis: World Wide, 1975.

Ebeling, Gerhard. *Word and Faith.* London: SCM, 1963.

Elliott, Lawrence. *I Will Be Called John: A Biography of Pope John XXIII.* London: Collins, 1974.

Evans, Robert P. *Let Europe Hear*. Chicago: Moody, 1963.

Flannery, Austin, ed., *Vatican Council II: The Conciliar and Post Conciliar Documents*. Dublin: Dominican, 1975.

Flynn, Thomas. *The Charismatic Renewal and The Irish Experience*. London: Hodder and Stoughton, 1974.

Forem, Jack. *Transcendental Meditation*. New York: Dutton, 1974.

Fuchs, Ernst. *Studies of the Historical Jesus*. London: SCM, 1964.

Goodall, Norman, ed. *The Uppsala Report 1968*. Geneva: World Council of Churches, 1968.

Heldt, Joachim. *Gott in Deutschland*. Hamburg: Nannen, 1963.

Henry, Carl F. H. and Mooneyham, W. Stanley, eds. *One Race, One Gospel, One Task*. Minneapolis: World Wide, 1967.

Hutten, Kurt. *Seher, Grübler, Enthusiasten*. Stuttgart: Quell-Verlag, 1966.

Jenkins, Daniel. *The British: Their Identity and Their Religion*. London: SCM, 1975.

Kahl, Joachim. *Das Elend des Christentums*. Hamburg: Rowohlt, 1968.

Käsemann, Ernst. *New Testament Questions Today*. London: SCM, 1969.

Kirby, Gilbert W., ed. *Evangelism Alert*. Minneapolis: World Wide, 1972.

Külling, Samuel. *Das Übel an der Wurzel Erfassen*. Bettingen: Privately published, 1966.

Küng, Hans. *The Church*. London: Burns and Oates, 1967.

––––––. *Infallible? An Enquiry*. trans. E. Mosbacher. London: Collins, 1971.

––––––. *That the World May Believe*. Translated by Cecily Hastings. New York: Sheed and Ward, 1963.

Meyendorff, John. *The Orthodox Church: Its Past and Its Role in the Church Today*. Translated by John Chapin. New York: Pantheon, 1962.

Moltmann, Jürgen. *Theology of Hope*. London: SCM, 1967.

Moore, John Allen, ed. *Baptist Witness in Catholic Europe*. Rome: Baptist Publishing House, 1975.

New International Dictionary of the Christian Church. Grand Rapids: Zondervan, 1974.

O'Connor, Edward P. *The Pentecostal Movement in the Catholic Church*. Notre Dame: Ave Maria, 1974.

Packer, J. I., ed. *Guidelines: Anglican Evangelicals Face the Future*. London: Falcon, 1967.

Pannenberg, Wolfhart, *Jesus—God and Man*. London: SCM, 1968.

Rahner, Karl. *The Christian of the Future*. New York: Herder and Herder, 1967.

———. *The Priesthood*. Translated by Edward Quinn. New York: Seabury, 1973.

Rinvolucri, Mario. *Anatomy of a Church: Greek Orthodoxy Today*. Bronx: Fordham University Press, 1966.

Robinson, John A.T. *Can We Trust the New Testament?* London: Mowbrays, 1977.

———. *The Difference in Being a Christian Today*. London: Fontana, 1972.

———. *Honest to God*. London: SCM, 1963.

Schaeffer, Francis A. *The Church at the End of the Twentieth Century*. London: Norfolk, 1971.

———. *The Church Before the Watching World*. London: Inter-Varsity Press, 1972.

Schillebeeckx, Edward. *The Mission of the Church*. Translated by N.D. Smith. New York: Seabury, 1973.

———. *Vatican II: The Real Achievement*. London: Sheed and Ward, 1967.

———. *Vatican II: A Struggle of Minds and Other Essays*. Dublin: Gill and Son, 1963.

Stratmann, Hartmut. *Kein Anderes Evangelium*. Hamburg: Furche-Verlag, 1970.

Ware, Timothy. *The Orthodox Church*. Baltimore: Penguin, 1963.

Weckerling, Rudolf, ed. *Jenseits vom Nullpunkt?* Stuttgart: Kreuz, 1972.

Wells, David F. *Revolution in Rome*. London: Tyndale, 1973.

Index